"[A] marvellous collection of essays testifying to the vitality and timeliness of Lacan's ideas."
Adrian Johnston, *Distinguished Professor, Department of Philosophy, University of New Mexico.*

"The contributions in this volume, meticulously edited, show how the practice of philosophy looks like, when Lacan's challenge is taken seriously, that is, beyond provocation."
Samo Tomšič, *Professor of Philosophy, University of Fine Arts Hamburg.*

"Moving across fields as diverse as neuroscience, theology, mathematics, continental philosophy, linguistics and politics, this incredible collection – a veritable dream team of Lacanian thinkers and scholars – demonstrates how the multiple trajectories of Lacanian anti-philosophy have inflected contemporary thought today in a way which is both irreversible and profound."
Derek Hook, *Associate Professor of Psychology, Duquesne University; editor, Lacan on Depression and Melancholia (with Stijn Vanheule).*

Philosophy After Lacan

Philosophy After Lacan: Politics, Science, and Art brings together reflections on contemporary philosophy inspired by and in dialogue with Lacanian theory.

Rather than focus on the thinkers who came before Lacan, the editors maintain attention on innovations in contemporary philosophy that owe their emergence to complimentary, critical, direct, or tangential engagement with Lacan. This collection makes one of the first concerted efforts to expand discussions between psychoanalysis and more recent philosophical thinkers while gathering chapters by some of the leading philosophical voices of the present moment. With contributors from around the world, this book has international appeal and is unique in its emphasis on contemporary philosophies inspired or influenced by Lacan.

Philosophy After Lacan will appeal not only to psychotherapists and psychoanalysts, but also to students and professors of philosophy, critical theory, psychology, politics, history and literature.

Alireza Taheri is a psychoanalytic psychotherapist based in Toronto, Canada. He is a faculty member of Persepolis Psychoanalytic and the Boston Graduate School of Psychoanalysis. He is the author of *Hegelian-Lacanian Variations on Late Modernity: Spectre of Madness* (Routledge) where he develops a novel dialectical theory based on Hegel, Lacan and Žižek.

Chris Vanderwees is a psychoanalyst, registered psychotherapist, and clinical supervisor at St. John the Compassionate Mission in Toronto, Canada. He is a member of the Lacanian School of Psychoanalysis and an affiliate of the Toronto Psychoanalytic Society.

Reza Naderi is a computer scientist and an author and researcher in the areas of logic, mathematical philosophy and theories of the subject.

The Lines of the Symbolic in Psychoanalysis Series

Series Editor
Ian Parker, Manchester Psychoanalytic Matrix

Psychoanalytic clinical and theoretical work is always embedded in specific linguistic and cultural contexts and carries their traces, traces which this series attends to in its focus on multiple contradictory and antagonistic 'lines of the Symbolic'. This series takes its cue from Lacan's psychoanalytic work on three registers of human experience, the Symbolic, the Imaginary and the Real, and employs this distinctive understanding of cultural, communication and embodiment to link with other traditions of cultural, clinical and theoretical practice beyond the Lacanian symbolic universe. *The Lines of the Symbolic in Psychoanalysis Series* provides a reflexive reworking of theoretical and practical issues, translating psychoanalytic writing from different contexts, grounding that work in the specific histories and politics that provide the conditions of possibility for its descriptions and interventions to function. The series makes connections between different cultural and disciplinary sites in which psychoanalysis operates, questioning the idea that there could be one single correct reading and application of Lacan. Its authors trace their own path, their own line through the Symbolic, situating psychoanalysis in relation to debates which intersect with Lacanian work, explicating it, extending it and challenging it.

A Lacanian Conception of Populism
Society Does Not Exist
Timothy Appleton

On the History and Transmission of Lacanian Psychoanalysis
Speaking of Lacan
Chris Vanderwees

Lacan and Capitalist Discourse
Neoliberalism and Ideology
Jorge Alemán

Philosophy After Lacan
Politics, Science, and Art
Edited by Alireza Taheri, Chris Vanderwees, and Reza Naderi

For more information about the series, please visit: https://www.routledge.com/The-Lines-of-the-Symbolic-in-Psychoanalysis-Series/book-series/KARNLOS

Philosophy After Lacan

Politics, Science, and Art

Edited by
Alireza Taheri, Chris Vanderwees and
Reza Naderi

LONDON AND NEW YORK

First published 2024
by Routledge
4 Park Square, Milton Park, Abingdon, Oxon OX14 4RN

and by Routledge
605 Third Avenue, New York, NY 10158

Routledge is an imprint of the Taylor & Francis Group, an informa business

© 2024 selection and editorial matter, Alireza Taheri, Chris Vanderwees, and Reza Naderi; individual chapters, the contributors

The right of Alireza Taheri, Chris Vanderwees, and Reza Naderi to be identified as the authors of the editorial material, and of the authors for their individual chapters, has been asserted in accordance with sections 77 and 78 of the Copyright, Designs and Patents Act 1988.

All rights reserved. No part of this book may be reprinted or reproduced or utilised in any form or by any electronic, mechanical, or other means, now known or hereafter invented, including photocopying and recording, or in any information storage or retrieval system, without permission in writing from the publishers.

Trademark notice: Product or corporate names may be trademarks or registered trademarks, and are used only for identification and explanation without intent to infringe.

Designed cover image: René Magritte, "La Lampe philosophique" ["Philosopher's Lamp"], 1936

British Library Cataloguing in Publication Data
A catalogue record for this book is available from the British Library

Library of Congress Cataloging-in-Publication Data
A catalog record has been requested for this book

ISBN: 978-1-032-54646-9 (hbk)
ISBN: 978-1-032-54645-2 (pbk)
ISBN: 978-1-003-42595-3 (ebk)

DOI: 10.4324/9781003425953

Typeset in Times New Roman
by Taylor & Francis Books

Contents

Acknowledgements	viii
List of Contributors	x
Preface	xiii

	Introduction	1
1	Lacan's Lesson for Philosophy: Why True Atheism has to be Indirect	7
	SLAVOJ ŽIŽEK	
2	My Transference with Lacan as a Thinker	27
	SERGIO BENVENUTO	
3	The Psychiatrist Despite Himself	45
	ALIREZA TAHERI	
4	How Not to Kill a Hysteric	68
	JAMIESON WEBSTER	
5	Feed My Desire: Occupy Wall Street and the Prospect of a Lacanian Gay Science	83
	DANIEL ADLEMAN	
6	Doomsday Fantasy: The Logic of Logistical Blocking of the Left	95
	ARIAN BEHZADI	
7	Real Ethics and the "Ethics of the Real" after Lacan and Wittgenstein	109
	PAUL M. LIVINGSTON	
8	Lacan with Derrida	127
	CHRIS VANDERWEES	

viii Contents

9 "Lacan is Our Hegel": Dialectic from Hegel to Lacan to Badiou   142
REZA NADERI

10 The Place of Mathematics: Badiou with Lacan   167
JELICA ŠUMIČ RIHA

11 The Logic of Institutions in Lacanian Psychoanalysis   197
GABRIEL TUPINAMBÁ

Index   213

Acknowledgements

We thank Ian Parker for his generous support of this project. We also thank Susannah Frearson for her help throughout the publishing process. This work was born out of a fraternal bond with our dear friends and comrades Arian Behzadi, Hossein Zarassi and Doug Orr, with whom we enjoyed regular discussions around philosophical and psychoanalytic readings. We owe them many thanks for inspiring exchanges over the last few years.

Contributors

Daniel Adleman is an Assistant Professor of Writing and Rhetoric at the University of Toronto, where he teaches Digital Rhetoric, A Brief History of Persuasion, Writing for Social Change and Rhetoric of Health and Medicine. He has published articles in *Cultural Politics, Cultural Studies, Communication +1, Canadian Review of American Studies* and *European Journal of Psychoanalysis.* Along with Chris Vanderwees, he is the co-author of *Psychoanalysis and the New Rhetoric: Freud, Burke, Lacan and Philosophy's Other Scenes* (Routledge, 2023).

Arian Behzadi is an attending psychiatrist and trauma clinic lead in the Mental Health and Addiction Program, Scarborough Health Network in Toronto, Canada. He is also a psychoanalyst in training with the Toronto Psychoanalytic Society and Institute. He teaches at the University of Toronto and the Toronto Psychoanalytic Society.

Sergio Benvenuto is a psychoanalyst in Rome, president of the Institute for Advanced Studies in Psychoanalysis, founder and former editor of the *European Journal of Psychoanalysis* and a researcher in psychology and philosophy at the National Research Council in Rome. He is a member of the Institute of Sciences and Technologies of Cognition at the Italian Council for Scientific Research. He teaches psychoanalysis at the International Institute of the Psychology in Kiev and at Esculapio Specialization in Psychotherapy in Naples. He is a contributor to cultural and scientific journals such as *Lettre Internationale, L'évolution psychiatrique, DIVISION/Review.*

Paul M. Livingston lives in the Sandia Mountains of New Mexico and teaches philosophy at the University of New Mexico. He is the author of several books, most recently *The Politics of Logic: Badiou, Wittgenstein, and the Consequences of Formalism* (2012), *The Problems of Contemporary Philosophy* (co-authored with Andrew Cutrofello, 2015) and *The Logic of Being: Realism, Truth, and Time* (2017). His current project is an investigation of several logics of the one and the many, primarily as these appear in the traditions of Platonism, Madhyamaka Buddhist philosophy and twentieth-century analytic philosophy, and of their implications for contemporary life and practice.

Reza Naderi has a Ph.D. in philosophy from the European Graduate School and a B.Sc. in computer science and pure mathematics from the University of Toronto. Reza's doctoral supervisor and committee chair was Alain Badiou. Reza is a computer scientist and practitioner interested in mathematics, mathematical philosophy, logic, politics and psychoanalysis. His research focuses on the cross sections of the theory of large cardinals and the theory of the subject. He has authored a book titled *Badiou, Infinity and Subjectivity − Reading Hegel and Lacan after Badiou*, which Lexington will soon publish. He has also published articles about fuzzy logic, model theory and politics. Reza is a member of the international research collective Subset of Theoretical Practice (STP) and has contributed to several publications by STP, including *Atlas of Experimental Politics* (Šuma #17, 2021).

Jelica Šumič Riha is a Professor of Philosophy at the Postgraduate School of Research Centre of the Slovenian Academy of Sciences and Arts and a Senior Research Fellow at the Institute of Philosophy, Research Centre of the Slovenian Academy of Sciences and Arts. She was a visiting professor at the University of Essex, University Paris 8, Universidad de Buenos Aires and University of São Paulo. In 2000–02 she conducted a seminar, "Le pour tous face au réel" at the Collège international de philosophie in Paris (together with Rado Riha). She has published a number of philosophical works, including *Politik der Wahrheit* (with Alain Badiou, Jacques Rancière and Rado Riha), *Turia+Kant* (Vienna, 1997), *Universel, Singulier, Sujet* (with Alain Badiou et al., Kimé, Paris, 2000); *Mutations of Ethics* (Založba ZRC, 2002); *Večnost in spreminjanje. Filozofija v brezsvetnem času* (*Eternity and Change. Philosophy in the Worldless Time*, Založba ZRC, Ljubljana 2012); *A política e a psicanálise: do nao-todo ao para todos* (Lume editor, São Paulo, 2019). Currently she is working on a forthcoming volume entitled *Volonté et Désir* (Harmattan).

Alireza Taheri wrote his doctoral dissertation on Nietzsche, Freud and Lacan at the University of Cambridge. He currently provides psychoanalytic psychotherapy and clinical supervision in Toronto where he is also actively involved teaching psychoanalysis at the Toronto Psychoanalytic Institute and Society. Alireza is a faculty member of Persepolis Psychoanalytic where he teaches psychoanalytic theory and practice to students in Tehran (Iran). He is also a faculty member of the Boston Graduate School of Psychoanalysis where he teaches Lacanian theories of psychosis as well as courses on philosophy and psychoanalysis. He is engaged in writing articles and books on philosophy, psychoanalysis, film and literature. Alireza has recently published a monograph with Routledge entitled *Hegelian-Lacanian Variations on Late Modernity: Spectre of Madness*, where he develops a novel dialectical theory based on readings of Hegel, Lacan and Žižek. Alireza's current research focuses on Lacanian theories of psychosis and autism about which he is preparing a monograph.

Gabriel Tupinambá is a practicing psychoanalyst in Rio de Janeiro, Brazil. He is also the Head of Social Strategy at the Alameda Institute and a member of the international research collective Subset of Theoretical Practice. He is the author of *The Desire of Psychoanalysis* (NUP, 2021) and the co-author of *An Architecture of Edges: The Left in times of world peripherization* (Autonomia, 2022) and *Hegel, Lacan, Žižek* (Atropos, 2013).

Chris Vanderwees is a psychoanalyst, registered psychotherapist and clinical supervisor in Toronto, Canada. He is the author of *On the History and Transmission of Lacanian Psychoanalysis* (Routledge, 2024), co-author with Daniel Adleman of *Psychoanalysis and the New Rhetoric* (Routledge, 2023), co-editor with Kristen Hennessy of *Psychoanalysis, Politics, Oppression and Resistance* (Routledge, 2022) and translator of Betty Milan's *Analyzed by Lacan* (Bloomsbury, 2023). He is also an affiliate of the Toronto Psychoanalytic Society and a member of the Lacanian School of Psychoanalysis.

Jamieson Webster is a psychoanalyst in New York City. She is the author of *The Life and Death of Psychoanalysis* (Karnac, 2011), *Conversion Disorder* (Columbia University Press, 2018) and *Disorganization & Sex* (Divided, 2022); she also co-wrote, with Simon Critchley, *Stay, Illusion! The Hamlet Doctrine* (Pantheon, 2013). She contributes regularly to *Artforum, Spike Art Magazine, Apology* and the *New York Review of Books*.

Slavoj Žižek is a Hegelian philosopher, a Lacanian psychoanalyst and a communist. He is the International Director at the Birkbeck Institute for Humanities, University of London, UK, a Visiting Professor at the New York University, USA, and a Senior Researcher at the Department of Philosophy, University of Ljubljana, Slovenia.

Preface

Psychoanalysis concerns itself with otherness, and encounters many other kinds of others in its engagement with the field of the symbolic, marking itself out as a distinctive form of practice if not knowledge; one of the most powerful other forms of supposed knowledge and reflective questioning we encounter is philosophy. What 'philosophy' is exactly, however, is as apparently numinous as psychoanalysis; at the one moment philosophy appeals to commonsensical understandings of the self and external reality, dabbling in imaginary appeals to what is felt or said, and at the other, sometimes even in the self-same philosophical paradigm, it delves deep, aiming to touch something that cannot be put into words, something of the real. In its manifold forms, then, philosophy is often an alluring temptation to psychoanalysts that promises to complete psychoanalysis and answer the questions that psychoanalysis cannot.

This multi-faceted volume sticks with the questions, with the reflective questioning that is at the heart of psychoanalytic practice, rather than pretending to come up with answers, rather than pretending to triumph over philosophy; this is crucial, for to engage in that kind of battle would be to fight on the field of the enemy and so, from the start, to lose everything. What there is of psychoanalysis to hold steadfast to is marked in the title of this book in three terms, 'politics', 'science' and 'art', and in a fourth term that is presupposed, operating, as it were, in the shadows; this fourth term, 'love', is hinted at in the introduction to the book as an opening to either a philosophy or an anti-philosophy.

Each of the authors in this field of work – a field adjacent to, if not immediately on the same terrain of philosophy – is mindful of a risk, that the kind of coordinates that Lacanian psychoanalysis gives us to speak about 'philosophical' questions should thereby lead us into making claims about others that would either obey their precepts or attempt to subsume them under psychoanalysis operating as a totalising worldview. In the case of 'politics', for instance, the question must be held open, rather than answered, as to whether it is possible to provide a psychoanalysis of politics – a reductive trap – or whether we should attend to the politics of psychoanalysis.

There is an equivalent risk in relation to 'science', a risk that has a long history in academic and informal philosophy, symbolic and imaginary, which is that as psychoanalysts we might attempt to answer the same kinds of questions that many philosophers have grappled with. There lie the pitfalls of empiricism and positivism which would tie down what reality is, even specify what is real and what is not. So here, again, the question must be kept open as to whether psychoanalysis must become scientific or whether science must be subjected to psychoanalytic scrutiny.

In the case of 'art' we are tasked with asking what kind of practice psychoanalysis is if it is not to be defined as a science. This question pertains not only to the aesthetic aspect of psychoanalysis, an aspect that does draw many practitioners and adepts close to it, but also to the more austere logical structure of psychoanalytic argument. Just as the philosophy of art has tended to obscure the ways in which philosophical argumentation as such has an alluring artistic quality, so we also need to be aware of the difference between turning psychoanalysis into an art practice and subjecting art to a psychoanalytic grid.

This book holds in abeyance, while suggestively hinting at the place of 'love' as a fourth 'truth procedure'. Here is a driving force in psychoanalytic theory and practice, one that manifests itself in the attempt by psychoanalysts to explain exactly what love is – an explanation that philosophy has also attempted to provide and failed at – and in the transferential hold that psychoanalysis has over so many of us, the love of psychoanalysis.

Psychoanalytic clinical and theoretical work circulates through multiple intersecting antagonistic symbolic universes. This series opens connections between different cultural sites in which Lacanian work has developed in distinctive ways, in forms of work that question the idea that there could be single correct reading and application. The *Lines of the Symbolic in Psychoanalysis* series provides a reflexive reworking of psychoanalysis that transmits Lacanian writing from around the world, steering a course between the temptations of a metalanguage and imaginary reduction, between the claim to provide a God's eye view of psychoanalysis and the idea that psychoanalysis must everywhere be the same. And the elaboration of psychoanalysis in the symbolic here grounds its theory and practice in the history and politics of the work in a variety of interventions that touch the real.

Ian Parker
Manchester Psychoanalytic Matrix

Introduction

Throughout his teaching, which spanned over several decades, French psychiatrist and psychoanalyst Jacques Lacan put forward a novel reading of Freud while drawing upon numerous fields including linguistics, anthropology, mathematical formalisation, topology, philosophy and literature. Many academic papers and books have been dedicated to Lacan's complex and intricate relationship with the philosophers that shaped his thinking such as Socrates, Aristotle, Descartes, Kant, Hegel, Koyré and Sartre. These major figures among others comprise the long list of Lacan's philosophical interlocutors. There are several texts, for instance, that engage with Lacan and philosophy including Ellie Ragland's *Jacques Lacan and the Philosophy of Psychoanalysis* from 1986, but this book mainly focuses on Lacanian psychoanalysis as a kind of philosophy and concerning historical philosophical ideas. Ruth Ronen's recent *Lacan with the Philosophers* (2018) also does not emphasise Lacan's contemporary influence and instead takes up canonical thinkers including Plato, Aristotle, Descartes, Pascal, and Hegel. Although Russell Grigg's *Lacan, Language, and Philosophy* (2008) does discuss the work of Slavoj Žižek and Alain Badiou, this book mainly limits its scope to Lacan's work to the "linguistic turn" in psychoanalysis. Finally, French-language edited volumes and monographs also consider the Lacanian corpus concerning its philosophical inheritance rather than what Lacan has himself bequeathed to contemporary thinkers. We are thinking specifically about Juranville's monograph entitled *Lacan et la philosophie* and the collection of papers entitled *Lacan avec les philosophes* where contemporary thinkers reflect once again on Lacan's engagement with previous philosophers. Therefore, the project we propose is unique in its focus on contemporary philosophies inspired or influenced by Lacan.

In this edited collection, *Philosophy After Lacan: Politics, Science and Art*, we bring together reflections on contemporary philosophy inspired by and in dialogue with Lacanian theory. Rather than focus on the thinkers who came before Lacan, we maintain our focus on innovations in contemporary philosophy that owe their emergence to complimentary, critical, direct or tangential engagement with Lacan. This collection makes one of the first concerted

DOI: 10.4324/9781003425953-1

effects to expand discussions between psychoanalysis and more recent philosophical thinkers while gathering chapters by some of the leading philosophical voices of our present moment.

In "Lacan's Lesson for Philosophy: Why True Atheism Has to Be Indirect", Žižek explores the basic premise of atheists today, which is that materialism is a view which can be consistently exposed and defended in itself, in a positive line of argumentation without references to its opposite (religious beliefs). But what if the exact opposite is true? What if, if we want to be true atheists, we have to begin with a religious edifice and undermine it from within? To say that God is deceiving, evil, stupid, undead etc. is much more radical than to directly claim that there is no god: if we just posit that god doesn't exist, we open up the way towards its de facto survival as an idea that should regulate our lives.

In "The Transference with Lacan as a Thinker", Sergio Benvenuto confesses his dissatisfaction with those philosophies that refer directly to Lacan, while he appreciates the many criticisms and analyses of philosophers who have measured themselves with Lacan's work (i.e., Derrida, Nancy, Lacoue-Labarthe, and others). In particular, he rejects what he calls Freudo-Lacanian Marxism, recalling how much Freud and Lacan distanced themselves from the Communist Gospel. Lacan's reintegration into militant (anti-capitalist, feminist, queer, avant-garde...) thought took place by inscribing Lacan's work in an essentially Hegelian vision, in short, by making it a modernist variant of idealism. Benvenuto exposes what seems to him important about Lacan's contribution beyond psychoanalysis – he does not label himself at all as Lacanian – proposing a "realist" reading of his thought and reading it against the backlight of Wittgenstein's thought. In particular, he valorises concepts that even Lacanians often tend to abandon, such as the power of the signifier, the crucial problematique of après-coup, the subject/ Other opposition, the emergence of the real in its correlation with the symbolic, the centrality of the category of enjoyment. Instead, Lacanian logocentrism should be abandoned. The author does not consider Lacan's as a complete and closed system, but as a tormented and always self-dissatisfied reflection on psychoanalysis and its practice. He does not believe that Lacan's teaching is a Revelation that provides answers but is an original (and sometimes mistaken) way of posing the crucial questions of psychoanalysis in a fresh and new way.

In "The Psychiatrist Despite Himself: How Sganarelle Parodied the University Discourse without Knowing It", Alireza Taheri delivers his message in the form of a play inspired by Jean-Baptiste Poquelin Molière's *Le Médecin malgrè lui* (*The Doctor Despite Himself*). The original piece by Molière satirises medicine by showing how an uneducated working-class man (Sganarelle) dupes people into thinking he is a learned doctor by feigning knowledge. In a similar vein, Taheri creates a play where Sganarelle is summoned to pretend to be a psychiatrist through a similar ruse of posturing erudition. The aim of the play is to parody not only the follies of modern American psychiatry but, more generally, the idiocies of what Lacan has termed the "university discourse", namely the covert use of power in the guise of knowledge and science. A call is made in the play to move beyond the limitations of the university discourse not only in mental health but also in economics, metaphysics, ethics, and matters pertaining to justice. A thinking that places the notion of the *symptom* at its heart is heralded as the remedy freeing modernity from the clutches of the university discourse.

In "Listening to Hysteria", Jamiseon Webster argues that there is something annoying about the celebrated (or denigrated) muteness, disappearing acts, or unspoken bodily protest attributed to hysterical women at this point in psychoanalytic history. Any analyst who has worked with a hysteric knows the intense intricacy of what comes to be said, the incredible work of analysis that she performs, no less the process of encountering, again and again, some kernel of trauma, the very limits of understanding, that tends to bring the analysis towards> its final moments. Why emphasise what is merely the symptomatic starting point? Why not describe the ferocious intelligence of some hysterical patients when it comes to analytic work, no less their intelligence in relation to their analysts, something that has often been called clairvoyant, even if defensive − let's talk about you? What other treatments are as maddening, mystifying, and magical? And what about the hysteric's politics, so variably celebrated as radical, feminist, or disparaged as submissive, conservative? This also seems to miss the mark of what takes place in analytic work; though the question, no less how it is conceptualised, is not impertinent for the future of the institution of psychoanalysis. What could a more hysterical psychoanalysis look like, and is that even something we want in the 21st century? In this chapter, looking at an analyst analyzing hysteria (Kristeva), a hysterical analyst (Montrelay) and the hysterical analysand turned analyst (Tustin) Webster will try to get closer to this vision.

In "Feed My Desire: Occupy Wall Street and the Prospect of a Lacanian Gay Science", Daniel Adleman argues that the 2011 Occupy Wall Street (OWS) protest was a remarkable watershed for radical subjectivity and political theorisation. His chapter examines Lee Edelman's application of Lacanian theory to this momentous event. Bringing Lacan's formulation of the death drive into conversation with Herman Melville's "Bartleby the Scrivener", Edelman alleges that the antisocial Real dimension of OWS was, in fact, the mainspring of its political efficacy. Against the grain of popular wisdom, Edelman argues that if OWS were to be absorbed into the dominant order of things and translated into a campaign to improve humanity's lot, the movement would lose its thanatotic potency in the process of assimilating into the homogenizing capitalist network it was meant to short circuit. According to Edelman, the "queer" drive function of the event must be understood as a "negativity that prefers not to pledge itself to the goal of a

4 Philosophy After Lacan

new community and declines its positivization in a recognizably political agenda". Adleman argues that while Edelman's breathtaking psychoanalytic critique of shallow neoliberal discourse cuts deep, his prescriptions neglect the manifold ways that the Occupy movement has already metamorphosed into a project oriented towards a better future for the 99%. Adleman's chapter makes the case that, in mapping his model of antisocial queerness onto social movements, Edelman perhaps overhastily dichotomises OWS's itinerary as either potently disruptive (yet without an agenda) or counterproductively oriented towards a future that reproduces the neoliberal conditions its progenitors revile. Looking to the psychoanalytically-informed political theories of Jodi Dean, Žižek, Glen Coulthard and others, Adleman presents an alternate array of Lacanian perspectives on the significance of OWS and subsequent waves of twenty-first-century political activism.

In "Doomsday Fantasy: The Logic of Logistical Blocking of the Left", Arian Behzadi asks if it is possible that something that has not yet been signified, something that is 'blocking' the full emergence of its significance in the political field, is connected to the repetitive puritanism of the Left? Could this 'something' be a very private state of essential hopelessness, a secret, delusional, and melancholic state – something we are compelled to call a fantasy, specifically, the 'doomsday fantasy'? This is the melancholic belief that not only will everything end but that 'things are already over'. The Lacanian structural analysis of the subject will be applied to elaborate on the melancholic state within the left: 'the left-wing melancholia'.

In "Philosophical Ethics and Real of Ethics after Lacan and Wittgenstein", Paul M. Livingston refers to Lacan's 1959–60 seminar *The Ethics of Psychoanalysis*, who notably specifies the psychoanalytic perspective as one on which "the question of ethics is to be articulated from the point of view of the location of man in relation to the real". Livingston argues that in the *Tractatus Logico-Philosophicus,* Wittgenstein declares that "ethics is transcendental" and, while holding that there can be no propositions of descriptive or normative ethics, he nevertheless interrogates sympathetically "drive to run up against the boundaries of language", which he associates with the ethical tendency in the 1929 "Lecture on Ethics". The aim of this chapter is to articulate how both conceptions of ethics as occupying a liminal position with respect to the totality of the symbolic can succeed in formulating what might be called (in contradistinction to "academic" or "philosophical" ethics) a *real* ethics: that is, an ethics that can comprehend and find terms to respond to the real ethical problems of global sociopolitical organisation today, including those involved in the global dominance of capitalism and anthropogenic violence over non-human forms of life. Livingston argues that, for both Lacan and the early Wittgenstein, the drive to the ethical evinces an essential tendency, inherent to our situation as speaking subjects as such, to witness the implications of our position as such subjects with respect to the totality of the symbolic. The articulation that both give to this limit-position with respect to the symbolic allows their respective analytic projects to evince the terms in which a real ethics might begin to respond to the systematic real and symbolic violence, grounded in the totalizing effects of capitalism and symbolic enframing, that dominates collective planetary life today.

In "Derrida with Lacan", Chris Vanderwees turns our attention toward Derrida's presentation entitled "For the Love of Lacan", which is a text that posits provocative exclamations about the Lacanian archive. From the position of deconstructionist, Derrida asks us to call into question what we think we know about Lacan. Here, Vanderwees explores Derrida's personal encounters with Lacan and the question of the Lacanian archive. In this text, Derrida takes aim at several theorisations of Lacanian psychoanalysis including the notion of the proper trajectory of the letter as returning to the place that reinscribes lack, the motif of truth being formulated as an unveiling, the transcendental place assigned to the phallus, and the phono-logocentrism or *phallogocentrism* contained in Lacan's work. Vanderwees follows Derrida's lead to raise new questions for the contemporary scene.

In ""Lacan is Our Hegel": Dialectic, from Hegel to Lacan to Badiou", Reza Naderi hones in on the quotation by Badiou in his 1982 book *Theory of the Subject* where Badiou states that Lacan is our Hegel. His statement is meant in terms of admiration for Lacan's work to advance the Hegelian dialectic and critical reading of Lacan. Contrary to the popular belief that Marxism was the heir to Hegel's dialectical thought, Badiou believed Lacan was the only true heir to Hegel's dialectic. More importantly, in the same way, that Lacan split Hegel to extract the rational kernel of the Hegelian dialectic, we must split Lacan to extract the rational kernel of the Lacanian dialectic. In this chapter, Naderi reviews Badiou's account by focusing on the splitting operation of Hegel by Lacan and of Lacan by Badiou. Naderi will also show why this early interest in dialectics played an essential role in forming Badiou's later thoughts toward ontology and the theory of the discipline.

In "The Place of Mathematics in Badiou and Lacan", Jelica Šumič Riha attempts to give an account of two different ways of relating to mathematics: Lacan's and Badiou's. Riha's starting point is Badiou's and Lacan's interpretation of Russell's infamous definition of mathematics, according to which mathematics is a discourse in which no one knows what one is talking about, nor whether what one is saying is true. While for Badiou, the ignorance that is supposed to characterise mathematics according to Russell only concerns the role philosophy assigns to it, namely, its being identified with the science of being qua being, for Lacan the ignorance constitutive of mathematics is rather to be seen as a symptom resulting from the reduction of truth to a mere truth value. In discussing the detected divergences in these two readings, this chapter shows how the access to psychoanalysis as well as the access to philosophy coincides with a certain access to mathematics, although we are not dealing with the same type of access.

In "A History of the Big Other: Lacan, Anthropology and Historical Materialism", Gabriel Tupinambá enquires into why did psychoanalysis emerge when it did – and what is its debt to these historical conditions? In this chapter, Tupinambá proposes a philosophical hypothesis which includes psychoanalysis in the history of the transformations of the logic of affinity and kinship under the consolidation of capitalist modernity. In a critical dialogue with anthropology and Lacanian psychoanalysis, Tupinambá suggests that one of the characteristic traits of modern sociality is that kinship structures organizing human social reproduction do not constitute a common "world", conditioning the emergence of social practices that recognise and intervene upon what Lacan called "individual myths" that we need to create in order to suture our fractured kinship histories into social reality. This thesis is quite acceptable in its content, but it is the form in which it is proposed – using resources from Kojin Karatani's theory of the modes of intercourse and Badiou's formal theory of world-logic – that claims some originality, especially since it allows us to derive some crucial ideas, such as Lacan's theory of the real, symbolic and imaginary registers, or his theory of sexuation, out of a more general conceptual framework, itself compatible with the basic tenets of historical materialism.

The vast spectrum of themes in this collection addresses some of the most pressing philosophical questions today. Some chapters engage directly with questions pertaining to psychoanalytic theory and practice while others delve into social, political, and institutional perspectives in light of psychoanalytic theory and contemporary philosophical influences. In direct dialogue with Lacanian psychoanalysis, these chapters put forward the full spectrum of Badiouian truth procedures, namely love, science, art and politics. While some papers focus more on the truth "conditions" of philosophy, others are more directly philosophical. While this Badiouian twist is an unintended outcome of the collection, we welcome it as a serendipitous result, signalling to us the intimate kinship between psychoanalysis and philosophy and heralding the idea of a future collection on Badiou and psychoanalysis as a specular mirror to this volume.

Chapter 1

Lacan's Lesson for Philosophy

Why True Atheism has to be Indirect

Slavoj Žižek

I am not only politically active but often, as they say, also perceived as politically radioactive. The idea that political theology necessarily underpins radical emancipatory politics will for certain add to this perception. The basic premise of atheists today is that materialism is a view which can be consistently exposed and defended in itself, in a positive line of argumentation without references to is opposite (religious beliefs). But what if the exact opposite is true? What if, if we want to be true atheists, we have to begin with a religious edifice and undermine it from within? To say that god is deceiving, evil, stupid, undead... is much more radical than to directly claim that there is no god: if we just posit that god doesn't exist, we open up the way towards its *de facto* survival as an idea(l) that should regulate our lives.

Why political theology? Why are so many essays entitled "politico-theological treatise"? The answer is that a theory becomes theology when it is part of a full subjective political engagement. Let's mention three examples: love, religion, Marxism. If there is a free choice it is that of a love object, love cannot be imposed; however, once fully in love, we experience love as our fate – it holds us in its clutches, no matter how hard we try we cannot escape it. This is why we can (usually) enumerate reasons why we fell in love, but these reasons appears as reasons only after we are already in love – we are never in a comfortable external position in which we can compare reasons to fall in love with different persons and decide whom to choose. Kierkegaard says exactly the same about faith: I do not acquire faith in, say, Christ after comparing different religions and deciding the best reasons speak for Christianity – there are reasons to choose Christianity but this reasons appear only after I've already chosen it, i.e., to see the reasons for belief one already has to believe. And the same holds for Marxism: it is not that, after objectively analysing history, I became a Marxist – my decision to be a Marxist (the experience of a proletarian position) makes me see the reasons for it, i.e., Marxism is the paradox of an objective "true" knowledge accessible only through a subjective partial position. This is why Robespierre was right when he distrusted materialism as the philosophy of decadent-hedonist nobility and tried to impose a new religion of the supreme Being of Reason. The old

DOI: 10.4324/9781003425953-2

8 Philosophy After Lacan

reproach to Marxism that its commitment to a bright future is a secularisation of religious salvation should be proudly assumed.

Here I am ready to use Lorenzo Chiesa's term of an irreducible oscillation[1]: radical emancipatory politics is condemned to oscillate between moments of ecstatic religious commitment where we suspend "reality principle" and try to actualise the impossible, and the long hard "pragmatic" process of transforming revolutionary goals into moments of ordinary social reality of the majority. The point is not that moments of ecstatic commitment are simply utopian/destructive and have to be "normalised": they are essential since they clear the ground and prepare a new base for pragmatic solutions. They are also not illusory since we, the engaged agents, are fully aware that our "impossible" striving will eventually subside, and this awareness only strengthens our commitment. So we don't oscillate between the One of full engagement and the cynical acceptance of not-One, of the messy reality: a true believer can be (and mostly is) ruthlessly cynical about his/her predicament, but this awareness only strengthens his/her commitment – this is the political version of Tertullian's *credo qua absurdum est*.

Most of us know well the culminating moment of *A Few Good Men* (Rob Reiner, 1992), when Tom Cruise addresses Jack Nicholson with "I want the truth!", and Nicholson shouts back: "You can't handle the truth!" This reply is more ambiguous than it may appear: it should not be taken as simply claiming that most of us are too weak to handle the brutal reality of things. We have to get rid of the metaphor of the Real as the hard core of reality (the way things "really are in themselves") accessible to us only through multiple lenses of how we symbolise reality, of how we construct it through our fantasies and cognitive biases. In the opposition between reality ("hard facts") and fantasies (illusions, symbolic constructs), the Real is on the side of illusions and fantasies: the Real, of course, by definition resists full symbolisation, but it is at the same time an excess generated by the process of symbolisation itself. Without symbolisation, there is no Real, there is just a flat stupidity of what is there. Another (perhaps the ultimate) example: if someone were to ask a witness about the truth of the holocaust, and the witness were to reply "You can't handle the truth!", this should not be understood as a simple claim that most of us are not able the process the horror of holocaust. At a deeper level, those who were not able to handle the truth were the Nazi perpetrators themselves: they were not able to handle the truth that their society is traversed by an all-encompassing antagonism, and to avoid this insight they engaged in the murdering spray that targeted the Jews, as if killing the Jews would re-establish a harmonious social body. What nonetheless complicates the things even more is that the "truth" evoked by Nicholson is not simply the reality of how things stand but a more precise fact that our power (not just the military) has to follow illegal unwritten rules and practices (the "Code Red" in the film) to sustain its legal system – this is the truth soft liberals are not able to handle.

We are thereby touching the delicate topic of the relationship between truth and lie. A rather boring sexual joke nonetheless concludes with an interesting final spin. A wife asks her husband to run to a nearby drugstore to buy her a package of cigarettes. He goes there, but since it is already late evening, the store is closed, so he goes to a nearby bar to get a package. A voluptuous young woman is serving at the bar, they get into a flirting conversation and end up in a bed in her nearby apartment. After a couple of hours of passionate love making, he begins to worry how he will explain his long absence to his wife; then he gets an idea – he asks the woman if she has some baby powder, and rubs it into his hands. When he arrives home, the wife is furiously awaiting him and asks where he was; he replies: "The drugstore was already closed, so I went to a nearby bar to get the package. I got into a flirting conversation with a voluptuous young woman who was serving at the bar, and we ended up in a bed in her nearby apartment. After a couple of hours of passionate love, I finally returned home..." "You dirty liar!" interrupts him the wife: "You think I didn't notice the powder on your hands! You did what you wanted for a long time but I prohibited it, you went to a night session of bowling with your friends!" This is a correct Hegelian reversal: when one is in a situation where even an outright lie will not be convincing, one should tell the truth and create conditions which will guarantee that the truth itself will be perceived as a lie...

Adrian Johnston addresses precisely this concoction of truth and lies in his question: "Is atheism condemned to remaining eternally, in Hegelian terms, a determinate negation of Christianity – and, hence, permanently dependent or parasitic upon what it negates? Can one move from sublating (as *Aufhebung*) religion to finally outright negating it? Is Judeo-Christian monotheism the disposable ladder of a thoroughly historical possibility condition for atheism? Or, is it an indispensable logical necessity for making possible all future atheisms?"[2] The answer to this question should be a resounding YES: atheism cannot stand on its own, a detour through religion is necessary – not only religion as such, but specifically Christianity is indispensable. If we throw away the ladder, we lose the thing itself which we arrived to through this ladder. This is why, in contrast to Freud for whom religiosity is a curable symptom, for Jacques Lacan it is an incurable *sinthome*.

So why is the detour through Christianity indispensable? Lacan said that "the Holy Spirit is a notion infinitely less stupid than that of the subject supposed to know"[3] – why? Because the Holy Spirit does not have to rely on a subject-supposed-to-know: it can function as the immanent community (the protestant *Gemeinde*) which already is what its members are looking for or devoted to. Chiesa writes: "Christianity transforms such a structural oscillation into a static dogma, that is, the neat separation between the abjection of our world and the perfection of the world to come that will have redeemed it". However, what if we read the return of Christ as something that already takes place in the Holy Spirit (the community of believers)

10 Philosophy After Lacan

which takes place in this earthly abject world? There is no oscillation here, Holy Spirit is an event which just changes the entire constellation.

Such a role of the Holy Spirit affects the identity of God himself. Lacan asserts that "God does not believe in God", and he immediately spells out the implications of this claim by way of equating "God does not believe in God" with "There is something (of the) unconscious (*y a d'l'inconscient*)".[4] The move we have to accomplish here is thus the move from our doubt about God to God doubting his own divine status, not believing in himself as God. But where is his non-belief located? Does God consciously doubts his own divinity? This would have meant that we assert a substantial unconscious God whose existence is too deep even for his own consciousness. So we should rather assert the opposite: God cannot consciously doubt himself, he has to believe he is God, it is unconsciously that he doesn't believe in himself (or, more precisely, that he knows he is not a God).

This tension in God himself complicates the status of the divine prohibition – to quote Chiesa: "for Freud, if the Father of the horde is dead, then nothing is permitted anymore, since he is turned into God; however, if God is dead, then everything is potentially permitted, at least in the direction of the species' collective self-annihilation". However, the God who prohibits everything is NOT the God of the real (parallel to the primordial Father) but precisely the symbolic dead god. When god is proclaimed dead, he returns in a whole series of pseudo-atheist shapes in which permissiveness itself is ultra-regulated – just recall how the Political Correctness imposes numerous prohibitions and regulations to guarantee our sexual freedom… This is why, when Lacan says that "we can do without [God] provided that we use [Him]",[5] this claim is also open to two opposite readings: a cynical one and an authentically-ethical one. It can mean: we know there is no God but we manipulatively "use" him as a spectre which enables our peaceful coexistence. Or it can mean: fully aware of the God's inexistence, we endorse this spectre as a Cause to which we commit our life.

What one should advocate is thus the materialist procedure of the immanent self-undermining of a religious edifice − the claim that god is evil or stupid can be much more unsettling than the claim that there is no god since the first claim destroys the very notion of divinity. Let's take *The Rapture* (1991, written and directed by Michael Tolkin) in which Mimi Rogers superbly plays Sharon, a young LA woman who works during the day as a phone operator endlessly repeating the same questions in a small cubicle among dozens of others, while in the evenings she engages in swinging orgies. Bored and dissatisfied at leading such an empty life, Sharon becomes a member of a sect which preaches that the end of times and the Rapture are imminent; turning into a passionate believer, she begins to practice a new, pious lifestyle, gets married to Randy, one of her previous swinging partners, and has a daughter Mary with him. Six years later, when Randy, now also a devoted Christian, is shot to death by a madman, this senseless catastrophe makes her and her daughter even more convinced that the Rapture is soon approaching. Sharon believes god told her to go with Mary to a nearby desert camping place and wait there until the two are taken into heaven where they will be united with Randy. Foster, a well-meaning, nonbelieving patrol officer, takes care of them there during their long wait when they run out of food. Mary gets impatient and proposes to her mother that they simply kill themselves in order to go to heaven and join Randy immediately. After a couple of weeks, Sharon also loses patience, decides to do the unspeakable and follows Mary's advice to stop her suffering; however, after shooting Mary, she is unable to take her own life afterwards, knowing that suicides are not allowed into heaven. She confesses her act to Foster who arrests her and takes her to a local jail...

Until this point, the story moves along "realist" lines, and one can easily imagine a possible "atheist" ending: bitter and alone, deprived of her faith, Sharon realises the horror of what she had committed, and is maybe saved by the good policeman. Here, however, events take a totally unexpected turn: in the jail cell, Rapture happens, literally, in all naivety, including bad special effects. First, deep in the night, Mary appears with two angels, and then, early in the morning, while Sharon sits in her cell, a loud trumpet blast is heard all around and announces a series of supranatural events − prison bars fall down, concrete walls fall apart, etc. Escaping from the jail, Sharon and Foster drive out into the desert, where signs of Rapture multiply, from dust storms up to the horsemen of the apocalypse running after and around the car. Next, Sharon and Foster are both "raptured", transported to a purgatory-like landscape where Mary approaches them from heaven and pleads with Sharon to accept god, to declare that she loves god − by just doing this she will be able to join Mary and Randy in heaven. Foster, although until now an atheist, quickly seizes the opportunity, says that he loves god and is allowed entrance to heaven, but Sharon refuses, saying that she cannot declare her love for a god who acted so cruelly towards her family for no reason at all. When Mary asks her if she knows for how long she will be confined to the purgatory, condemned to be there alone, Sharon replies: "Forever". Sharon's resistance to God, her refusal to declare her love for him, is thus an authentic ethical act. It would be totally wrong to say that she rejects the *false* god and that, in an authentically Christian version of the film, the true Christ should appear at the end, proclaim her a true believer precisely because she refused to declare that she loves the false god. The true temptation to be resisted is thus to declare our love for a god who doesn't deserve it *even if he is real*. For a vulgar materialist, all this cannot but appear as an empty mental experiment; however, for a true materialist, it is only in this way that we really renounce god − by way of renouncing him not only insofar as he doesn't really exist, but even if he is real. In short, the true formula of atheism is not "god doesn't exist" but "god not only doesn't exist, he is also stupid, indifferent, and maybe outright evil" − if we do not destroy the very fiction of god from within, it is easy for this fiction to prolong its hold over us in the form of disavowal ("I know there is no god, but he is nonetheless a noble and uplifting illusion"). Lacan's programmatic claim, in *Seminar X*, that "the atheist, as combatant, as revolutionary, is not one who denies God in his function of omnipotence, but one who affirms oneself as not *serving* any God"[6] fits perfectly this final gesture of the heroine in *Rapture*: even when she directly confronts the divine dimension, she refuses to serve him.

The song *The Night They Drove Old Dixie Down* (best known version by Joan Baez) is a first-person narrative relating the economic and social distress experienced by the protagonist, a poor white Southerner, during the last year of the American Civil War; it does not glorify slavery, the Confederacy, or Robert E. Lee, it rather tells the story of a poor, non-slave-holding Southerner who tries to make sense of the loss of his brother and his livelihood.[7] As such – as an attempt to render the experience of a poor white man sympathetic to the Southern cause but dismayed at the horror of his suffering for the interests of the rich slave owners – it is much more effective in dismantling this cause than a direct abolitionist critique, in exactly the same way as endorsing a religion but then demonstrating how its God is evil/ stupid is much more effective than a direct atheist critique. But does this mean that this detour through religion is just epistemological, owing to the limitation of our knowledge, or does it also refer to God himself? Chiesa opposes Lacan when the latter allegedly "insinuates" (Chiesa's strong word) that "the truth of incompleteness can only be half-said, *but* the not-One really *is* all there is, the problem is simply we cannot *say* it":

> such a blind reliance on an ultimate ontological not-Oneness supposedly obfuscated by the finitude of our linguistic-logical condition only reinforces weak atheism through the very endeavor to defuse it. If, beyond the wall of language, and the illusory fabrications of the One it gives rise to, the not-One is *all* there is, then this *a fortiori* requires the deceiving God, one who is now being specified as not only deceiving us but also, *extra*-linguistically, the whole of Creation – as still seen from an *intra*-linguistic perspective (Lacan's).

The basic thrust of Chiesa's argumentation is accurate: the position he rejects is the one of naively opposing our perspectives on reality-in-itself to the (not-One) reality out there, beyond our walls of language. Chiesa correctly points out that the position of enunciation of such a claim exempts itself from reality, as if the speaker can elevate itself into the One who can compare reality with our limited visions of it. This means that the speaker regresses into general ontology, an all-encompassing vision of reality. However, does the fact that we don't have an access to general ontology beyond our historically-specified transcendental horizons really compel us to leave the possibility open that not-One is Not "all there is", that there may be a divine transcendent entity above/beyond it? This is also why I find problematic Chiesa's claim that "what science should instead seriously consider as modern physics is the *hypothesis* that 'the real is not everything', or better, that *the real not-all is itself not necessarily all there is – although it might well be*" – problematic because, for Lacan, "not-all" means precisely a multiplicity which, since it cannot be totalised, allows for no exception: "not-all" means that, since it is never all, there is no exception to it. In other words, Chiesa regresses here to the commonsense notion of the real "not all" as "not everything there is" – he regresses to the Kantian notion of a possible unknown In-itself beyond the sphere of phenomena.

My Hegelian solution is here that there is a crack in reality which makes it non-totalisable, "not-all", but everything that we project beyond this gap is our fantasy formation. The only way to avoid agnostic scepticism is to transpose this gap into reality itself: the gap we are talking about is not the gap that separates reality-in-itself from our approaches to it but an impossibility which gapes in the heart of reality itself. Let me quote here again the well-known passage from the "Foreword" to his *Phenomenology of Spirit* where Hegel provides the most elementary formula of what does it mean to conceive Substance also as Subject:

> The disparity which exists in consciousness between the I and the substance which is its object is the distinction between them, the *negative* in general. This can be regarded as the *defect* of both, though it is their soul, or that which moves them. That is why some of the ancients conceived the *void* as the principle of motion, for they rightly saw the moving principle as the *negative*, though they did not as yet grasp that the negative is the self. Now, although this negative appears at first as a disparity between the I and its object, it is just a much a disparity of the substance with itself. Thus what seems to happen outside of it, to be an activity directed against it, is really its own doing, and substance shows itself to be essentially subject.[8]

We should be very precise here: this in no way implies that there is nothing beyond the phenomena accessible to us – of course there is an infinity of entities and processes we haven't yet discovered, but they are not "transcendent" in the sense of an In-itself beyond the phenomenal sphere. Our claim is that when we will discover new aspects of reality up to alien lives, we will not cross the boundary of impossibility that constitutes our reality. We will not discover God or anything of this order because such figures are a priori, constitutively, or (as Hegel would have put it) in their very notion, fantasy formations destined to fill in a gap – as Hegel put it long ago, "behind the so-called curtain, which is supposed to hide what is inner, there is nothing to be seen unless we ourselves go behind it".[9] So yes, our epistemological uncertainty is irreducible, but whatever awaits us "out there" is NOT anything resembling our figures of "God" – to bring this point to extreme, even if we'll eventually encounter something whose features appear to us "divine", this will NOT be what we call "God".

But does Chiesa's insistence on agnosticism not rely on his doubt in the possibility of our full scientific self-objectivisation? Thomas Metzinger[10] agrees with him, but he sees this as a limit of our self-experience: we cannot help experiencing ourselves as "selves", i.e., it is impossible for us to phenomenologically imagine a selfless experience: one can know (in the purely epistemic sense of objective knowledge) that there is no substantial Self (this is what Metzinger develops in his PSM theory of subjectivity), but *"you cannot believe in it"*:

"The PSM is a theory of which *you cannot be convinced*, in principle.... . This fact is the true essence and the deepest core of what we *actually* mean when speaking about the "puzzle" – or sometimes even about the "mystery" – of consciousness.... . If the current story is true, there is no way in which it could be intuitively true".[11]

However, Metzinger goes a step further here: there is one caveat that he allows, the Buddhist Enlightenment in which the Self directly-experientially assumes his own non-being, i.e., recognises himself as a "simulated self", a representational fiction. Such a situation in which the phenomenal dream becomes *lucid to itself* "directly corresponds to a classical philosophical notion, well-developed in Asian philosophy at least 2500 years ago, namely, the Buddhist conception of 'enlightenment'".[12] Such an enlightened awareness is no longer self-awareness: it is no longer I who experience myself as the agent of my thoughts, "my" awareness is the direct awareness of a self-less system, a self-less knowledge. In short, there effectively *is* a link, or at least a kind of asymptotic point of coincidence, between the radical brain-sciences position and the Buddhist idea of an-atman, of the Self's inexistence: the Buddhist subjective stance of "anatman" is the only subjective stance which really assumes the result of cognitivism (no Self), and which (in certain versions, at least) is fully compatible with radical scientific naturalism.

What should interest us here is the link between purely biochemical processes (attacking our brains with so-called "psychedelic" substances) and the highest spiritual "inner" experience uncannily close to what Lacan designated as "subjective destitution", the disintegration of the fundamental fantasy which sustains our ego – we can biochemically cause the death of our ego. People who are doing this are as a rule attacking their depression, hoping to reinvent themselves completely – or, as Rorick put it: "Ego death can be really humbling and really important for some people, there's some people that need to have their egos killed; but at the same time, it's a scary thing to go through". He's had friends who have experienced ego death and never returned to drug use – they just needed drugs as a powerful tool for subjective change.[13] It is all too easy to try and distinguish such biochemical "death of the ego" with the "authentic" subjective change caused by symbolic work. But there is a limit to this biochemical procedure: it just brusquely erases the symbolic network the subject relies upon without "working through" it and made it implode from within, i.e., without making the subject confront its antagonisms, its points of impossibility – a nice paradox of how a direct intervention into the biogenetic Real serves as a way to avoid confronting the Real immanent to the symbolic order itself.

And this holds even for traumatic events like the Holocaust: any prosaic description of the horrors of holocaust fails to render its trauma, and this is why Adorno was wrong with his famous claim that after Auschwitz poetry is no longer possible: it is prose which is no longer possible, since only poetry can do the job. Poetry is the inscription of impossibility into a language: when we cannot say something directly and we nonetheless insist in doing it, we unavoidably get caught in repetitions, postponements, indirectness, surprising cuts, etc. We should always bear in mind that the "beauty" of classic poetry (symmetric rhymes, etc.) comes second, that it is a way to compensate for the basic failure or impossibility.

Does then the Buddhist meditation, interpreted in Metzinger's sense, enable us to evade this basic failure or impossibility? I think it doesn't – why not? This brings us back to our topic of mediation and indirectness: Buddhism's goal is nothing less than to circumvent every form of symbolic mediation/indirectness and rejoin the pre-symbolic flow of the real. I'll try to make this clear by way of a belated reply to my critics. In the last decades, critiques of my reading of Buddhism abound – even those who are otherwise sympathetic to my general approach claim that I miss the point when I target Buddhism. Representative of my critics is "Nagarjuna and ecophilosophy" by Adrian J. Ivakhiv[14] who also relies on John Clark's "On Being None With Nature: Nagarjuna and the Ecology of Emptiness"[15]. Ivakhiv's starting point is the core Buddhist concept of "dependent origination": every identity is process-relational position, which means that, say, a tree's existence as a unitary object, as opposed to a collection of cells, is conventional: "Removing its properties leaves no core bearer behind". In other words, "the thing we call a 'tree' is, as Buddhists say, empty of inherent self-existence; its essence is nothing other than the properties and conditions of its self-manifesting".[16] This goes against Graham Harman's (and others') argument that there is something more to any object than its properties, relations and conditions. For Buddhism, there is nothing (no-thing) left over. "But that is not to say that there is, in fact, *nothing*... There is the process-relational flux of what Clark calls "nature naturing", the continual coming into existence and passing away of the experiential bits of the world, all of which is quite real".[17] What this implies is that the "negative" and "deconstructive" project that Nagarjuna is best known for "goes hand in hand with an affirmative, 'reality-based' project of the sort that, in current continental philosophy, is best represented by Deleuze" – or, to quote Clark:

> For Buddhism the negative path of the destruction of illusion is inseparably linked to the positive path of an open, awakened, and compassionate response to a living, non-objectifiable reality, the 'nature that is no nature.'

This brings us to what I see as the central challenge for Buddhism: how do we, humans, get caught into "a dream world of illusory, deceptively permanent objects and egos, and a futile quest to defend the ego and dominate reality"? Is it enough to say that this is a "fundamental human predicament", i.e., a trans-historical invariant? Clark makes here a surprising move into a Marxist direction:

> Where most analyses (including most Buddhist analyses) of egocentric consciousness and the egoic flight from the trauma of lack stop short is in failing to investigate the social and historical roots of these phenomena. We must understand that the ego is not only a psychological and epistemological construct, *but also a historical one.* Its roots are to be found in the development of large-scale agrarian society and regimented labor, the rise of the state and ancient despotism, the emergence of economic class and acquisitive values, the triumph of patriarchy and warrior mentality – in short, in the evolution of the ancient system of social domination and the domination of nature. To put it in Buddhist terms, our true karmic burden, both personally and collectively, is our profound historicity and our deep materiality.[18]

But the question remains: how far can we go in this direction of historicity? Were individuals in pre-class societies dwelling in a "living, non-objectifiable reality, the 'nature that is no nature'", and should the possible post-capitalist society also be conceived as a liberation from the "wheel of desire"? Another question lurks beneath this one: "Why should the destruction of illusion lead to compassion rather than to cynicism as it often seems to in everyday life, or to social conservatism as it has in the case of Humean and other forms of philosophical skepticism?"[19] I think that, in spite of all desperate attempts to demonstrate that the way to Buddhist enlightenment goes through modesty and compassion, the only honest answer is that of D.T.Suzuki: Zen is a technique of meditation which is compatible with any political orientation, liberalism, fascism, Communism...

This brings us back to me and to the Buddhist critique of my work. For Ivakhiv, this is the point where Buddhism meets psychoanalysis: "The key difference between Freud/Lacan/Žižek/et al. and Nagarjuna is that the former presuppose that this /rise of dominating ego/ is unavoidable – the best we can do is to come to terms with the ego (etc.) process and try not to get too caught up in the delusional tricks it plays on us".[20] This is why my work totally ignores "the real potential of actually reading Western

Buddhism not just in light of Lacan, but the teachings of the Buddha and their lineage".[21] This "real potential" is, of course, the affirmation of the flux of positive life – Ivakhiv introduces it by way of a long quote from D.T. Suzuki:

> D.T. Suzuki, whom Žižek has probably never read[22], a trained Zen Buddhist, as well as professor of Buddhist philosophy and delightfully fluent writer and speaker of English, echoes Vajjiya when he writes about Zen as life as 'absolute affirmation': 'we live in affirmation and not in negation, for life is affirmation itself; and this affirmation must not be the one accompanied or conditioned by a negation, such an affirmation is relative and not at all absolute. With such an affirmation life loses its creative originality and turns into a mechanical process grinding forth nothing but soulless flesh and bones. To be free, life must be an absolute affirmation ... Zen does not mean a mere escape from intellectual imprisonment, which sometimes ends in sheer wantonness. There is something in Zen that frees us from conditions and at the same time gives us a certain firm foothold ... Zen abhors repetition or imitation of any kind, for it kills. For the same reason, Zen never explains but only affirms. Life is fact and no explanation is necessary or pertinent. To explain is to apologise and why should we apologise for living? To live – is that not enough? Let us then live, let us affirm. Herein lies Zen in all its purity and in all its nudity as well'.
>
> (An Introduction to Zen Buddhism)[23]

Ivakhiv's "Lacanian" reading (supplemented by a critique of Lacan) is obvious here: far from advocating a renunciation to our desires, Buddha "is suggesting that staying true to our desire will yield the satisfaction of that (and all) desire, whereas Lacan is less interested in what it would mean to satisfy our desire, if it is once we have properly identified it". How can this be? Ivakhiv introduces here sexual difference: he interprets (what Lacan calls) the impossibility of the sexual relationship as the impossibility to reach the goal of the masculine phallic subject which is to swallow/dominate entire reality; from this phallic standpoint, Buddhism:

> appears as a fantasmic spectre in the West, where masculine jouissance is predominant. Buddhism at once promises and threatens with the Other, dark, feminine jouissance. Buddhism is only conceivable in what Žižek might call the Western ideological matrix as this testament to its very failure to be conceived. Žižek's critique of Western Buddhism, therefore, has much less to do with the teachings of the Buddha than he has made it seem, and significantly more to do with the mystical, feminine *jouissance* it suggests, which seems to be beyond and for that reason threatening to Žižek.[24]

18 Philosophy After Lacan

But is this equation of the Buddhist enlightenment with the assertion of the mystical feminine *jouissance* not totally unfounded? Chiesa convincingly characterises it as "an *inverted mysticism*":

"Unlike Eastern polytheisms and their stress on enjoyment, Buddhism is thus in this sense a religion of desire, but it organises it in a way that is very different from that of Judeo-Christianity. More precisely, Buddhism short-circuits 'all the variations of desire' (as poly-desire, we might add), which appear in it ,in a most incarnate fashion, 'with the ,ultimate apprehension of the radically illusory character of all desire'".[25]

The formula of Buddhism would thus be: not the mystical "one with the world" (my immersion into the divine One bringing full enjoyment) but the "none with the world": I identify the void of my (in)existence, the nothing-ness of my Self, with the void of reality itself which lacks any substantial (id) entity. While mysticism aims at the subject's full immersion into the divine *jouissance*, Buddhism focuses on desire as the ultimate cause of our suffering: desire is inconsistent, it cannot ever be fulfilled, fully satisfied, because its nature is inconsistent – since its object is illusory, the false appearance of a void, the moment of desire's fulfillment is the moment of its defeat. Bud-dhism draws the radical consequence from this insight: the only way to avoid suffering is to step out of (gain a distance towards) the "wheel of desire", to avoid attachment to any object of desire, which means to accept (not only as a theoretical statement but also as an existential stance) that desires are illu-sory because all objects (of desire and in general) are non-substantial fluctu-ating appearances. Such an existential detachment is the only way for us to attain peace.

The key question that arises here is, of course: so where does desire come from? How do we get caught into its illusion? Desire cannot be accounted for in the terms of the opposition between reified particular objects and the void beneath them, so that it arises when we get excessively attached to particular objects. The object-cause of desire (what Lacan calls *objet a*) is not an empirical object, it is a virtual element which disturbs the harmonious nat-ural circuit described and celebrated by my Buddhist critics. So the vision, advocated by my critics, of a desire purified of its excess, is for Lacan totally illusory: desire is in itself a "pathological" excess, a de-stabilisation of any balanced natural order. Suzuki seems to imply that what makes a desire mortifying is its "intellectualisation", its submission to rational categories that reify the fluid life experience of reality into a world of fixed substantial objects. However, desire is at its most basic not an effect of mechanic intel-lectual imprisonment, it is a "deviation" inscribed into life itself. In other words, if we subtract desire from life we don't get a more balanced life, we lose life itself. To put it succinctly: Buddhism celebrates the stepping out of the "wheel of desire", while Lacan celebrates the subject's very fall into this "wheel": "not compromising one's desire" means a radical subjective engagement in a crazy desire which throws entire reality out of balance.

Or, to put it in yet another way, Buddhism accepts the common view that the purpose of life is happiness (to quote Dalai Lama, "the purpose of our lives is to be happy"), it just defines this term differently – here are a couple of statements by Dalai Lama which make this difference clear: "Happiness is not something readymade. It comes from your own actions". / "When we feel love and kindness toward others, it not only makes others feel loved and cared for, but it helps us also to develop inner happiness and peace". / "We don't need more money, we don't need greater success or fame, we don't need the perfect body or even the perfect mate. Right now, at this very moment, we have a mind, which is all the basic equipment we need to achieve complete happiness". / "Human happiness and human satisfaction most ultimately come from within oneself".[26] Following Freud, Lacan, on the contrary, asserts death drive as the basic component of our libidinal lives which operate beyond the pleasure-principle: what Lacan calls enjoyment (*jouissance*) emerges out of a self-sabotage of pleasure, it is an enjoyment in displeasure itself.

A Lacanian view is much closer to dr. House who, in one of the episodes of the series, when he tries to diagnosticise a patient with his group and one of his collaborators mentions that the patient radiates happiness, immediately adds "happiness" on a list of the patient's symptoms of his illness to be explained and abolished. The feeling of happiness is a dangerous symptom, not something we should strive for. And one should add here that the same goes for what is also considered the most spontaneous parental feeling: the immense love of one's own small child. Small children are horror embodied: stupid, annoying, smelling bad, breaking our sleep... so the feeling of love for them is a clear case of what is called the "Stockholm syndrome": a coping mechanism to a captive or abusive situation, when people develop positive feelings toward their captors or abusers over time. Isn't this the exact mechanism of how we cope with small children?

So what about the desperate Lacano-Buddhist attempt to read what Buddhism calls nirvana as grounded in what Lacan calls "traversing the fantasy"? We cannot simply dismiss it as a gross misunderstanding of Lacan because there is a grain of truth in it: desire is metonymic – every empirical positive object that we desire is a trap (in the sense that, if we get it, our desire is not fully satisfied but disappointed, we experience a *"ce n'est pas ça"* (this is not *that* what we really desired), so let's drop our attachment to particular objects and just persist surfing along from one object to another. In other words, a true betrayal of our desire is precisely our full attachment to a particular object as its true object – if we renounce this, if we maintain a distance towards every object, we attain peace, we are faithful to our desire, i.e., to the void in its heart which cannot be abolished by any object... But this logic ultimately fails: for Lacan, desire in its "purity" (considered without an empirical object of desire) cannot be transformed into a peaceful integration into a non-substantial changing multiplicity of our reality because desire is as

20 Philosophy After Lacan

such a gesture of breaking up the balance of reality. If we subtract particular objects, we get the gesture of breaking-up, of disturbing the balance, as such. What any particular empirical object of desire obfuscates is not the balance of a void but this negative gesture as such: any particular object particularises this rupture as such, transforming it into a desire for something that positively exists as a particular object... But where is here the dimension of intersubjectivity? In her "Relational Dharma", Jeannine A. Davies deploys a "liberating model of intersubjectivity" – her starting point is the basic goal of practicing dharma, which is:

> to discern the distinction between conventional and ultimate realities through direct experience. A simple example of the distinction between conventional and ultimate reality is the difference between the concept of water and the physical sensation of water. Its salient characteristics are of wetness and of a cool, warm, or hot temperature. As awareness discriminates between the concept of water and water's physical sensations, an insightful penetration into the nature of conceptual ideation occurs. Concepts are then seen as abstractions within consciousness, mental overlays born through prior conditioning.[27]

Davies, of course, has to concede that the practice of meditation is primarily focused on solitary, introspective methods, where stages of insight unfold within a climate of extreme mental seclusion and interpersonal isolation – her aim is to demonstrate how dharma can also be achieved through new practice of social interaction. In order to deploy this claim, she has to engage in the opposition between two main orientations of Buddhism, Mahayana and Theravada: Theravada concentrates on achieving dharma by means of individual practice of introspection, while Mahayana emphasises dharma achieved by social interaction. Say, when an individual is afflicted by a trauma which threatens to destroy her/his psychic balance and ability to interact with others, Mahayana practices the Relational Dharma approach, which:

> mediates and attunes within an environment of empathic union, nourishing an atmosphere that assuages anxiety and facilitates the generation of trust and safety to flow in the in-between. This process allows for the possibility of transforming negative or life-diminishing 'filters' into associations that widen and deepen identity. In this experience, the appearance of something 'foreign,' 'not part of,' or 'too much,' is relaxed, so that one's sense of what constitutes a 'whole person' naturally broadens and evolves, and a deeper understanding of oneself and the relationship between oneself and others emerges.[28]

In such an approach, one achieves "the inner liberty to feel another's suffering as inseparable to one's own and the compassion to seek to alleviate it, thus respecting the freedom of others as inseparable to one's own freedom", a freedom to "forgive others for their transgressions. In order to forgive, the ability to 'step back' and recognise the conditions that gave rise to his or her actions versus reacting from a place of personalising these actions, must be developed. As awareness into the causal relationships that led this individual to be wounded and act in a harmful ways becomes recognised, relational objectivity emerges and compassion becomes possible".[29] Such a stance opens up a path to peacefully revolutionise our world beset by violence and non-sustainable action. Our

> insight into the conscious engagement of interrelatedness may be one of the most important in terms of its spiritual, social, and political implications. It is only when we see with greater clarity the intimate causation of how 'we,' citizens of the Whole, affect totality that we find the inspiration to take personal responsibility for our presence and fine tune our physiological, emotional, and physical resonance within the Whole.[30]

Suffering and obstacles to freedom do not simply vanish, they are not simply left behind; in an almost Hegelian way, they are re-experienced as vehicles for growth and freedom. They are deprived of their substantial identity and put in their relational context in which they arise and disappear in co-dependence, resonating within the Whole.

Another difference between Theravada and Mahayana concerns the accessibility of nirvana which makes the subject a bodhisattva: in Theravada, encountering somebody who already is a Buddha is needed to truly make someone a bodhisattva – any other resolution to attain Buddhahood may easily be forgotten or abandoned during the long time ahead. Theravada thus held that the bodhisattva path was only for a rare set of individuals and has to be transmitted through exclusive lineage, in contrast to Mahayanists who universalised the *bodhisattvayana* as a path which is open to everyone and is taught for all beings to follow.

To maintain this universality, the Mahayana tradition has to introduce a distinction between two different notions of a bodhisattva's relationship to nirvana. The basic goal is to become arhat ("the one who is worthy"), a perfected person, one who has gained insight into the true nature of existence and has achieved nirvana (spiritual enlightenment): the arhat, having freed himself from the bonds of desire, will not be reborn. While the state of an arhat is considered in the Theravada tradition to be the proper goal of a Buddhist, Mahayana adds to it an even higher level:

> a kind of non-dual state in which one is neither limited to samsara nor nirvana. A being who has reached this kind of nirvana is not restricted

from manifesting in the samsaric realms, and yet they remain fully detached from the defilements found in these realms (and thus they can help others).[31]

We thus obtain the distinction between two kinds of nirvāṇa: the nirvāna (Buddhism)"nirvāṇa of an arhat and a superior type of nirvāṇa called apratiṣṭhita (non-abiding) that allows a Buddha to remain engaged in the samsaric realms without being affected by them. However, the predominant Mahayana notion of bodhisattva silently concedes that to arrive at such non-dual state is practically impossible, so he heroically sacrifices his own dharma and postpones his awakening until all living beings will be liberated – bodhisattvas take the following vow: "I shall not enter into final nirvana before all beings have been liberated", or "I must lead all beings to Liberation. I will stay here till the end, even for the sake of one living soul".

The bodhisattva who wants to reach Buddhahood for the sake of all beings, is more loving and compassionate than the sravaka (who only wishes to end their own suffering): he practices the path for the good of others (*par-ārtha*) while the sravakas do so for their own good (*sv-ārtha*). I find this distinction between *par-ārtha* and *sv-ārtha* potentially very dangerous: although Mahayana appears more "democratic", allowing everyone to attain dharma, does its notion of bodhisattva who refuses to enter nirvana not conceal a new form of elitism: a selected few who remain caught into our ordinary reality (in the wheel of desire), legitimise their special privileged position by the fact that they could have reached nirvana but postponed it to help all others to reach it. In some radical sense nirvana thus becomes impossible: if I reach it, I act as an egotist, caring only for my own good; if I act for the good of others, I postpone my entry into nirvana... I consider this privileged position dangerous because it remains caught in a dualism that authentic Buddhism promises to leave behind: the realm of nirvana becomes a Beyond which we strive to reach. The danger resides in the fact that this position relies on what one could call the basic syllogism of self-sacrifice: I want all living beings to overcome their suffering and achieve the supreme good; to do this, I have to sacrifice my own happiness and accept suffering – only in this way my own life has meaning... Again, the danger is that a short-circuit necessarily occurs here: I automatically take my own suffering as a proof that I am working for the good of others, so that I can reply to anyone who criticises me: "Can't you see my suffering? Who are you to criticize me when I sacrifice myself for you?" This is why the only authentic nirvana means that I fully remain in this world and just relate to it differently: "non-abiding" nirvana is the ONLY full and true nirvana. So where does even this authentic nirvana fail?

Buddhism ignores the radical intersubjectivity of desire, the fact that desire is always reflexive (a desire for desire, a desire for being desired) and that the primordial lacking object of desire is myself, the enigma of what I am for my others. What this means is that, as Hegel clearly saw it, domination of others and violence towards them is a key moment of the painful process of inter-subjective recognition. This violence is not an expression of my egotist self-interest, it relies on an "evil" for which I am ready to put at risk my own welfare and even my life. Relational dharma is not enough to account for this "evil" since this dimension of "evil" is constitutive of how I experience an Other: as an impenetrable abyss which cannot be dissolved in a fluid network of appearances. At is most basic, "evil" has nothing to do with my egotist interests: it is more spiritual than simple self-interest – the Buddhist notion of samsara ("the wheel of desire") ignores this spiritual aspect of "evil".

This is where the already-quoted passage about the "key difference between Freud/Lacan/Žižek/et al. and Nagarjuna" – "the former presuppose that this /rise of dominating ego/ is unavoidable – the best we can do is to come to terms with the ego (etc.) process and try not to get too caught up in the delusional tricks it plays on us"[32] – totally misses the point: Buddhism describes how we can gradually get rid of the egotist stance of domination over others and of being enslaved to our desires which both cause suffering; our goal is to reach dharma in which our ego dissolves in the flux of appearances and loses its substantial identity. Within this space, Freud and Lacan can only appear as going half-way: they clearly see the self-destructive nature of the dominating Ego, but they ignore that there is a domain beyond the ego and its paradoxes, the domain of inner peace and happiness, so their ultimate reach is to escribe the paradoxes of the ego. For Freud and Lacan, on the contrary, there is nothing beyond the antagonisms of our reality, nothing but a gap of impossibility that thwarts it from within: everything that we perceive as its Beyond we project it there. What this means is not that what Buddhists describe as nirvana or dharma is an illusion or a fake: it is a profound experience of subjective destitution, but it nonetheless functions as the obfuscation of a more radical experience of a gap out of which our reality appears.

Since dharma is as a rule described as the highest freedom accessible to us, one should point out that, to anyone who knows a little bit about Hegel, the radical opposition between the Buddhist and Hegel's notion of freedom cannot but strike the eye: for Buddhism, we are truly free when we liberate ourselves from the rational categories which cut into pieces and thus mortify the pure non-substantial flux of reality, while for Hegel, the basic form of freedom is precisely the infinite power of abstraction that pertains to our Understanding (not Reason), the power to interrupt the smooth flow of reality and to cut mechanically reality into it species. The very idea that there is something (the core of the substantial content of the analysed thing) which eludes Understanding, a trans-rational Beyond out of its reach, is the fundamental illusion of Understanding. In other words, all we have to do to get from Understanding to Reason is to *subtract* from Understanding its

24   Philosophy After Lacan

constitutive illusion – Understanding is not too abstract/violent, it is, on the contrary, as Hegel put it apropos of Kant, *too soft towards things*, afraid to locate its violent movement of tearing things apart into things themselves. In a way, it is epistemology versus ontology: the illusion of Understanding is that its own analytic power – the power to make "an accident as such – that what is bound and held by something else and actual only by being connected with it – obtain an existence all its own, gain freedom and independence on its own account" – is only an "abstraction", something external to "true reality" which persists out there intact in its inaccessible fullness. In other words, it is the standard critical view of Understanding and its power of abstraction (that it is just an impotent intellectual exercise missing the wealth of reality) which contains the core illusion of Understanding. To put it in yet another way, the mistake of Understanding is to perceive its own negative activity (of separating, tearing things apart) only in its negative aspect, ignoring its "positive" (productive) aspect – Reason is Understanding itself in its productive aspect.

The common counter-argument is here: but is for Hegel such mortifying abstraction not just a negative moment followed by a notional mediation by means of which we return to a higher form of organic unity? Yes, but this higher organic unity in no way returns to the reality of direct experience: in it, any reference to direct experience is obliterated, we move entirely within notional self-mediation. This doesn't mean that Hegel does not allow for something that echoes the practice of meditation which (within Theravada Buddhism) "has primarily focused on solitary, introspective methods, where stages of insight unfold within a climate of extreme mental seclusion and interpersonal isolation". However, while, in Buddhism, through such practice the mind "experiences a kind of current of quiet peace", for Hegel introspection confronts us with an awful space in which ghastly apparitions of partial objects float around – here is his most famous and often quoted passage of this "night of the world":

> The human being is this night, this empty nothing that contains everything in its simplicity – an unending wealth of many representations, images, of which none belongs to him – or which are not present. This night, the interior of nature, that exists here – pure self – in phantasmagorical representations, is night all around it, in which here shoots a bloody head – there another white ghastly apparition, suddenly here before it, and just so disappears. One catches sight of this night when one looks human beings in the eye – into a night that becomes awful.[33]

One should not be blinded by the poetic power of this description, but read it precisely. The first thing to note is how the objects which freely float around in this "night of the world" are *membra disjecta*, partial objects, objects detached from their organic Whole – is there not a strange echo between this passage and Hegel's description of the negative power of Understanding which is able to abstract an entity (a process, a property) from its substantial context and treat it as if it has an existence of its own? "That an accident as such, detached from what circumscribes it, what is bound and is actual only in its context with others, should attain an existence of its own and a separate freedom – this is the tremendous power of the negative".[34] It is thus as if, in the ghastly scenery of the "night of the world", we encounter something like *the power of Understanding in its natural state,* spirit in the guise of a *proto-spirit* – this, perhaps, is the most precise definition of horror: when a higher state of development violently inscribes itself in the lower state, in its ground/presupposition, where it cannot but appear as a monstrous mess, a disintegration of order, a terrifying unnatural combination of natural elements. And Hegel's ultimate lesson is to learn to "tarry with the negative", not to dissolve its unbearable tensions into any kind of natural positive flux of appearances – in short, Hegel's ultimate lesson is that even the highest directness of the Absolute is a retroactive product of its mediation.

Notes

1 See Lorenzo Chiesa, "Psychoanalysis and Agnostic Atheism," in Lorenzo Chiesa and Adrian Johnston, *God Is Undead: Psychoanalysis Between Agnosticism and Atheism,* Evanston: Northwestern University Press, 2023 (to appear, quoted from the manuscript). All quotes from Chiesa are from this source.
2 See Adrian Johnston, "Modest Absolute," in op.cit. All quotes from Johnston are from this source.
3 *Le Séminaire de Jacques Lacan, Livre XV: L'acte psychanalytique,* session of February 21, 1968 (quoted from the manuscript).
4 Jacques Lacan, *Seminar XXI (The Non-Dupes Err),* the May 21, 1974 session (quoted from the manuscript).
5 *The Seminar of Jacques Lacan. Book XXIII: Le sinthome,* Paris: Editions du Seuil, forthcoming, p. 116.
6 *The Seminar of Jacques Lacan. Book X: Anxiety,* Cambridge: Polity Press, 2015, p. 309.
7 The Night They Drove Old Dixie Down (Wikipedia).
8 G.W.F. Hegel, *Phenomenology of Spirit,* Oxford: Oxford University Press 1977, p. 21.
9 PhG English GERMAN (marxists.org).
10 See Thomas Metzinger, *Being No One: The Self-Model Theory of Subjectivity,* Cambridge: The MIT Press, 2003.
11 Ibid., p. 627.
12 Ibid., p. 566.
13 Why more people are seeking out "ego death" via psychedelic drugs | Salon.com.
14 Nagarjuna, ecophilosophy, & the practice of liberation (uvm.edu), and Nagarjuna, ecophilosophy, pt. 2 (uvm.edu).
15 See "On Being None With Nature: Nagarjuna and the Ecology of Emptiness" | John Clark (Academia.edu).
16 Ivakhiv, op.cit.
17 Op.cit.
18 Clark, op.cit., p. 28.

26 Philosophy After Lacan

19 Ivakhiv, op.cit.
20 Op.cit.
21 Žižek's Western Buddhism (Redux) | And Now For Something Completely Different (wordpress.com).
22 Incidentally, I DID read Suzuki, not only in my youth (when he was a key point of reference of the hippie movement) but also later, when I learned that, in the 1930s and early 1940s, he fully supported Japanese war against China and elaborated how a Zen training can make individuals much better soldiers.
23 Ivakhiv, op.cit.
24 Op.cit.
25 Chiesa, op.cit. Quotes within the quote are from *The Seminar of Jacques Lacan. Book X: Anxiety*, Cambridge: Polity Press, 2016, p. 226.
26 Inspirational Quotes About Happiness From Dalai Lama (Lifehack).
27 Relational Dharma: a Modern Paradigm of Transformation − A Liberating Model of Intersubjectivity (DocsLib).
28 Op.cit.
29 Op.cit.
30 Op.cit.
31 Bodhisattva (Wikipedia).
32 Ivakhiv, op.cit.
33 G. W. F. Hegel, "Jenaer Realphilosophie," in *Frühe politische Systeme*, Frankfurt: Ullstein, 1974, p. 204; translation quoted from Donald Phillip Verene, *Hegel's Recollection*, Albany: Suny Press, 1985, pp. 7–8.
34 G.W.F. Hegel, Phenomenology of Spirit, p. 19.

Chapter 2

My Transference with Lacan as a Thinker

Sergio Benvenuto

There will be something spurious about what I will say here on the subject of Lacan and philosophy, because I practice as a psychoanalyst. This means that, unlike certain philosophers, I think I know how psychoanalytic concepts are constructed and used, I do not take them as *ready-to-wear* concepts. I am close to the philosophical movement that seeks the sense of concepts in the way they are produced. The true meaning of a concept is given by the form of life it expresses (Wittgenstein[1]).

I confess that I am quite dissatisfied – apart from a few exceptions – with philosophies that fully take up some of Lacan's concepts referred to as post-structuralist or as French Theory. Paradoxically, I find the *critical* analyses of both Freud and Lacan by philosophers ranging from Wittgenstein to Derrida, from Borch-Jacobsen to Nancy and Roustang, far more interesting. In short, I prefer to deconstruct Lacan rather than use him as an accomplished construction. This is because I have long since overcome transference towards Lacan, and transference – as he said himself – is based on the *sujet supposé savoir* [the subject supposed to know]. I do not suppose Lacan's knowledge, nor do I suppose Freud's. I do not take their doctrines to be revelations. My reading of these authors is *laïque*, lay, not ecclesiastical; there are no sacred texts involved.

I smile when I see philosophers taking as gospel every word psycho-analysts say, as if a clinical practice were enough to conceptualise the unconscious. It would be like saying that because a couple has given birth to several children, they have special knowledge about the biology of reproduction! Theorising a practice is an entirely different thing from the theory that describes a practice.

Too often we are seduced by the theoretical talent of certain thinkers – and Lacan's theoretical talent was remarkable – and believe that they ipso facto speak the truth. Aristotle's *Physics* is one of the most brilliant intellectual constructions in the history of thought, but today we think that it was rather the atomists who stated the truth about the structure of nature, even if we can find Aristotle cleverer than Democritus or Epicurus. The intellectual seductiveness of a theory does not guarantee its truthfulness. The music of

DOI: 10.4324/9781003425953-3

28 Philosophy After Lacan

concepts is not actual proof of truth. There is a deviation between truth and enjoyment.

Though I no longer have a transference towards Lacan, I do find some of his concepts extremely useful, not only for understanding analytic practice but also for formulating certain speculative problems acutely.

The Idealist Argument

Much of the 'Lacanian' philosophy that flourishes in the sheltered garden of university campuses leads Lacan back into the tradition of German idealism and of Marx. A Hegelian-Marxist-Freudian-Lacanian thought, from which I feel estranged, thrives today. In fact, Lacan was very much influenced by Kojève's seminars on Hegel in the 1930s, and his originality consists in having transferred what I would call the standard *idealist argument* to psychoanalysis.

This argument already began with bishop Berkeley, who intended to exclude matter from a philosophical ontology (and Lacan acknowledged his debt to Berkeley[2]). Berkeley said: our only contact with reality is through perceptions, we can therefore conclude, following Occam's conceptual economy of sorts, that reality is the totality of perceptions: *esse est percipi*. German idealism took up this argument in a much more sophisticated key: given that we always understand the world through concepts, we can conclude that we can see the world and its history as a dialectical set of concepts, themselves moments of a single *Geist*, spirit. This idealist argument is irrefutable. If someone, such as the Kantian philosopher Krug[3] says "how can I deduce the pen with which I am writing through a historical phenomenology of spirit?", the idealist will always have an easy time saying that Krug is talking about a pen because he already has the concept of a pen, without which he would not be able recognise that specific pen. And the pen is contingent because he already possesses the concept of contingency. In the end, everything is resolved in concepts, even pure chance.

Lacan thought of applying the following argument to psychoanalysis: psychoanalysis is always a logotherapy, i.e., it acts essentially through words. We can hence conclude that the unconscious itself is logos, discourse. Words have an impact on the unconscious because it is of the same stuff of which words are made. But, on the other hand, Lacan knows that the Freudian unconscious is not made up of concepts, it is something material, which can, for example, produce somatic effects. For him, therefore, the logos that counts is not the concepts but the signifiers, that is, the opaque, the material side of the concepts. The signifier, concretised as the *letter*, is an ambiguous entity, a centaur, which has something of the logos and something of thingness. Hence Lacan's physiognomic slogan: "The unconscious is structured as a language". Language replaces the Hegelian *Geist*.

Derrida criticised Lacanian theory as logocentric, which is another way of saying idealistic. Some also pointed out that not everything in language is structured. It is strongly structured at the two extremes of phonology and syntax[4]. In between we have the chaos of the lexicon, which Saussure had already put on the tab of diachronic linguistics and geographical linguistics. At the unstructured level of words and sounds, fluid processes operate in space and time. Two opposite categories dominate current thinking: system versus flows.

But what Lacan meant to say was: "the unconscious is as structured as a language is", hence not everything in language and not everything in the unconscious is structured. And here the problems begin. Lacan put the unstructured or weakly structured part of the unconscious on the tab of the *imaginary*. For him, the imaginary is the animal, i.e. non-*log*-ical, part of subjectivity; it is what properly concerns psychology. For Lacan, psychology is always animal psychology, even when it deals with humans.

"The unconscious is structured like a language" should therefore be taken in a weak, philosophical, sense: the unconscious is signification. And it is a non-analogue signification, it is essentially digital. Yet the logos introduces the negative and time into the world. How to put this in agreement with Freud's 'analogical' image of the unconscious, as something without negation and without time? The logic-isation of the unconscious leads to a reversal of original Freudianism.

In any case, I reject what most Lacanians ascribe to Lacan: having de-naturalised our relationship to the body and to the drives. For the simple reason that I have ceased to believe in the nature versus culture binarism, which amounts to their opposition. In my view, the distinction/opposition *nature* versus *nurture* is the modernist form of the old metaphysical opposition of matter versus spirit. In fact, culture is seen as a collectivisation of the spirit. I think it is time to finally overcome this opposition, and to think of culture as the non-deterministic unfolding of nature, and a part of nature as already fully penetrated by negation and time, inventions of the logos.

Today we de facto label as natural anything that resists our plans. If we try to teach a child mathematics, for example, and he absolutely refuses to learn it, then we simply give in and say that "the child has a natural learning deficit". But the symptom formed by the unconscious is precisely that which resists the subject's project, so in this sense we can consider the Freudian unconscious part of nature. Unless we completely abandon the nature/nurture opposition.

Towards the real

The fact that the idealist argument is irrefutable does not ipso facto imply that we must accept it. I personally do not. It is an argument that glorifies philosophical narcissism to the utmost, as it makes the real world appear entirely homogeneous to the philosopher's essential medium, which is language/thought. Idealism is the seductive professional bias of the philosopher, like that of a mason is to see the whole world as a construction (see Freemasonry) or like that of musician is to see the whole world as sound vibrations... Philosophers feel hurt when they have to admit that something is unthinkable and yet real. Rationalist philosophers assume that all the real is rational (the principle of sufficient reason, *nihil est sine ratione*, nothing is without a reason) and all the rational is real. They perceive an extra-rational real as the troublesome Gallic village of Asterix, which manages to evade the domination of the Roman empire. The empire of thought – the acme of which is philosophical – admits no pockets of resistance. It excludes the possibility of thinking that something is unthinkable, that we can say that something is unsayable. But to name the unsayable is not to say it... Just as being able to say "I shall die" does not at all mean to have defeated our death.

This does not mean that in rejecting idealism we must ipso facto return to a naive form of realism, whereby the effort of thought has to be that of describing the "real relations" between things outside ourselves. Relations are products of our systems of thought, particularly our languages (in the plural), and the relations between things are relations that depend on different systems of thought.

The real-ism I intend to uphold against idealism is not therefore a return to positivism, according to which reality is something that language/thought can describe more and more faithfully. It is not a question of seeing language/thought as a more or less faithful mirror of the world (Rorty). The historiographic reconstruction of scientific thought itself, mainly by the Austro-American epistemological current (Popper, Kuhn, Lakatos, Feyerabend), shows that knowledge about nature proceeds discontinuously according to *paradigm shifts*. That is, the relationship between language/thought on the one hand and nature on the other is by no means linear or specular. To put it brutally, the image we have today of scientific knowledge is not that of a mirror but rather of a biological organism that more or less manages to survive in a natural environment. Theories fight for survival like beasts running to arms. Rather than representing, science survives and reproduces itself, and it helps us survive and reproduce ourselves. It is a conception of knowledge that I would call bio-pragmatist.

The whole so-called post-structuralist season has been dominated by a profound historical relativism. In *The Order of Things*, Foucault[5] tried to show that words are not the mirror of things, but that things are formatted, as we would say today, by words. Are we then sliding back into idealism? No, a third way between speculative idealism and positivist realism is possible. To say that facts are always interpreted as facts does not imply the conclusion that "there are no facts, only interpretations", as per the slogan of hermeneutic nihilism. We always interpret, true, but what do we interpret? Facts, even if these are in turn interpreted facts.

I believe that in the course of time Lacan increasingly distanced himself from his Hegelian roots, and his admiration for Heidegger is a trace of this detachment. Significantly, in Lacan a gentle shift would occur from the primacy of desire, which evokes the philosophical tradition of the primacy of eros (Plato's *Symposium*), to the primacy of *jouissance*, which is something *accomplished*. (Earlier the so-called 'psychopathology' was a matter of persistence of a lack, later it is a matter of a sort of addiction.) Above all, an increasing primacy of the register of the real over that of the symbolic would occur. His later reference would therefore be less and less linguistics and more and more a mathematical topology, which is a structure of real space. For the late Lacan, the unconscious was topologically structured. But we have no room here to analyze this shift in depth.

Lacan's philosophical knots

In my opinion, the important cues for philosophy in Lacan's thought are the following:

(A)   The power of the signifier
(B)   The cause as après-coup
(C)   The primacy of difference
(D)   The real as correlative to the symbolic
(E)   The *jouissante* essence of the humans
(F)   The ethical and political nature of psychoanalysis

Power of the signifier

What follows may seem contradictory. In other words, on the one hand it is necessary to overcome Lacan's logocentrism, on the other it is important to apply to fields even very different from psychoanalysis a power that has largely been ignored: the power of the signifier in society and in history.

Two fundamental readings of society have emerged in modern culture, the Marxist and the liberalist, which share an essential axiom: that the key to explaining human history is ultimately economic. The struggle between economic classes for Marxism, the freedom or non-freedom of the market for liberalism. These are two sides of the same theoretical coin that places the production, reproduction and distribution of goods as the primary cause of historical fortunes. Liberalism and socialism see the social being essentially as a producer or as a consumer.

Instead, Lacan prompts us to see in history the extraordinary power of signifiers. The human community is largely *désoeuvrée*, inoperative, as Jean-

Luc Nancy called it[6]. Human beings become excited, sacrifice themselves, kill and are killed for signifiers. For signifiers like the nation or democracy, socialism or fascism, or like their religious faith or ethnic 'identity'... But, as Ernesto Laclau[7] would say, all signifiers are empty deep down.

Over the years I have had the opportunity, having taught regularly in Kyiv for over 20 years, to follow the development of Ukrainian patriotism. Early on, being Ukrainian or Russian was irrelevant; they spoke the same language; having ended up within Ukrainian or Russian borders was purely coincidental. But then, over time, the Ukrainian signifier began to fill with meaning, as did being Russian, to the point that both sides engaged in a horrifying war. It's not as if a flag represents the country to which we belong, it's the flag itself that gradually creates a country that recognises itself behind it.

The signifier has a semantic opacity. For example, when we say 'Ukraine' or 'Ukrainianness', what is the sense of the terms? *Sense* is one thing; the *referent* is another. We can certainly say what *Ukraine* refers to – a certain portion of territory, a portion of population, mostly Slavic... – but not its sense. Of Ukraine, at least initially, we can only say that it can be distinguished from Russia and its neighbouring countries... Even though, given what is happening, the term is filling with meaning. But the sense here is an effect of the signifier, it is not the signifier that is summarising a sense. I would say that Ukraine has become a massive signifier precisely because other signifiers – primarily *Russia* – Ukraine *was not recognised any more as a signifier.*

By this I am certainly not trying to say that the resistance of the Ukrainians against the Russians is futile, that it is a struggle between mere symbols. Symbols constitute our *cause*, something for which we can give up our lives; making signifiers our cause gives meaning to our lives.

Since structural linguistics points out that signifiers are defined by oppositions, political conflict is very often a consequence of the oppositional character of signifiers.

This by no means reduces the importance of economic conflicts in history, but they are mostly effects of signifying oppositions rather than being the matrix of even armed oppositions.

Perhaps the most terrifying case of the power of the signifier is the 1994 genocide in Rwanda, when the Hutus killed over half a million Tutsis in three months. What was the difference between Hutu and Tutsi? A purely signifying difference. Had it not said 'Hutu' or 'Tutsi' on their identity cards, it would have been very difficult to exterminate the latter.

The will to power certainly explains much about politics. But *whose* will to power? Always that of subjects identified with certain signifiers.

The power of the signifier reveals, in my opinion, the essentially transcendentalist nature of the human being, who never lives in mere immanence. We all live for the Other, for example by having children. Our values survive us, because they are always the values of the Other. Human lives are completely immersed in transcendence.

The cause as après-coup

Lacan had a merit for which even his most ardent opponents give him credit: emphasising in Freud's thought the notion of *nachträglich, après-coup*, afterwardness, one that readers of Freud before Lacan had not seen. Now, *après-coup* is interpreted in various ways. For me, après-coup is a crucial concept in psychoanalysis, the one around which its plausibility is at stake.

The après-coup consists of two scenes: an earlier one and a later one, with the second scene seemingly giving a traumatic meaning to the first. In The Wolf Man, for example, the scene of the dream with the wolves sitting in the tree, which the subject had at the age of four, reveals as traumatic a scene that Freud supposes to be an earlier one, that of the vision of his parents' coitus when he was one and a half years old.

Now, Lacan's highlighting of the Freudian après-coup has given this notion, après coup, a disturbing sense. That is, après-coup gives substance to a *'coup'* that would not exist without the après-coup.

There are at least four interpretations of après-coup, which I would call positivist, hermeneutic, relational and magical-mythological. The positivist sees the two scenes in a line of cause and effect: the après-coup is like a bomb that explodes at a later time. The hermeneutic interpretation is based on the idea that the present re-signifies the past on a line of backward projection of meaning. The relational line makes the second scene a reinterpretation of what another (an adult) wanted in the first scene: the subject thus questions what the other wanted of him. "Après-coup is a phenomenon that is not played out within the intrapersonal but within the interpersonal"[8]. It is the enigma of the other's desire that presents itself again afterwards.

The magical-mythological explanation (sometimes illustrated through sophisticated philosophical tools) relies on the inversion of the cause-and-effect relationship in time, as in certain science fiction stories (the *Back to the Future* series, for example): that is, a posterior effect can act retroactively on the anterior cause by inverting the arrow of time[9]. This thesis puts psychoanalysis completely outside scientific rationality.

I proposed a further reading[10].

The inversion of the arrow of time means that the *nachträglich* is a process thanks to which *the sense* of a later event gives a previous one a *causal force*. There is a causal primacy of the later scene, in the sense that its sense makes an earlier scene the aetiology of later symptoms. Now, this feedback of the present on the past is only possible in a human world.

An imaginary example: a subject crosses a bridge and then reads that years earlier that bridge had been destroyed; but this doesn't trouble him much. Years later he witnesses a house collapse in an earthquake, after which he

34 Philosophy After Lacan

develops a phobia of... bridges. He cannot cross them, because he fears they will fall. In this case, the first experience of crossing the bridge only became the cause of the phobia through the meaning that the second event gave to the first: *collapsing*. An event 1 becomes a cause through a sense given après coup by an event 2.

This is indeed an inversion of the arrow of time, but not of the magical or miraculous sort, because the previous event is not modified in its reality: it is its *power* that is modified.

The après-coup is a special case of sense causing events: it is not the sense of an event that is directly causal, but it causes a previous event, with a different sense, to take on causal force.

The way Lacan promoted the concept of après-coup had something scandalous about it: that the cause does not come before but after, by a recalling of the past. In this way, there is no longer any *primacy*, in the sense that there is no absolute *before*.

In any case, this uncertainty about cause and meaning seems to place psychoanalysis in a marginal space of knowledge and action. But we could show that the après-coup also characterises other human activities such as politics, education, the law... Cause and sense are *entangled* (like particles in quantum physics) in a way that is not only complex but open: causal effects and effects of sense intertwine in an often uncanny way.

Psychoanalysis therefore occupies a space, which some find impossible, between positive realism, hermeneutics and intersubjectivism, without ever reducing itself to any of these.

Psychoanalysis becomes banal when, in order to overcome its perplexities, it opts for one of the three interpretations of its knowledge and power. Psychoanalysis is neither positive science (something Lacan often repeated), nor interpretation in the sense of hermeneutics (re-significations of the world that can change the world), nor interpersonal dialectics, but something that seeks a space situated at the crossroads of all these concepts. At the constant risk of being identified as, downgraded to, a magical and superstitious practice. This is the extraordinary importance of Lacan's insistence on après-coup.

Even if Lacan does not say so explicitly, the après-coup reveals that every analytic reconstruction hangs on a crucial uncertainty: with my analysand have I, the analyst, reconstructed the subject's original experiences, or have I constructed them today, projecting them into a past history that in this way ipso facto takes on the form of a myth? It is this uncertainty, or conditionality, that lies in every future perfect. Rather than saying "Like everyone else, I've had my Oedipus", I ought to say 'If I do analysis, *I will have had* my Oedipus'.

In fact, the concept of après-coup is fundamental precisely because that of which the après-coup is an *after* refers back to a *before* that remains suspended, an unknown. The paradox of après-coup is that there is an after at the beginning, never a prima-cy. It is an after without a before. It does not lead us to the primacy of the other like in Laplanche, but to the *primacy of the after.*

The primacy of difference

Lacan does not aim at the systemic character of subjectivity, but on its differential grain. It is often said that Lacan's thought is an aspect of the philosophical turn that had its epicentre in France, that of the *primacy of difference.* A primacy taken up by Saussure when he says that signifiers are not full realities but *distinctions*: the essence of logos is to hinge on distinctions, not on full concepts. (Saussure does however set forth a theory of language as a system that Lacan does not take up). From 'distinction' the philosophers of that season slid towards a primacy of Difference.

Difference, as we said, is intrinsic to signifiers. What identifies a Ukrainian and a Russian? The fact that the Ukrainian signifier is distinct from the Russian signifier. Nothing more.

This means that there is no *primum movens* in human affairs, be it the will to power, or modes of production, or the alienation of nature in culture, or the need to survive, or the optimisation of biological fitness... History flows because differences emerge everywhere; randomly, I would say, blindly.

But if difference is at the root of all human reality, this means that any homogenisation of humans is doomed to failure: differences continuously reproduce, as, after all, they do in biological life. All biological evolution is differentialistic: a life history exists because there is a continuous stochastic production of differences. But this wrecks any egalitarian ideologies: formal equalities between human beings are certainly possible (equal rights and opportunities), but the *formal equalities produce actual differences* [11]. Differentiation is the very dynamic of life; it is the tragic side of life that no political Good News will ever be able to erase.

And is it really a coincidence that the most modern cosmology reaches a purely differentialistic hypothesis of the origin of the universe, according to which our universe originated from a sudden rupture in the symmetry of the void? In other words, the void divides itself, thus producing fullness. The whole that makes up the universe is a differentiation of nothingness.

The real as correlative to the symbolic

Today, Lacanians tend to confer more and more value to the register of the real, to the detriment of the register of the symbolic. This expresses a general slant of Western thought in recent decades: going beyond the *linguistic turn* with a 'return to the real'. Today, for example, biological metaphors are more intellectually appealing than linguistic ones. Hence the success of categories such as biopolitics (taken up by Foucault) or the concept of bare life (taken up by Agamben).

Should we think of Lacanian real in idealistic terms as something that the symbolic itself posits as its own other-than-oneself? In the same way as Fichte said that the I posits the non-I (external reality), we could say that language posits non-language as the real. In this way Lacan's doctrine would be reduced to an idealistic reading of psychoanalysis.

What I think, instead, is that the real should be seen as a topological place correlative to the symbolic, but not created or posited by the symbolic. There is no before and after between the real and the symbolic. The difference between the two is primal. The real is what every discourse supposes as other-from-discourse; and let us also add that it is the transcendence of every discourse. But not the transcendence of intentional consciousness in Husserl's sense: it is a transcending that always misses that towards which one is transcending. Like an ostension with no object. This real, therefore, unlike the reality of positive realist thought, is not something to be symbolised, to be reproduced in human knowledge: it is something that will always be topologically *other* from human knowledge, *other* from rationalising comprehension. It is like what lies *beyond any horizon of mine...* Of course I can widen my horizon out of all proportion, but there will always be a horizon, a line beyond which... there is nothing for-me. What we see within a horizon always assumes something that is beyond it and that by its structure will never be *within* that horizon.

The Lacanian theory of psychosis, according to which what is *foreclosed* in the symbolic appears as a hallucination in the real, would seem to refute this. The voices the schizophrenic hears are symbolic snippets that subjects can only know to the extent that they find them in *their own* real, i.e., in a topological space of the non-subject. So, we each have our own real; that is to say, a point from which our own thinking and our own 'own' are interrupted to make way for an unthinkable. It is in this sense that Lacan, I believe, understands Freud's 'primal repression' (*Urverdrängung*): an original division from which each subject constitutes itself in a fundamental difference from the non-subject; that is, from the real.

This approach essentially contradicts the Hegelian 'what is rational is real, and what is real is rational'[12], which radicalises the principle of sufficient reason (*nihil est sine ratione*). Here, instead, the real is precisely what evades rationality, what threatens and limits it, what I would call a *principle of insufficient reason*. Scientific thought certainly relegates the real, it tends to rationalise everything in ever more sophisticated ways, using the calculation of probabilities and accepting indeterminacy... but, while being relegated, the real perseveres and insists in questioning us. Something that makes knowledge an infinite process: being itself is at the bottom of every possible explanation, the fact that things are as they are and not otherwise. We can even say that the real is *the pure event*. But the totality of the being is always pure event.

Hence Lacan's provocative assertion that "the real is the impossible", which overturns the philosophical common sense. The Lacanian desire to provoke common sense was linked to the idea that essential truths can be told through paradoxes. What he means is that if something is real, it is so because it contradicts... what is it that it contradicts? I would say the pure necessity of logic. After all, according to logic the real is not possible, yet it is there.

The jouissante *essence of the humans*

The way Freud described the origin of his doctrine – as the result of objective unbiased clinical research – is a self-misconception of his work caused by his positivist prejudices. Instead, I think Freud directed his clinical practice, albeit unconsciously, through a genealogy of human singularity.

For Freud, the essence of the human is *die Lust*, which in English becomes *lust*. The term is ambiguous in German, because it means pleasure and enjoyment as well as desire and drives. In other words, for Freud the human being is an organism that seeks enjoyment above everything else. Even when it is merely trying to survive, it seeks to continue to enjoy life.

Lacan grasped this Freudian axiom about the essence of humanity. In fact, the guiding concepts of Lacanian thought, desire and enjoyment, articulate the two possible slopes of the German *die Lust*. Human beings are desiring beings, or rather, insofar as they derive pleasure from their desire, they desire to perpetuate their pleasure. *Lustprinzip* should therefore be translated as 'desire-pleasure principle' and not simply, as has been done, 'pleasure principle'.

Thus, Freud's doctrine separates itself *ab initio* from the current cognitive sciences, according to which human beings are instead the result of subsequent adaptations, according to the strictly neo-Darwinian view. The human being that interests Freud is not the adaptive human being, but the desiring and enjoying, pleasure-seeking, human being. Psychoanalysis is interested in what Gould and Lewontin – biologists who wished to correct rigid Neo-Darwinism – call, by analogy, *spandrels*, the left-over spaces of evolutionary construction[13]: a part of the organism that means nothing, yet stands there as a zero-degree by-product of adaptive history. The spandrels are actually a slice of wall left behind by the arch structure.

Spandrels are an example of noise in any meaningful construction, even if we disguise them with wonderful and meaningful figures.

Can we believe in the Freudian genealogy today? Should we prefer it to other meta-anthropologies, such as the Darwinian (the most influential today), or the Marxist, or the phenomenological and 'empathic' (see the mirror neuron theory), or the existentialist? We can in any case say that Lacan, unlike most psychoanalysts, is more purely Freudian precisely because for him *die Lust*, desire and *jouissance*, is the essential element of

38 Philosophy After Lacan

human subjectivity. Even if this *Lust* is always articulated, he believed, in the differential terms of symbolism.

In Freud and Lacan, objects are essential insofar as they are *Lust-Objekte*, objects of desire and pleasure. The difference between Freud and Lacan on this point is that for the former the *Objekt* is what every drive or desire finds on its path, often incidentally, whereas for Lacan the object *a* (the object-other) is the *cause of* desire. In other words, for Lacan what attracts us comes from the world and not from the internal dynamics of our psychic organism. What rouses us comes from the real. Lacan most probably took this idea from phenomenology. Sartre said that "if we love a woman, it is because she is lovable"[14]. It is a case of eliminating any analysis of love as a profound interiority, it is a case of seeing my love *in* the woman I love and not as if didn't concern that woman but only me.

I believe that the human being is not just *lust*, desire and enjoyment. There are various other 'psychological' functions to take into account. But beyond the social and biological variables, the analyst's interest tends to concentrate on just one thing: *understanding in what way the subject derives pleasure*. It is only a spandrel, but the essential one for the analyst. This seems to me the bone of Lacanian clinic practice. Understanding how an individual derives enjoyment also therefore means understanding the origin of their suffering, because to suffer is the price to pay for something in them that derives enjoyment.

The point is that for Freud affects are always conscious, whereas the representations related to affects are unconscious, except... pleasure, *Lust*. Pleasure is something that lies between the subjective and the objective, between affect and process, between perceiving and being.

The great initial paradox of Freud's doctrine is that *die Lust*, desire and pleasure, can be unconscious. Unlike all other affects, desire and pleasure are the *arché* of the psyche; what came first and is commander. Lacan does not resolve this primal paradox, he inhabits it to the fullest.

But we should say that *jouissance* is still an affective metaphor, that what has been called unconscious pleasure is *the very fact of repetition as such*. Lacan rightly included repetition among the four fundamental concepts of psychoanalysis (and not desire and jouissance): human beings tend towards repetition as if they were unable to detach themselves from a certain pleasure... But is then the unconscious as a whole just repetition?

The point is that the unconscious, in both Freud and Lacan, is also the creative matrix of humans – think of the jokes and quips. Art and literature are creative when they come from the unconscious, that is, when they break a repetition. Getting pleasure lies in repetition, but also in breaking a repetition.

I believe that the fundamental problem of analytic thought and practice lies in this glitch; a problem that is still completely unsolved, but one which Lacan had the merit of highlighting.

It is also important to grasp social and political conflicts, and within cultural conceptions, the economics of enjoyments as well as the power of the signifier. Even when we follow scientific protocols, what is ultimately decisive is the way we get pleasure. Even objective research is a way of enjoying. Of course, the will to power counts too, but also the fact that power is a source of enjoyment.

For some time, I have decided to stop saying "I reject that philosophy" or "that psychoanalytic theory states the truth" and saying instead "that philosophy gives me no pleasure" or "that psychoanalytic theory gives me pleasure". What then becomes extremely interesting is to understand why certain theories afford more or less pleasure than others. And to understand why they afford *me* that pleasure.

But if finding pleasure amounts to breaking a repetition, we could say that the theories that give us authentic pleasure are the ones that break the repetition of what has been said and thought again and again... and instead open us up to a real.

Here arises the unsolved problem of what makes it possible to link the desire and enjoyment of power to what I would call the desire or need for unveiling; that is, for truth. From where does this strange tropism of humans towards the real, i.e. towards the unthinkable, arise?

The ethical and political vocation of psychoanalysis

Freud said that there are three impossible professions: politics, education and psychoanalysis. What do all these 'impossibilities' have in common? That none of them tend towards truth as science does, but towards a certain effectiveness. Towards an effectiveness that is not technological but instead stems from what Lacan calls, using a Greek word, *tuké*, the good encounter[15].

Psychoanalysis is not essentially a technique, just as politics and education are not (exclusively) techniques. They are all ethical activities, something that does not exclude that they need to be realistic; Realpolitik, Realbildung. Psychoanalysis too has to be a Realpsychologie. It lies between art and science, between construction reconstruction and deconstruction.

Though I still find an overly mythical way of looking at psychoanalytic practice in Lacan (he believed that the right theory led to good clinical practice, which is not the case), his way of looking at psychoanalysis seems to me quite convincing. One that makes it futile to turn it into an Evidence Based Medicine, basically into a practice based on incontrovertible results. Psychoanalysis is not a scientific theory, it is the theory of a practice – precisely as in the case of political or pedagogical theories, which never produce incontrovertible results.

Some may say: we effectively do judge the validity of political and educational theories according to the results. For example, if we vote for a party that follows a certain political theory and then it governs for five years, by the end of that time we will have judged whether the conditions in our country have improved or deteriorated. This is the justification of democracy: the people is called upon to judge whether a certain idea of politics has performed well or not. But we know that this is not the case. What is it that entitles us to say "the government has done a good job"? If things are going better or worse, we cannot say to what extent this better or worse depends on what the government in question has actually done. We can notice that during that term the economy of the country has improved or declined, but in either case can we really say it was due to the effects of the government's measures? It could be that in the meantime there's been a worldwide economic crisis that hasn't spared the country... On the contrary, a booming economy of the country could be due to reasons involving a whole set of countries. Furthermore, certain government measures can benefit certain social classes and harm others: the assessment of these measures will then depend on the specific interests of these classes. In short, nothing is more complex than objectively assessing the effects of policies. And the same applies to educational strategies.

In the same way, there may be multiple factors leading to the improvement of an individual in analysis, something which makes any validations extremely difficult. Many patients, for example, are manifestly better after months of analysis, but often attribute this improvement to other factors. What causes what?

In other words, so-called analytical technique is inseparable from an ethical project. Lacan said that the ethical project of psychoanalysis is to ensure that subjects do not give up on their desire, on their *thing*. But if our thing is destructive, nefarious? My "thing" can be also sadistic. Does the Sadian hero not pursue his thing? "Ethics" in Lacan can be "the good ethics, to reject evil" but also "my ethics, which can be destructive". Can you say that a mafioso, for example, has his own ethics? In any case, Lacan's ethics is not a normative one. The question remains suspended, unresolved.

Negativistic realism

Is it possible to philosophically conceptualise the real in the Lacanian sense, so that it becomes a concept that can also be used outside of a psychoanalytic orthodoxy?

I will attempt to do this by evoking the biological approach of Jakob von Uexküll[16], which also influenced Heidegger. Here, the biologist, in a Kantian-style gesture, clearly separates the *Umwelt*, the environment of an animal, from the world-in-itself to which the animal has no access. Every species, and perhaps even every organism, has an environment of its own, but beyond this environment (which for the human being is also a symbolic one) there will always be a pure real, which constitutes the background *noise* of the living experience. There is therefore an unavoidable dose of incommunicability between organisms.

Information theory distinguishes between signal and noise. In a vinyl record the signal is the music recorded on it, the noise is the annoying sounds produced, for example, by warps on the surface of the record. Psychoanalysis is interested precisely in noise, in what breaks the meanings of a signal, as in the case of the spandrels. Humans have always tried to integrate noise into a wider field of signals. For example, in the case of records, the practice of scratching in music. But no matter how much one tries to enrich the world of signals by integrating noise, the possibility and interference of noise always remains. I believe that what Lacan calls the real is precisely this unavoidable residue of noise, "that which has gone wrong". The very moment Lacan says that the unconscious is structured like a language, he is suggesting that the unconscious is just what the structure has dismissed as pure noise.

The transcription of idealism in biological terms would be "there can be no real beyond *our* environment". Whereas what I would call *negative realism* – to distinguish it from the usual positive realism – acknowledges this rift between the environment and the real, the paradoxical dimension of the human trying to ponder its own human limit. We can then say that philosophy lays bare the *Epimenidean* fate (from the Cretan Epimenides) of the human relationship to being.

And it is insofar as for Lacan psychoanalysis loves the real like an amateur that it cannot be a science; and analysis is not a technology either. Science seeks to be an ever more adequate mirror of nature, but the real always is a hole in the mirror, which evades knowledge and calls us to a praxis.

But I would add that even if psychoanalysis is by no means a science (Lacan agreed with Popper), it has nevertheless sprung from the *scientific spirit* of our times, which is *analytical*: according to which, a whole must be 'opened' into its constituent parts in order to be understood.

If Lacan ceases to be Hegelian, then he somehow accepts Kantian assumptions. In Western philosophical culture the ridge between Kantianism and Hegelianism is represented by Anselm's ontological argument, even in its most modern and 'pragmatistic' forms: those who accept the argument are Hegelian, those who reject it are Kantian.

Lacan's seminar that marked a turn towards a broader Kantianism is the seventh, *The Ethics of Psychoanalysis*. Lacan said that in his doctrine the real is not the Kantian thing-in-itself, yet the ethics Lacan describes is an entirely Kantian 'categorical' ethics, and it is in this seminar that Lacan speaks of *das Ding* (the thing). Note that Lacan would develop the concept of the Thing exclusively in this seminar; it was a conceptual butterfly that was to fly only for one year. It is as if the *Ding* of pure reason had been transferred into practical reason: this Thing can only be represented through a void; in other words, it is not representable, yet it directs all our objects of desire. Indeed, the Kantian thing today cannot simply be the unknowable, what today we call an *event*, but a transcendental condition by which all objects are arranged before us as objects-for-us, i.e. invested by our desire and occasions for enjoyment.

Unlike positivism, Lacan does not think that everything in the world is positive. Positivism radically separates the world from the logos, and negation is only a thing of the logos not of the world, even though from another point of view the logos is part of the world. There is no 'not' in things. After all, for physics there is no such thing as time even in nature[17]. When Freud said that there is neither negation nor time in the unconscious, it is because he ultimately considered it a fact of nature. But this cannot be true for the processes of human life related to language. If we look at nature as an all-positive entity, we can at most use the metaphor of 'conflict' to explain some of its processes; for example, animals are often in conflict. But we can never say that nature contradicts itself. Contradiction is uniquely a logical thing. Now, since the human world is permeated by the logos, we need to see the negative and the lack in the human world. We can say that Lacan added the following to what Freud said: that what the latter described as conflicts is rewritten by the former as contradictions. The original contradiction can be described as that between being and sense.

Does admitting negation and contradiction – and thus time – as part of the world then mean being Hegelian? I do not think so. The fact that logos, and hence negation, are part of the world does not imply that all being is logic-al. We must admit that logos somehow divides being, at least as far as we human beings are concerned: on the one hand the *Welt*, the world, on the other *das Ding*, the thing that exceeds the world.

Political masquerades

Most Lacanians have remained tied to a Marxist-libertarian left, to which I adhered myself in my youth. The model is Louis Althusser, a Marxist-Leninist, a structuralist and a Freudian through Lacan. Yet one fact is incontrovertible: neither Freud nor Lacan were Marxists, neither believed in socialism. Why do then some of Freud's followers and most of Lacan's identify with the radical left, the sanctuary of which is the Ljubljana School?

Like Freud and Lacan, I do not believe in the communist gospel. Certainly, there are affinities between Marx's thought and Freud's – both understood that certain reasons are rationalisations, that behind the discourses certain drives and interests need to be reconstructed – but there are also extraordinary differences that should not be ignored. One essential difference is that whereas Marx proposes a solution to the dramas of humanity in a millenarian vision, when everyone will have according to their needs, Freud sees no solution to subjective dramas, only a sober way of living with them. Freud is a reformist, not a revolutionary, of psychism. A reformism as well-known as his pessimism. Pessimists can never believe in a final Revolution, they can only hope that certain reforms will bring us some relief.

Like Freud, Lacan too thought that Marxism was a gospel; fascinating, but full of illusory promises. And for the same reason Lacan thought Marxism was a lesser substitute for religion: for him, the real challenge to psychoanalysis came from religion, especially from Roman Catholicism. Well before the fall of the Berlin Wall, Lacan understood that communism had proved to be a historical failure, and that we would return to the original Hope, not its secularist facsimile.

We always find the same figures in mass political discourse, which we can see as fixed topological locations: The Persecutor, the allied Friend, the Liberator, the Führer, the Plotter, the manipulating Exploiter. These characters are predetermined to concrete political dynamics, and need therefore to be considered as signifiers, that is, as positions of the Other. Lacan could never have believed in socialism because he did not believe that the Other exists. Hence, what functions as the Other in politics does not exist, even though I define myself through it. The power of the Other is not to be demolished, because it is an imaginary power. Political revolutions are always, to some extent, masquerades.

Notes

1 L. Wittgenstein, *Philosophical Investigations*, Macmillan, London, 1953.
2 J. Lacan, *The Seminar, book XX. Encore*, transl. by B. Fink, W.W. Norton & Co. (1998), ch. VIII, p. 102.
3 W. T. Krug, *Schelling und Hegel oder die neueste Philosophie im Vernichtungskriege mit sich selbst begriffen* (1835).
4 The phonetic system of different languages has been described by structural linguistics, the syntactic structure of language in general has been reconstructed by Chomskyan transformational grammar.
5 M. Foucault, *The Order of Things: An Archaeology of the Human Sciences*, Pantheon Books, 1970.
6 J.-L. Nancy, *The Inoperative Community*, University of Minnesota Press, Minneapolis, 1991.
7 E. Laclau, *On Populist Reason*, Verso, London, 2007.
8 J. Laplanche, *Après-coup*, The Unconscious in Translation, 2017.
9 Effects certainly do retroact on causes in a complex networked system: the relationships between cause-points and effect-points are relative, because in a network there really is no before and after. But the individual histories with which psychoanalysis deals do not concern networked systems, but stories, which must necessarily follow the arrow of irreversible time. Any reversibility of time is a fairy tale.
10 S. Benvenuto, "The Après-Coup, après coup: Concerning Jean Laplanche Problématiques VI", *Language and Psychoanalysis*, vol. 7, no. 2, 2018, pp. 72–87. www.academia.edu/38022201/ Language_and_Psychoanalysis_Volume_7_Issue_2_2018.
11 This is the main thesis on social inequalities by R. Dahrendorf, (1959), *Class and Class Conflict in Industrial Society*, Stanford University Press, California, 1959.

44 Philosophy After Lacan

12 G. W. F. Hegel, *Preface to the Philosophy of Right*, Berlin, June 25, 1820. Translated by S.W. Dyde, 1896.

13 S.J. Gould and R.C. Lewontin, "The Spandrels of San Marco and the Panglossian Paradigm: A Critique of the Adaptationist Programme", *Proceedings of the Royal Society of London*, Series B, vol. 205, no. 1161, 1979, pp. 581–598.

14 J.P. Sartre, *La transcendance de l'Ego et autre textes phénoménologiques*, Vrin, Paris, 2003, p. 89.

15 J. Lacan, *The Seminar, book XI: The Four Fundamental Concepts of Psychoanalysis.* W.W. Norton & Co., New York, 1998.

16 J. von Uexküll & G. Kriszat, *Streifzüge durch Umwelten von Tieren und Menschen. Ein Bilderbuch unsichtbarer Welten. Bedeutungslehre*, Rowohlt, Hamburg, 1934.

17 If anyone is in any doubt about this statement, I would suggest reading the letter Einstein wrote to Michele Besso's widow: "People like us, who believe in physics, know that the distinction made between past, present and future is nothing more than a persistent, stubborn illusion".

Chapter 3

The Psychiatrist Despite Himself[1]

How Sganarelle Parodied the University
Discourse Without Knowing It

Alireza Taheri

Characters

Sganarelle, husband of Martine, imposture psychiatrist
Martine, wife of Sganarelle
Sofia Leclaire, critic of psychoanalysis
Lucian's father
Lucian's mother
Lucian, young schizophrenic man
Young man suffering of trichotillomania
Middle-aged man suffering of insomnia
Teenage boy suffering of dyscalculia
Line up of patients visiting Sganarelle for their psychiatric session
Dr. Andrew Oates, neurobiologist seeking Sganarelle's teaching
Psychologist, the first clinician whom Noah's mother consults
Noah, little transgender boy identifying as a girl
Noah's mother
Psychiatrist, the one who welcomes Noah and his mother at the clinic
Justin Krieger, film director of *Wonder Girl*
The sheriff
The sheriff's two underlings
The jury comprised of 12 men
The judge
The audience in court
The executioner
The Absolute, a spectre-like apparition
Dr. Molar, the psychoanalyst
John Copelin, Dr. Molar's patient
The chorus comprised of 15 men

DOI: 10.4324/9781003425953-4

46   Philosophy After Lacan

Scene 1: Martine Beats Her Husband Sganarelle

[Martine holds a shoe in her hand as she angrily chases after her husband Sganarelle]

MARTINE: Get over you here you little rascal
You're nothing but a scoundrel and a vandal
You spent all our savings on gambling and beer
I'm sick of watching you sit on your rear
You haven't made a farthing in months
We're nearly broke and all out of funds
If only I get my hands on you ...

[Sganarelle runs cowardly away from her. She puts him down and beats him physically]

SGANARELLE: Please have mercy on a soul meek as mine
I was born this way, 'twas not my design
I promise to change and do as you tell
To old Sganarelle, we shall say farewell.
MARTINE: Before I leave you, I'll give you one chance
To earn money and rekindle romance.
SGANARELLE: My love, you are so clement and kind
I promise to work and not lag behind
I'll find a job and bring home the pennies
I'll spoil my fair queen and her progenies.
MARTINE: You need to be loftier in aim
And set your ambitions aflame
Why do you speak of pennies and a job
Such aspirations are fit for the mob
You need to look for a what they call a career
Jobs are for the masses, let us be sincere
Why don't you pretend to be a physician?
That would command respect and adoration
You need only sharpen your skills as an actor
And no one will know that you're not a doctor
Just feign the solemn airs of one who knows
And the people will confess their woes
And at your thralls they shall remain
Treat them with arrogance and disdain
They will kneel at your feet and sing your praise
Shower you with gold and beautiful bouquets
Acquire some jargon and wear a white gown
In today's world, tis like having a crown.

Scene 2: Sganarelle Performs Faecal Microbiota Transplantation

MOTHER: Our son is schizophrenic. I am devastated.

FATHER: This is a tragedy for the family.

MOTHER: We need to explain this to the other children.

FATHER: The psychiatrist said there is nothing we can do, and that Lucian will be on medication for the rest of his life.

MOTHER: I will do my best to provide him with the best life he can possibly have.

[Mother and father sob as they hold each other in a deep embrace. Sganarelle appears suddenly out of the blue]

SGANARELLE: Do I hear a parent's sad lament?
    The suffering child is a father's torment
    A mother knows no greater pain
    Then a son's life lived in vain
    Delusion and hallucination
    The fear of persecution
    The plight of alienation
    Routine medical sedation
    But behold there is a magical solution
    Faecal microbiota transplantation.[2]

[The mother and father jump up in curiosity and joy]

MOTHER: What is it you named? Is that a cure for schizophrenia?

SGANARELLE: Yes, there is no need for grief nor sorrow
    Your son shall be cured by the morrow.

FATHER: What is entailed by this Godsent remedy?

SGANARELLE: It's a simple and painless procedure
    A minor ingestion in the posterior.

FATHER: Ingestion? Posterior? Can you be more precise?

SGANARELLE: A sample of foreign faecal matter
    Stiff enough not to splatter
    But amply soft to cause no pain
    Shall be inserted in the rear domain.

FATHER: The rear domain? That's my son's arse you're talking about!

SGANARELLE: I recognize, it may seem foolish
    Perhaps even a tad bit brutish
    But if it brings forth future salvation
    We mustn't waste a moment's cogitation
    Rather than ancient remedies through the mouth

Let us dare to go down south
Have no fear of gay connotations
Tis 2023, it shall gain him salutations.

MOTHER: Where and when can this procedure take place?

SGANARELLE: I am ready to administer this very moment
The magical cure through rectal ointment
There will be a small cost for my labour
Forget not, my erudition is your saviour.

MOTHER: I will bring Lucian here immediately so we may begin the transplantation.

[The mother steps out and brings Lucian back with her. Lucian is dishevelled, tired and reticent]

LUCIAN: What's going on? Who's this guy [pointing to Sganarelle]?

MOTHER: This is the highly regarded Dr. Sganarelle.

LUCIAN: What's he here for? And why did you drag me out of bed?

MOTHER: He is here to cure you of your ailment. Remember, the psychiatrist said you have schizophrenia.

LUCIAN: That fool doesn't know what he's talking about? I'm just fine.

MOTHER: But Dr. Sganarelle knows many things and he can help you. He is no fool.

LUCIAN: Dr. Sganarelle? What a weird name? Sounds like "scam-arelle" [emphasizes the first syllable] or "scoundrel". He looks like a trickster to me.

MOTHER: Please Lucian. Don't talk like that about Dr. Sganarelle. He is an acclaimed physician praised for his healing hand.

LUCIAN: Acclaimed physician! Ha!
What non-sense mother.
Open your eyes.
What's his cure then? Another pill like all the others?

MOTHER: No. He will perform a new procedure called "faecal microbiota transplantation", also known as "stool transplant".

LUCIAN: Stool transplant? You mean he's going to rub poo on me? [He snickers mockingly].

MOTHER: I will let Dr. Sganarelle himself explain.

SGANARELLE: Fear not young man for I am here to console
To bring rest and peace to your tormented soul
Neither evil nor malice in me will you find
I am all healer, body, soul and mind
Nothing but your health is my concern
I ask merely for a small sum in return
The procedure in question lasts but a moment
But the reward is akin to atonement

You will be freed of delusion and hallucination
At the cost of a twinkling's penetration
A minor breach of your chastity's prized possession
Trust my word, I seek no pleasure from perversion
I am a man of science driven solely by rectitude
A male anus is but a site of decrepitude
I go there valiantly as a saviour
Driven by neither delinquency nor misbehaviour
So please lean forward as I prepare the balm
Tis like a sacred hymn and holy psalm
Once the faecal lotion has been ingested
Of smoky vapours, your mind shall be divested
In preparation I now slide on this rubber glove [grins mischievously to the audience]
To accomplish my physician's task ... with love.

[Lucian's parents hold him down as he resists. Sganarelle administers the faeces with his middle finger]
[He smiles devilishly to the audience, but the parents do not see].

SGANARELLE: And the transplantation is complete
With another's faeces you are now replete
Brimming to the tip with poo
For a few hours, please avoid the loo
You must wait for the brownish potion
To magically alter your state and emotion.

[The father and mother let go of Lucian who runs out of the room screaming]

MOTHER: We cannot thank you enough Dr. Sganarelle. You are a saint, an angel.
FATHER: Thank you, sir! We are forever indebted to you. What do we owe you for your precious work?
SGANARELLE: Feel free to donate what you deem right
However you value your son's health and might
If his wellbeing is to you of worth
Then by God, please donate the Earth
If in your eye, Lucian but a rascal be
A farthing will do, at most a penny.
FATHER: I give you all my wealth. Here is a cheque for everything I have.

[The parents leave after taking turns kissing Sganarelle's hands. Sganarelle is alone, and he gives a soliloquy to the audience]

50 Philosophy After Lacan

SGANARELLE: Ah poor simple folk so easily fooled
> By the attire of one so highly schooled
> The garments and trinkets of a learnèd mind
> Are smoke and mirrors that make men blind
> Barely a graduate of grammar school am I
> And yet my white gown deceived their eye
> Extravagant phrases and ornamental words
> Cast a mighty spell upon the herds
> Faecal microbiota transplantation
> Simply put, it's anal penetration
> But concealed in the jargon of science
> It numbs the lay man to silence
> Pupils dilate, jaws drop in admiration
> Knowledge is a tool of intimidation
> Ah! What a blessing to be taken for a physician
> We may blunder in blind omission
> But ne'er are we seen as liable
> As our faults are always deniable
> To logic and reason our patients bid farewell
> When upon their minds we cast a spell
> You saw it happen in this occurrence
> It's the magical curse we call transference.

Scene 3: Sganarelle Consults Patients in His Psychiatric Office

[A long queue of people waiting to be seen by Sganarelle as he sits behind a desk with a white robe assuming the aura of authority as a psychiatrist. He holds a pipe in hand]

SGANARELLE: What is your symptom young man?
YOUNG MAN: I pluck out my hair nervously all day long.
SGANARELLE: That's a simple diagnosis. You have trichotillomania, also known as hair pulling disorder.

[He hands him prescription after scribbling something on a paper]

SGANARELLE: Next!
MIDDLE-AGED MAN: I cannot sleep at night.
SGANARELLE: Easy. You have insomnia, from the latin "in" and "somnus". The negation of sleep.

[He hands him prescription after scribbling something on a paper]

SGANARELLE: Next!

TEENAGE BOY: I have problems with mathematics at school.
SGANARELLE: We call that dyscalculia, to "count badly".

[He hands him prescription after scribbling something on a paper. This repeats with a few more people. We don't hear anything. We just see him hand out prescriptions. There are no more patients left and Sganarelle gets up and gives another soliloquy]

SGANARELLE: What fools they are in awe of empty gestures
　　　　They take for truth such rash conjectures
　　　　Silly words with Latin and Greek root
　　　　It's all meaningless jargon, to boot
　　　　Everyone seeking a label and diagnosis
　　　　Easier than the exploration of neurosis
　　　　Whatever is inscribed in the holy DSM
　　　　No mortal would ever dare condemn
　　　　A new Bible has been written
　　　　To disagree is strictly forbidden
　　　　It is likewise with other psychologies
　　　　They too are a nesting ground of ideologies
　　　　Introversion, extroversion, intuition, and sensing
　　　　Not to mention judging and perceiving
　　　　INTJ or ISTP
　　　　Who cares about your history?
　　　　Myers-Briggs and Enneagrams
　　　　Assessed by multiple choice exams
　　　　It is indeed a strange situation
　　　　If you recall the hermeneutics of suspicion
　　　　Nietzsche, Freud and Marx
　　　　Their thought has vanished like a spark
　　　　We stand on the threshold of oblivion
　　　　Honour only to those who are Darwinian
　　　　Psychoanalysts and German Idealists
　　　　Are labelled dreamers and surrealists
　　　　Though deep truths therein lay hidden
　　　　Revealing realities so far forbidden
　　　　Freud, Lacan and Hegel have shown
　　　　That the truths of humans can be known
　　　　Only through the arduous struggle
　　　　Of deciphering jouissance as in a puzzle
　　　　Lacan has shown with his barred $
　　　　That the path to rigorous progress
　　　　Is to reject all intrinsic traits
　　　　As we are all blank and empty slates

Born into a symbolic world
Into which we are unfurled
We are the products of relations
Libidinal attachments and separations
But it is today's ideology
To reduce humans to biology
But honestly, I really do not mind
Let all and everyone of them stay blind
I will deceptively play along
And pretend to the world I see no wrong
May psychiatry and pharmaceutics prevail
To challenge them is of no avail
I have profited amply from the system
And this, I feel, is highest wisdom.

[He laughs wickedly as he holds a wad of cash in hands and lecherously looks at it. As he laughs, he hears its loud echo and then it seems like the laughter continues independently from the heavens. He looks up in fright and leaves the stage in haste]

Scene 4: Dr. Andrew Oates Seeks Sganarelle's Teaching

[Sganarelle is sitting majestically on a throne with his legs crossed. Dr. Andrew Oates bows to him]

DR. ANDREW OATES: O great Doctor, I come to seek your schooling
My soul needs wisdom, my mind refuelling
I plan to teach happiness to humanity
There is none with your insight and acuity
What is the secret of eternal elation
Through science alone, not religious persuasion?
You are the great materialist of the time
You err not into folly, ne'er into the sublime
Rational cogitation at its best
Of flights of mental fancy, you are bereft
O wise Sganarelle, give me the key to bliss
The world will be a heaven and I, famous.
SGANARELLE: A few basic principles are all it takes
There's no need for potions, no oil, no snakes
It's all proven by novel neuroscience
Psychoanalysis is a pseudoscience
All that is needed is a good night's sleep
If it comes not easy, just count some sheep

The Psychiatrist Despite Himself 53

And get some sunlight in early daylight
This will set your soul and your heart aright
Just make sure the sun shines at the right angle
Not too wide, not too narrow, just ample
Forty-five degrees is the most accurate
Others may differ, this is how I calibrate
Serotonin, cortisol and endorphins
Will absolve you of all evils and your sins
Add pharmaceutical meds to your diet
Pain will disappear, you will find peace and quiet.

[Sganarelle is interrupted by advertisement for a greens supplement. He resumes after the ad]

SGANARELLE: Fear not biohacking accusations
These are petty, envious recriminations
Follow my lead, superhuman you will be
Henceforth, Andrew Ubermensch the world shall see [he touches Dr. Andrew Oates' muscles as he says that].

Scene 5: Sofia Leclaire Seeks Sganarelle's Advice on How to Critique Psychoanalytic Approaches to Autism

SOFIA LECLAIRE: Doctor Sganarelle, my name is Sofia Leclaire
I seek your help about a difficult affair
About autism, psychoanalysts know naught
But here in France that's all that's taught
In America, there are other options
Avoiding Freudian-Lacanian concoctions
I would like to expose to the earth
That psychoanalysis has no worth
It's a system and bundle of lies
That must soon meet its deserved demise
O Great Sganarelle, give me guidance
On how to debunk this false pseudo-science.
SGANARELLE: My dear Sofia, you are wise as your name
Here is the way to encourage disdain
Against psychoanalytic tyranny
Hindering American epiphany
A good platform for expressing your creed
A documentary, guaranteed to succeed
I suggest you interview some analysts
Pretend they are the true protagonists

Do not be afraid to lie and mislead
In this day and age, tis the way to proceed
Ignore the context of sentences said
This is how human minds are misled
Expose their weird ideas about incest
That will outrage the masses and make them incensed
People are generally apt to receive
Only that which they already perceive
Psychoanalysis is very weird
Let it be tarnished, dirtied and smeared
Insist in your film, all is biology
All else is akin to astrology
Argue that the mention of parenting
Is just for blaming and finger pointing
Who knows what is true in this twisted affair
What matters is to destroy beyond repair
The reputations of Lacan and Bettelheim
Reduce their efforts to the level of slime
Forget the contributions of generations
Simplify all, ignore the complications
Depict the psychoanalysts as evil
Leave no room for nuance or retrieval.

SOFIA LECLAIRE: [in a jubilatory tone while also eyeing herself in the mirror proudly]
O great Sganarelle, you are a genius
I am wonderstruck, utterly speechless
I love all your tricks, what wonderful ruse
What a bliss to attack, destroy and accuse
Time to put an end to this outdated "science" [she gestures scare quotes with her fingers"]
These old farts must be cast deep into silence
Through my film, the French shall open their eyes
And wake from this slumber of falsehood and lies.

[Sofia Leclaire continues to be jubilant in front of the mirror. It borders on the sexual. The curtain closes]

Scene 6: Sganarelle Takes Noah to the Clinic for Gender Disphoria

[A psychologist's office. A middle-aged woman consults the psychologist]

WOMAN: My 3-year-old son, Noah, wants to become a girl. Indeed, he says that he is a girl. I don't know how this happened.
PSYCHOLOGIST: During pregnancy did you perhaps wish for a daughter?

WOMAN: I had a daughter who passed away before Noah's birth and I really wanted another daughter. I think I gave him the mixed name "Noah" for this reason. Could my desire be at the root of my child's gender confusion?

[A moment of silence. The psychologist looks nervous. The woman is getting more anxious, She grabs a knife and is about to blind herself. The scene freezes as she holds the knife close to her eye. The chorus begins to chant while everyone else is still frozen]

THE CHORUS: A mother is plagued with guilt and despair
To see her child maddened beyond repair
What caused gender dysphoria, no one knows
Is the mother's guilt a clue to her woes?
Drowned in self-reproach, she grabs the knife
To blind herself rather than take her life
She could no longer bear contrition
And sought in blindness, her redemption
Oh, woeful mother and child, our hearts are with thee
May divine miracle set you free!

[The chorus is silent and the scene unfreezes. The woman is about to stab herself. Out of nowhere, Sganarelle flies down to the office and enters through a window with a white cape. He grabs the woman by the wrist as she is about to blind herself]

SGANARELLE: No need to wallow in sorrow and remorse
The root of the problem is of unknown source
Your desire for a daughter is of no import
All this self-questioning, you must abort
Most likely, it is a genetic affliction
Your guilt and self-reproach have no foundation
It is a simple matter of choice and taste
We will not allow Noah to be disgraced
The ailment lies neither with you nor Noah
But rather with those who have transphobia
They are the culprits in this affair
Their narrow minds stifle our air
Pause and breathe a sigh of relief
So we may take a moment to debrief.

[Justin Krieger suddenly appears]

JUSTIN KRIEGER: Thank you Dr. Sganarelle for the light you shed

56 Philosophy After Lacan

With the sweat of your brow, you earn your bread
I will film a documentary called *Wonder Girl*
Sweet as honey, pretty as a pearl [he does a kind of ballet leap in a
dainty and feminine way].
SGANARELLE: No need for thanks, my good friend
A helping hand, I will always lend
Let us lose no time and seek assistance
The specialists in the dysphoria of gender
Have brains so sharp and souls so tender
I will take you in my arms and fly us there
We shall make it, with time to spare.

[Sganarelle grabs the mother and Noah under his arms and flies off with
his cape. They land in the beautiful garden of a clinic. There is a psychiatrist
there]

THE PSYCHIATRIST: Welcome to our great institution
A place where you will find life's solution
Dr. Sganarelle told us that you are dysphoric
Rest assured, soon you shall be euphoric
All your desires shall be sated
The limits of the body are all outdated
[To the mother] Can you tell me a little more about your situation
So I may gather all the information.
MOTHER TO THE PSYCHIATRIST: Dear doctor, we seek your help in times of despair
Our family is in need of deep repair
One day, our little Noah solemnly decreed
That her anatomy and her mind disagreed
"When I am big, I will be a girl", she said
Is this madness, has she lost her head?
Or is it a natural wish for a child this age
To hold against her penis such deep rage
Noah hates her organ and wants a baby
I told her that's a "No", not even a "maybe"
She burst into tears, I ruined her life
I shattered her dreams, stabbed her with knife
The damage was done, she was forever condemned
I seek your assistance, what do you recommend
Did I put this idea in her head?
Which has now sunk into her mind like lead
Could her desire be tied to my wish for a daughter?
Please tell me honestly, most esteemed doctor.
PSYCHIATRIST: Set your worries aside, tender mother
The root of gender dysphoria is likely other

The Psychiatrist Despite Himself 57

We know not from where it comes
But it has naught to do with dads and mums.
MOTHER: Oh, what a relief to be freed of guilt
I now have the energy to rebuild
A new life for my child as a young lass
She will be pretty, she shall have class
I cast aside all my previous self-doubt
Against the evils of society, I shall shout
My bond to Noah is forever secured
We shall never be severed, rest assured
I am locked to you eternally, my child
While I live, your honour shall ne'er be defiled
I am your Antigone, you are my Polyneices
As she fought Creon, I will combat the disease
Of a society that condemns a child
If he wishes to change his gender with pride
I will dedicate my life to children's freedom
Sexual difference shall be relegated to a museum.
PSYCHIATRIST [TO NOAH]: Consider this place a modern Eden
With all the bliss, yet fully heathen
Worry no longer of the burden of gender
Simply enjoy life in all its splendour
Your mother is a beautiful soul indeed
She toils and labours so you shall be freed
We at the clinic will do our best
To make sure that you are blessed
With all the care that you require
To get you out of this quagmire
Feel free to do as you wish, life is boundless
All other arguments are simply groundless
This garden is full of exciting gems
You will enjoy them with family and friends
I warn you of only one danger that is near
If you do not obey, consequences will be severe
There is an apple tree a few yards yonder
It delivers lies dressed as knowledge and truth
It pretends to be a detective and cunning sleuth
The tree goes by the names of Lacan and Freud
Wherever there's pain, it says it's enjoyed
It's a cauldron of lies leading to despair
An antidote to joy and precious repair
A little snake may tempt you to speak
It's an evil ruse and wily technique
Avoid it at all costs and you shall find bliss

58 Philosophy After Lacan

Otherwise, you will fall into a deep dark abyss
The snake will tell you that despair is noble
That "common unhappiness" is universal
He will fool you into so-called "castration"
And then skewer you into "depressive position"
If you resist all these lies and stick to our story
You and mother shall find joy and glory.

Scene 7: The Chorus Chants About the Impasses of the Liberal Age[3]

THE CHORUS: Men and women of the current age
  Look upon this troubled stage
  The mother's struggle with remorse
  Was not allowed to run its course
  Rather than the exploration of the unconscious
  We have the clearing of her conscience
  Conflict is said to reside out there
  Of inner struggle, she is unaware
  Rather than a discourse of introspection
  And an effort at self-reflection
  A war is waged with the world
  Upon which the mother's guilt is hurled
  Tis a shame as insight was about to rise
  When the mother nearly plucked her eyes
  As she wondered, "why did I choose that name?"
  Is there a deeper meaning or is it all the same?
  Noah, a boy's name, and a girl's as well
  Whether it matters, tis hard to tell
  Psychoanalysis could help explain
  The role of mother's desire in this domain
  However, the era of bioengineering
  Forbids the unconscious to get a hearing
  The voice of subjectivity has been muted
  The pillars of speech are uprooted
  We witness the simplification of science
  Which forms, with the mother, a daunting alliance
  The complexity of symptoms is abolished
  Psychic causality is demolished
  To take the child's words as sovereign aspiration
  Is to forgo nuance and distinction
  Forget not, a child is a mirror of the mother

The Psychiatrist Despite Himself 59

Her desires are alienated in this Other
We live in the era of the tyranny of jouissance
It is a relapse, not a Renaissance
The child's words are taken literally
Rather than explored metaphorically
The space is thus barred for speech
Regarding the 1001 ways one may reach
The wished for state of sexual being
With or without biomedical tinkering
Could Noah not enjoy ballet as a lad?
Would it be so awkward, would it be so bad?
Science promises to lift the body's limit
If you protest, you must be a bigot
Soon we shall defy death as well
To all constraints, we say farewell
It is no wonder that we have an agreement
Twixt sexual ambiguity and medical treatment .

Scene 8: Sganarelle's Guilt and Confession to Martine

SGANARELLE: My love, this game I can no longer play
     I must stop this deceit without delay
     I have gathered wealth and station without merit
     Simply by repeating words as a parrot
     The money I have accrued far surpasses
     The combined wealth of most of the masses
     Tis not fair that I keep my lavish treasures
     When my brethren are nearly all beggars
     My conscience has awoken to this mess
     I see that happiness lies beyond success
     In this world where few are sated and many famished
     Extremes of opulence should be banished
     I beg you, allow me to quit this career
     Lest you wish to see me carried in a bier.
MARTINE: What non-sense do you speak my dearest
     You have achieved great things as a careerist
     The world is a jungle with predator and prey
     The winners survive and the rest go away
     Your cunning and ruse have brought you above
     The wretched losers who lack self-love
     Besides, don't forget that the greater your wealth
     The better for all the commonwealth
     Cutting edge economics has decreed

60 Philosophy After Lacan

That amassing of riches by those who succeed
Will trickle tasty crumbs to the rabble below
We enjoy French cake, let them have raw dough.

SGANARELLE: This economic theory that thou hast found
Does nothing more than innocent minds confound
It is a grand old mystification
To pretend that theft is gentle donation
Perhaps I am too weak for this jungle
Deep down I am meek, modest and humble.

MARTINE: You are a lowly slave without a spine
Tis no way to be, for a man of mine
To hear you speak this way is nauseating
I am of noble nature, I deserve a king
You have regressed to your cowardly ways
My lust and love for you were ablaze
But your lowly miserable condition
Has led to my passion's attrition
You are not the splendid lion I deserve
In you, an oppressed nature I observe
It makes me vomit, it makes me hurl
You dress as a man, but you are a girl
I sought a tiger who would inspire awe
Instead I got you, a pussy without a claw!

Scene 9: Sganarelle at the Mirror

[Sganarelle stands in front of the mirror and consoles himself]

SGANARELLE: I am all man, neither girl nor lass in soul
I stand by the mirror in order to console
My spirit bruised by harsh words of Martine
A deep depression, a melancholy spleen
Has colonized my spirit and occupied my mind
Could she not be more tender, a bit more kind?
Gaze at your image, noble man that you are
A king among men, a splendid and fine star [he holds a crown over his head]
In the kingdom of the wild, you are a valiant beast [he holds a mane over his head]
You have the courage of a knight, the wisdom of a priest [he alternatingly places a knight's helmet and priest's cap on his head].
Do not let a simple maiden cause you pain
Your wounded inner child, you must contain [he begins to sob but struggles to hold it in].[There is a loud knocking at the door]

The Psychiatrist Despite Himself 61

SGANARELLE: Who could it be that knocks at the door at night?
I am seized with terror, clutched by fright.

THE SHERIFF: [in a loud and deep voice]: It is the sheriff, we have a warrant
to arrest
Please comply with us and do not protest

[Sganarelle opens the door. The sheriff walks in with two underlings]

THE SHERIFF: We must take you in for examination
Tis a serious matter concerning salvation
You have been accused of fraud and deceit
Please follow, try neither escape nor retreat.[They handcuff Sganarelle
who complies. The scene ends as he is taken away]

Scene 10: Absolutum ex Machina

[We are in court. There is a judge and an audience. The jury is about to
announce the verdict]

JURY: We, the jury, find the defendant guilty as charged on counts of fraud.
He is sentenced to death. The execution shall take place immediately.

[Sganarelle is mute. Martine is there too. She is also silent. The executioner
walks him to the guillotine and prepares him for beheading. As he is about to
walk to the guillotine, an apparition emerges and delivers a speech to the court]

THE ABSOLUTE [IN AN OMINOUS VOICE]: I am the brainchild of Hegel,
Nietzsche and Freud
Through them the old worldview has been destroyed
Their thought invites us to view justice differently
Nietzsche has put it best, most succinctly
Yesteryear, actions were judged by their effect
Later, intention was deemed more circumspect
Now comes a time to consider that intent
Is itself a sign and symptom to suspect [the word "symptom" is
accentuated]
It needs attentive interpretation
To crack its overdetermined causation
With the help of this system of higher justice
I propose that we consider to dismiss
The previous verdict cast upon this human
And view his deeds with learnèd acumen
Sganarelle was delinquent, one cannot deny

That said, allow me to provide his alibi
We live in the time of constitutive deceit
Where the major scoundrels lie with conceit
That Sganarelle was a fraud, this is correct
But we should remind ourselves to reflect
On the discourse of the university
Which rules over all with hegemony
It mistily confounds knowledge and power
Against its ruse, we must not cower
I hold that Sganarelle unwittingly aimed
To unveil this modern evil without shame
"The way to hell is paved with good intentions"
That should be the core of our interventions
"No man is an island entire of itself"
The wrong of another reflects myself
As Barad has argued with deep lucidity
My entanglements are my responsibility
Through quantum physics she has finally thrown
Metaphysical individualism from its throne[4]
Sganarelle is a symptom of our predicament [the word "symptom" is accentuated]
With reflection, he may be its medicament
Through the wisdom of thinkers past and present
I ask for court and jury to humbly consent
As I declare with symptom-awareness [the word "symptom" is accentuated]
To punish Sganarelle would be unfairness
The crime is its own punishment, Hegel said
I thus command, let this man live and keep his head.

Scene 11: Martine's Anxious Soliloquy

MARTINE: O what deep despair takes hold of me
Old Sganarelle is destined to be free
From time immemorial, women have been blamed
For the errors and faults of men ill-trained
I am truly delighted that my man may live
And relieved to hear that judges may forgive
What I severely fear with my heart and soul
Is that the guilt of his deeds be shifted whole
On to me, with the pretext that I inspired
The fraudulent acts that transpired
Indeed, I may have pushed my man to stray

The Psychiatrist Despite Himself   63

But it was only to pull him out of decay
He sat around all day drinking beer and wine
Our life had no future, no form, no design
Tis truly a hell for a woman to dwell
Under one roof with a coward from hell
Tis natural for a woman to stir her man
A good life for the family, that was my plan
But now I live in trembling and fear
Lest the courts come and spank at my rear
And no Mr. Freud, my fright betrays no desire
Believe me, my unconscious is no liar
This old myth of feminine masochism
Is a remnant of patriarchal fanaticism
"Woman is the problem; man is virtue and good" [she gestures scare
quotes]
Pounded in our head till we understood
I know it all too well, the story from hell
"She put the innocent man up to it
He could not say no, he had to do it" [she gestures scare quotes]
It's an ancient tale as old as Eden
Woman is evil and man is all reason
Let it not be so, I fear condemnation
Lord, I entreat you, guard my salvation.

[The Absolute returns as an apparition with gentle voice]

THE ABSOLUTE: Fear not Martine, heaven's graces you will receive
The Absolute hears your pain, your words I believe
Indeed, you may have sinned in leading your man
Down a gloomy path without rigorous plan
If man is the head and woman, the neck
Steer him aright, not straight into wreck
Subtle feminine guile is entirely fair
A man unduped by woman is sure to err
For years, I have observed your life and your pain
To live with Sganarelle is a heavy strain
His debauchery made life into hell
You put up with him incredibly well
But his wanton ways led you to despair
You lost all your hope in life and in prayer
If you turned into a savage old shrew
The Absolute knows that tis not all of you
When a woman becomes cruel to her man
The Absolute knows: she's a symptom of man

64 Philosophy After Lacan

So, rest assured and sleep sound, without care
You shall ne'er be impugned for this affair.

Scene 12: The Concluding Soliloquy of the Chorus

THE CHORUS: O men, women and children of the day
Though this is not a Theban play
It stages the calamity and abomination
That has plagued the world and our nation
Through Sganarelle we have tried to show
The madness of the world in all its woe
The university discourse has prevailed
Sanity and reason have been derailed
We see the rise of dogmatic scientism
It heralds the dawn of gloomy nihilism
The transplanting of stool into the anus
By God, what could be more heinous?
How could there be a good prognosis
With a psychotic "remedy" for psychosis
We must gather the courage to condemn
American psychiatry and the DSM
They have become a collection of names
Without proper theoretical frames
A list of symptoms and traits without concern
For the suffering of those who mourn
The various losses that plague a life
Be it a father, mother, child or wife
The complexities of the human soul
Are managed by biochemical control
Tis all a part of contemporary hedonism
Which appeals to plebeian cretinism
The promise of eternal joy without pain
A life unscarred by mark or stain
Pop one pill and total bliss shall be
Regardless of the vicissitudes of destiny
Not to mention theories of autism
Where biology is the new theism
As for medical bodily transformation
It may lead to subjective liberation
But it may also hide omnipotent delusion
To wish for a magical solution
If biomedical intervention
Entirely replaces conscious reflection

We see omnipotence in various guise
Bare and naked, without disguise
Noah's mother projects her guilt outside
Her own responsibility is denied
A sturdy bond is formed with her child
She is captivated, rivetted and beguiled
Castration has been repudiated
A return to Eden is advocated
They will urge you not to bite the fruit
Lest awareness brings them disrepute
Psychoanalysis is what they oppose
Denial of the unconscious, they impose
"Sexual difference is a social construction"
Therein lies some truth but also confusion
Generational difference is forgotten
Parental authority is downtrodden
This is especially true of Noah's father
His words are but mirrors of the mother
A tender teddy bear without a claw[5]
Has he the power to proclaim the law?
A symbolic father must castrate the Other
Be it the doctors, science or the mother
Thereby freeing the child for fun and play
Not obsess over pronouns – "he", "she" and "they"
Today's masters are masked as liberators
They reproduce power, they are its perpetrators
The lust for domination and control
Has extended to the dominion of the soul
It's all disguised as knowledge and science
Don't be fooled, tis an unholy alliance
When power wears the cloak of truth
A cunning way to mislead the youth
It's the mark of university discourse
To sacrifice knowledge for power's sake
Its theories, cauldrons of error and mistake
Its dominion goes far beyond mental health
Into the sphere of economics and wealth
Deceiving the innocent without a clue
To settle for breadcrumbs out of view
Rather than enjoy the full loaf of bread
Let mere scraps and morsels fall on their head
This is the madness and folly that ensues
When Milton Friedman triumphs in his ruse
And the wise Karl Marx is cast away

His grand theories and visions left to decay
The idea of individualism is a lie
It leaves the poor down low and the rich up high
It denies entanglement and connection
True justice is achieved when there is reflection
Regarding how my neighbour is my symptom
He is not a distant Other but close kin
Thought adequate to the symptom is our salvation
Tis akin to Freudian overdetermination
It is a materialism that considers
Ghosts, spectres, and generational transmitters
All the things which exist but remain unseen
Language, the unconscious, that "Other scene"
Such philosophy born out of Lacan and Freud
Is the antidote against the modern void
The university discourse reifies the person
It's a kind of theoretical coercion
The human spirit will resist this plight
With illness and symptom, it will fight
"Sickness is the birth of spirit", Hegel claimed
It is the cross that we must bear unashamed
Let us chant together in universalist decree
Death to the discourse of the university
Goodbye false paradise, so deeply ingrained
With Freud and Lacan, we are symptom regained
Men and women, chant with us as we exclaim:
Of paradise lost and symptom regained
Of paradise lost and spirit regained
Of paradise lost and symptom regained
Of paradise lost and spirit regained
…

[The sound of the chorus fades away. We are in a psychoanalytic office with a patient on the couch and a psychoanalyst behind him. The psychoanalyst (Dr. Molar) touches the patient gently on the shoulder]

DR. MOLAR: Wake up John Copelin! Your time is up. Open your eyes.

JOHN COPELIN: Oh, I'm sorry Dr. Molar. I fell asleep. I had a crazy dream. There was a woman called Martina, I think.

DR. MOLAR: Who is Martina? [He slowly articulates the syllables of her name]

JOHN COPELIN: I don't know but it's definitely not my mother.

DR. MOLAR: Hmmm.
We'll continue tomorrow.

And please, remember to take your meds next time.
Hopefully it will help you keep your eyes open.

[John stands up and leaves. Dr. Molar is left pensively stroking his beard as the curtains close. The chorus is heard again faintly in the distance]

THE CHORUS: Of paradise lost and symptom regained
Of paradise lost and spirit regained
…

Notes

1 The title is a play on Molière's *Le médecin malgré lui* (*The Doctor Despite Himself*).
2 This is a treatment for schizophrenia involving the transplanting of faecal material from a "healthy" person into someone suffering from schizophrenia and other ailments, some physical and mental.
3 Some very insightful psychoanalytic insights of Francesca Biagi-Chai inform the chorus's chant. Her astute comments can be found here: www.youtube.com/watch?v=vlzy6UxZMFM.
4 In her masterpiece entitled *Meeting the Universe Halfway*, Karen Barad draws out the ontological and ethical consequences of quantum physics. On the side of ontology, she argues brilliantly that metaphysical individualism does hold because entanglement radically blurs the contours that would allegedly circumscribe an "object". On the side of ethics, Karen Barad argues that we must take responsibility for our entanglements. I translate this idea to mean that we must see in the Other a symptomatic reflection of ourselves, rather than a total stranger to be denied. If the Other commits a wrong, I am entangled to his/her act too.
5 Charles Melman (2022) refers to a particular transgendered child's father as a gentle teddy bear ("un gentil nounours") who repeats what the mother tells him.

References

Barad, K. (2007) *Meeting the Universe Halfway.* Duke University Press.
Melman, C. and Lebrun, J.-P. (2022) *La disphorie de genre. À quoi se tenir pour ne pas glisser? 20 ans après l'homme sans gravité.* Éditions érès.
Molière. (2013) *Le médecin malgré lui.* Folio.

Chapter 4

How Not to Kill a Hysteric

Jamieson Webster

There is something annoying about the celebrated (or denigrated) muteness, disappearing acts, or unspoken bodily protest attributed to hysterical women at this point in psychoanalytic history. Any analyst who has worked with a hysteric knows the intense intricacy of what comes to be said, the incredible work of analysis that she performs, no less the process of encountering again and again some kernel of trauma, the very limits of understanding, that tends to bring the analysis towards its final moments. Why emphasise what is merely the symptomatic starting point? Why not spend time describing the ferocious intelligence of some hysterical patients when it comes to analytic work, no less their intelligence in relation to their analysts, something that has often been called clairvoyant, even if defensive − let's talk about you?

What other treatments are as maddening, mystifying *and* magical? And what about the hysteric's politics, so variably celebrated as radical, feminist or disparaged as submissive, conservative? This also seems to miss the mark of what takes place in analytic work; though the question, no less how it is conceptualised, is not impertinent for the future of the institution of psychoanalysis. What could a more hysterical psychoanalysis look like, and is that even something we want in the 21st century? Looking at an analyst analysing hysteria (Kristeva), a hysterical analyst (Montrelay) and the hysterical analysand turned analyst (Tustin) we will try to get closer to hysteria.

Admittedly, one could even spend a great deal of time on the infamous aggression of these patients, how charmed and terrified we might be of them − Freud's "morbid craving for revenge". Or the impasses and virtues of such a direct display of hostility towards the world, and certainly, at times, towards the analyst. There seems so much left to do, technique-wise, around the important question of "negative therapeutic reactions" which, addressing what Freud called the bedrock of castration and the repudiation of femininity, seems to speak to a hysterical dilemma, at least in its final forms of resistance. We would have to be careful here to avoid the drift into denunciation, like Kernberg for whom they are simply, constitutionally, too aggro. Or the demand for something real, what Freud called, a woman who only tolerates "soup with dumplings" − not nice.

DOI: 10.4324/9781003425953-5

Or what about living with their amnestic problems that always make the analysis something that escapes – also, at times, a virtue, for who would want to remember all of *that*? And finally, there is the place or point where hysterical analyses get stuck, or fail, in the grand tradition of Freud's Dora. This is often the place we are taught the most as analysts, testing our elasticity to the hilt, challenging our lingering symptoms. How does the hysteric make you a partner, a symptom partner, and how does this effect an analysis. One could spend a lifetime figuring out how to describe the intricacy of this *danse macabre* – but that's also an hysterical trick.

Even if we hand to the hysteric the inspiration for the construction of new maladies that help create new social bonds – a vigilance for a connection to the Other different from what is on offer – how this is discovered, underlined, read and marked in the analysis, no less, what she comes to do outside, always seems to slide by the way side. And does the analyst even get to see the fruits of their labor with her? We've always wondered about Dora's bridge club that she ran with Frau K, a master of the game who taught it to other women, reuniting her with her object of love:

> It is as if, across the years, they had finally dispensed with the superfluous men who had previously been their partners in their complex social games and contracts, yet they had retained their love of those games whose skill lies in the secret of mutual understanding of open yet coded communication within and across a foursome.
>
> (Appignanesi and Forrester, *Freud's Women*, p. 167)

Such an unexpected and strange future of the case of Dora, also given the fact that bridge is Lacan's treasured game, the model of analytic technique.

Darian Leader, in an essay titled "Hysteria Today" remarks that the idea of hysteria today is an oxymoron. It's always the hysteria of today, and today, we psychoanalysts, may not actually be the object of transference any longer; that their conversion symptoms may not be addressed to the analyst. So try as one may – you won't get very far unless one manages in the opening act to become the point of address. Leader writes:

> referral to psychotherapists, let alone psychoanalysts, is quite rare here, and the symptoms tend to lead to rounds of consultation with specialists. The body remains Other, the site of an unexplained and pervasive misery. After months or years of inconclusive care, their symptoms may settle into chronicity or metamorphose into something else.
>
> (p. 31)

A group of psychoanalysts and myself tried to work with a group of women with chronic illness. The transference to the work of analysis was seemingly impossible as they had not exhausted the possibilities, which are endless today, of trying to force an intervention on the real of their bodies. I think many will return. Ever the optimist when it comes to hysteria.

Today we hear so much about mass hysteria, hysterical contagion, the destructive unveiling of the lack in the Other (the move from father as empowered to father as lacking to the mother as lacking), and so on, with respect to what is taking place socially. But we also know that hysteria is a very particular phenomenon in a transference between analyst and patient structured through the medium of speech; which is not the same thing as a social phenomenon and its amorphous appearance in groups of individuals via the mechanisms of identification and discourse with forms of panic that can dominate. And while in analytic work hysteria or hystericisation is the hinge mechanism for certain transformations, socially there is neither an analytic environment nor an analyst, and thus even less of a guarantee than that faced by the analyst.

Should we get rid of the term hysteria then? There is no end of encountering the sense of the word as used in a misogynist way – stop being so hysterical! – or, immediately condemned as misogynist, leaving us on the defense. And yet, as Vincent Dachy, says (trying to answer the question of whether we should keep the word or even the concept) that while it may be dangerous to discard the concept – for we always need a space to think about the new ways of "grasping, circumscribing, taming" the real of dissatisfaction – if we do get rid of it, we cannot let disappear the consideration of symptomatic arrangements and constructive solutions when it comes to speaking about dissatisfaction and the thorny problems of enjoyment. He reminds us that desire, enjoyment and love will never line up in the social field, and it is hysteria which is the most vocal about confronting this dimension of truth. And "who wants to do without that?" he finishes his piece. The conundrum being that everyone may want to do without it, even the hysterics!

What do analysts say about hysterics: she became a psychoanalyst. And then? What have these figures brought to psychoanalysis and its institution? What does this have to do with the strange splitting that seems to beset the analytic institution and its insistence on wandering off alone, ambivalent about its place at the margins? While the Other woman is seen as hidden behind the Father in hysteria, Darian Leader points out that it is often more useful to think of the horror-fascination the hysteric has with respect to an ideal of *jouissance* this woman is seen to have and which she sees as excluding her. No end of symptoms arise in this place. Psychoanalytic institutes then are basically eating disordered. Think of the approach-avoidance in relation to candidates in psychoanalysis, starving them or "killing their creativity" as Kernberg called it, by stuffing them with information and infinite tasks. Where is the transformation of this ideal which fosters the horror-fascination into the possibility of joy in analytic institutions and embracing of castration?

Think of how psychoanalysis cosies up to the phallic institutions it was meant to ward-off, like the university, or medicine, or psychiatry or even pharma, and then feeling abandoned by them? Importantly, wellness itself is now an industry, allied to capitalism and privilege more generally, with which psychoanalysis flirts in its 21st-century forms. And wellness, in its obsession with the body, is decidedly hysterical. Will this make for a more hysterical psychoanalysis? It depends, I suppose, on how we hook into the question of the body. If we do so but refuse to leave sexuality behind. Mind you, an ethos of wellness in relation to the body will certainly not mirror what is meant when we talk of the hystericisation of the patient in analysis, which is a deepening of the confusions around desire and enjoyment.

Lacan is a problem with respect to these questions – too specifically, historically and culturally French; though it's not as if psychoanalysis hasn't taken a huge hit in Paris. The documentary *La Muir* – The Wall – (about the Lacano-Freudian treatment of autism) made a mockery of the psychoanalysts who were all too eager to be interviewed, seemingly unaware of how their words might be taken – so sure of themselves and their theories. It is difficult to watch, cringe-worthy, as when an analyst proclaims that girls who are sexually abused by fathers may become a little stupid, but won't become psychotic, like a son with a mother. Or the analyst who is asked about what can be hoped for in the psychoanalytic treatment of an autist, and he replies, the enjoyment of soap bubbles.

This documentary was part of a wider attack on the hold psychoanalysis had institutionally in France, and while it is a story of rival theories and treatments, it is also a war waged via capitalism where the search for treatments is a search for what is economically viable and serves the interests of this machinery – fast and cheap and repressive – through which this or that modality of treatment and its adherents are swept up. It was sad to watch the psychoanalysts get drawn into this documentary that served these interests, only to be spit out quickly. Lacan, I do believe, takes up these changes he senses on the wind when he speak about capitalism and technology, but he was doing so well as a psychoanalyst that the threat being posed to the art, no less practice, remained an insider affair – and this is how all his affairs were. Who among you understands me? A hysterical ploy to be sure. The drama is local – a *famille*.

Sometimes it feels like a game of seduction with the women, and there are so many extraordinary French women analysts who produced voluminously for the love-hate of Lacan: from Julia Kristeva to Luce Irigaray, Colette Soler, Michèle Montrelay and Geneviève Morel, to Catherine Clément and Catherine Millot, Monique-David Ménard and Barbara Cassin, to name a few. But from another angle, one can see Lacan as a game for men, with all the trappings of a battle for recognition fueled in the transference cross-fires of the teachers and students from the École normale. Does it matter that

72 Philosophy After Lacan

Lacan begged the women in his audience to speak while inviting one boy-philosopher after another to formalise what he said?

The very fact that we've moved from a question of women analysts to the interrogation of men and Lacanian psychoanalysis seems hysterically apt. Why is it so hard to stay on the side of the women? This drift into exclusion is of course a Lacanian joke: "If there is one thing about which women have complained enough for the time being, this is it – only they don't know what they are saying, that's all the difference there is between them and me" (Se 20, *Encore*, p. 68). At first glance, the comment feels utterly misogynistic, until you realise what he is doing is reversing the polarity of the exclusion – he may know more about what he is saying, but she knows when she is enjoying, enjoys what she knows, even if she says nothing about it and complains about me, over here, with my pathetic explanations.

Everything in Lacan comes to a full-stop in the figure of women and their singular relationship to their own body. Exclusion is close to separation. Being with one's body that you can't really have, surely leaves one feeling separated out, a partner with one's own solitude, as Lacan said once of female *jouissance*. But where are all the solitary women now? Can we actually try to listen to what they have to say about analysis?

The Analyst of Hysterics

I decided to look at Kristeva though there were many others I considered, including Juliet Mitchell and Christopher Bollas who have long case studies and theorisation around working with hysteria. But I like Kristeva, which is why I was surprised by this case, and its sharing in a similar antipathy that, as Anne Worthington remarks in her essay "Beyond Queer?" creeps up constantly when analysts speak about hysteria – always brining the conclusion that there is something "deadly" there, whether it be the devil, evil, or the death drive.

Looking at the question of women as it punctuates Kristeva's book *New Maladies of the Soul*, she takes up the question of whether hysteria and other neuroses look different in the contemporary crisis of values that she says leave us without a soul, something she equates with the world of representation. The idea of the loss of our soul might not be a great starting point for the question of women. It leaves Kristeva oddly adrift in her work with hysterics without even the impasses that Freud thought could firmly be dealt with simply by the frame of analysis alone. There seems to be a doubt about whether these soulless women will take to a talking cure at this point in time. Many analysts theorising that the times are changing patients drastically, feel that psychoanalysis no longer works, whereas we always thought the idea was that we were to change with them – or at least that is what we thought the idea was.

Kristeva glides into her conundrum with hysterical anxiety, never-felt-as-such, which leads to all kinds of cognitive breakdowns in the form of vagueness, amnesia, somatic symptoms, affective outbursts, acting-out, para-suicidal gestures, erotomania, linguistic muteness, hostility, or even all of them at once. As she puts it:

> Hysterics seek a maximal symbolic and psychic *jouissance* while simul-taneously postulating the impossibility or futility of this desire. This dis-crepancy takes on some well documented forms: endless seduction *and* frigidity, an eroticization of the link with other people and the outside world *and* an untouchable autosensuality, verbal haste *and* the discredit-ing of speech, an erotomanic exaltation *and* an inexorable sadness with its underlying depressive tendencies, the incitement of the father and his knowledge *and* a spasmodic, angry and mute body that can even be morbid toward the rival, the double, the mother.
>
> (Kristeva, *New Maladies of the Soul*, p. 70)

While I would love to be the all and *and* of this hysterical conundrum, so well described, Kristeva finds it something of a challenge. Anyone who has worked with a hysteric, she says, will recognise in them precocious children – they are often described as sexually, verbally, intuitively, precocious. They are often caught at the threshold having arrived too early. This too-soon all too-soon grows ambivalent about what she knows and what she feels, putting her on separate tracks of development. Kristeva says the hysteric is caught between two kinds of reminiscing or memories, two systems of representa-tion, two sexualities, indeed, two parents, with competing interests. But is this really new? Is this an example of a contemporary form of soullessness?

Kristeva gets caught up in the "auto" aspect of the hysteric, not merely the automaticity of her unconscious mechanisms (what else would they be), but of her sensuality, what she calls auto-sexuality, a new version of Freud's auto-eroticism, as well as, auto-*jouissance*. The hysteric can't seem to join an intense sensualisation and auto-erotic excitability with genital or actual sexuality, what she calls desire and the knowledge attached to it. Again, this all sounds fantastic, as with all that the hysteric displays of the search for and sense of the futility of *jouissance*, but Kristeva says this, as if this wasn't the sheer truth of *jouissance*, of the disjunction of bi-phasic sexuality in Freud's *Three Essays, or* the difficulty of interpretation pure and simple as that which addresses the knot of *jouissance*, desire and love. She says it as if it is a real and chronic new deficit. Again remember here that the question of the disjunction between love, desire and enjoyment in a body, is the site, in a manner of speaking, of hysterical address.

Kristeva then moves to unequivocally state that the disjunction between these two shores *is* the very space of the unconscious, the site of transit or transference where the unconscious is discovered, along with the analyst.

74 Philosophy After Lacan

"As they both (unconscious desire and its analyst) are servants of the hysteric, they allow hysterics quite simply to exist. That is they allow them to exist within the speech that shapes hysterics, but also dissolves them" (p. 76). The hysterical ambivalence of the statement itself must be noted – not merely the question of being the hysteric's servant, a problem straight out of Freud's countertransference, but also the idea of dissolving hysterics in the language they abhor, while also venerating them for targeting the very arena that delimits the unconscious and the psychoanalyst. If you don't throw yourself at the feet of such a hysterical feat, you probably want to kill this hysteric.

A short while later in the chapter, Kristeva advises analysts to consider using anti-anxiety medications on hysterics, just before she goes into a section to discuss counter-transference problems with them. This recommendation is strange, especially when she goes on to iterate the difficulties of dealing with the oral-phallic hunger of hysterical patients, but she claims that their bodies, so excitable, sometimes need to be calmed in order to do the work of integrating their split halves. I have had so many of our hysterical patients come to us having had therapists who threw medications at them, sometimes by the dozen, since of course this only ups the ante as an act caught in the transference. Strange also, since Kristeva mentions how Lacan thinks of working with hysteria – namely that one has to work with not-knowing, especially with her not-knowing, and not rush to translate all of this into words or objects. What is medication if it is not an object, all too close to the object *a*. If you give it, you can't be it. That much seems categorical.

Kristeva understands that for Lacan, the analyst must part with any idea of "cognitive congruence" (read here integration) and use their ignorance to listen, becoming the object of the patient. With this gap firmly in place, the analyst can play a game of bridge – play with death, play dead, work with the cards that are on the table! But Kristeva says she doesn't understand how this strategy doesn't become complacency, apathy, or even a hidden phantasmatic union with the hysteric? Well, from my perspective, it doesn't because you don't let it – that is the job of the analyst. One must always to be attuned to the vicissitudes of separation and difference, how they are potentially being covered over or mismanaged.

That being said, working with any patient may enter complacency, apathy or hidden forms of gratification and identification, but we are meant to have faith that our listening to our own and the patient's unconscious would alert us to something going off-track. But what does this have to do with hysteria? Kristeva is worried about the sheer repetition of fantasy that the hysteric is want to evoke, worried that the transference takes such a hold on the analyst that they will never escape, like the fantasy of her body as what must be quieted so that she can give herself to the symbolic work she eschews and stop making everyone the slave of her *jouissance*. But isn't this such a

How Not to Kill a Hysteric 75

prototypical neurotic fantasy itself, both the desire born of a body and the disgust in the face of it? What is it then doing as Kristeva's fantasy of what can beset the analyst? Whose hysterical fantasy is this, namely, that someone is going to repeat their fantasy in you? She needs to calm down. Give Kristeva a Klonopin.

The patient Kristeva in fact speaks about in the chapter on hysteria, Claire, gets her to shut-up and stop Claire-ifying everything (Kristeva makes this pun herself) she says by becoming utterly confused about things having to do with the analysis – what the analyst said, their agreements, her vacations, all her points of reference. Kristeva said the patient worked to eject her from her mental framework. She also mentions that her turn to silence was a strategy to *make* the patient think that *she* was mistaken – I guess she wasn't – which seemed to work and keep the patient out of her prior states of confusion. The patient, Kristeva reports with pride, went on to say some important things, finally, about her father, and moved away from the maternal conflict. But perhaps this silence helped Kristeva be less confused and stop making unhelpful interpretations or, at the very least, left what she did say to the future where it could open of its own accord.

Why not give up one's "mental framework"? Isn't this the Bionian, no memory, no desire, starting point of every session? In a strange, final, misogynistic turn, in the chapter on "Women's time" looking at the question of female writing, Kristeva asks how the female and maternal can become a 'true' act of creation – without masochism, and without annihilating one's intellectual and professional personality. Again Kristeva is worried about the hysterical attack on the symbolic, the social contract and communication, which amount – I guess – to a less true act:

> Does women's literature consist of a morose rejection of the very 'male literature' that serves as a model for so much of women's writing? Thanks to the stamp of feminism, do we not sell many books whose naïve whining or commercialized romanticism would normally be scoffed at? Do female writers not make phantasmatic attacks against Language and the Sign, which are accused of being the ultimate mainstays of male chauvinist power, in the name of a body deprived of meaning and whose truth would only be 'gestural' or 'musical'? Nevertheless, however questionable the results of women's artistic productions may be, the symptom has been made clear: women are writing. And we are eagerly awaiting to find out what new material they will offer us.
>
> (Kristeva, *New Maladies of the Soul*, pp. 220–221)

I'm not really worried about *any* of these things, not the masochism or professional undoing, not the rejection of men, or even the whining or romanticism. I'm especially not concerned with the hysterical distaste for language capital L – in fact, it is more crucial than ever for psychoanalysts to acquaint

76   Philosophy After Lacan

themselves with what is beyond language, something Kristeva has written powerfully about and often. Finally, the attack on the social contract if done in earnest in the space of analysis is always an attempt to forge a new one, however vehement the attack. It is an attack on the analyst after-all and not the social. One way to steady the attacks of patients is not to be undone by them.

What seems most strange, in the end, is the idea that we are awaiting anything from women and what they have to offer. Women have been writing for quite some time (this essay was originally written in 1979, while the book was published in 1994 in English), there is much to be read, new material has long been on offer and has radically altered the landscape again and again.

The psychoanalyst, above all, in having treated women for over a century, has been there with her, reading these turbulent remains. The continued denunciation of the hysteric (or borderlines or whatever you want to call them) at least testifies, albeit negatively, to the continued conundrum. I was told by a close colleague in Paris that as far as feminine or Other jouissance is concerned, it is something difficult to open someone up to – they have to have, at the least, a taste for it. Otherwise it drives them crazy. What about the psychoanalyst's taste for it?

The Hysterical Analyst

In Michèle Montrelay's paper "Inquiry Into Femininity" she says that jouissance is extra-territorial and always subject to repression and discipline in a patriarchal world. Psychoanalysis moves in the opposite direction. Interpretation or work in analysis is a means of listening to the progression and rhythm of *jouissance* that is not a repression of the hysteric and instead produces infinite pleasure, transporting her unconscious, and her body, into the realm of the signifier. Turning to a clinical example of hers, it reads like a testimony of this infinite pleasure in the form of a listening psychoanalyst that can only be called hysterical.

Michèle Montrelay, in her paper "On Folding and Unfolding: An Example of Dream Interpretation in English", speaks about how she works as an analyst, especially in the direction of a re-enchantment of language, to give words back their value as sound and music, their visual graphic nature, their coenesthetic and motor value, their historical value, their semantic value pertaining to grammer, syntax, etymology. Everyday life, she says, restricts these values, and we want every word to say as much as it can – a slight twist on the law of free association.

Montrelay goes into great detail on a case and shows how she came to unlock several signifiers through close attention to the patients language, along with her own associations. She says this kind of work demands a lot of the analyst: the analyst regresses, and yet cannot let the states they are dragged into overwhelm them, they must work at the edge of language and with their own imagination and attentive listening. The analyst has to let the patient's words work on the analyst, not just in a session, but for days, maybe even years. All this, and yet the analyst must not think, must not reason, must not make arguments.

She says that she understands that one might want to object to her way of working, to say that she lets her imagination run wild, that maybe she subordinates the patient's fantasy to her own − in the dream text she was analysing she constellated a series of words used by the patient in order to locate what she felt were the repressed signifiers which amounted to a word that, for her, pointed to a fantasy of his mother's pregnancy, a kind of primal scene. This she saw as the source of the inhibition behind his premature ejaculation, current somatic asthmatic difficulties and breakdown after publishing his book. She also came upon a word that, by the end of analysis, seemed to touch on, but also break apart, the name of his father; a name that had been buried not only by his mother and her family that had erased it (and him) from the patient's life, but also in the patient's unconscious, held in a kind of suspension. This is why publishing with his father's name was not only a transgression against a maternal prohibition, but a point of real breakdown.

Montrelay didn't say any of this to him. She is clear on that in her detailing of sessions. She merely commented on the words, watched as the material unfolded, sometimes quite to the patient's bewilderment and even overt annoyance. A kind of − so what, these stupid words, what do you mean? But she was succinct about where her imagination took her and the importance that she accorded to this work in the unconscious that happened almost beyond her and the patient. Her response to the criticism that she is just making all of this up, letting her imagination run away with her is − "it must be so":

> In this space whose coordinates are the two rules − free association and floating attention − it is not up to us to decide where the separation comes between analyst and analysand. Let there be no misunderstanding on this point: I do not consider there is a fusion of two people here. No. There are processes of differentiation in this field − unless the analysand is psychotic, but in that case the practice of the two rules, and consequently that of words, is not advised, or should be handled with the greatest care. Thus there is differentiation, but it is not up to us, through a deliberate act of judgment, to localize what belongs to the analysand… and what belongs to us… Separating transference and countertransference would destroy both of them. The dynamics of analysis would disappear.
>
> (Montrelay, *On Folding and Unfolding*, p. 203)

She does not differentiate, she allows there to be differentiation by virtue of what comes to be said and heard. The method for her is in fact quite Freudian. How words lead by themselves to childhood, the body, sex, deploy and structure these earliest traces, act like condensed folded programs to be

78 Philosophy After Lacan

unfolded and brought into suspension in analytic work, often bringing painful experiences into the present, but also, eventually lifting inhibitions. This is the very question Freud asked in the opening of *his* first book – Studies in Hysteria.

Giving words back to themselves in the shuffle between patient and analyst often makes new meanings suddenly appear that are "surprising, multiple, unsuspected, and yet perfectly logical" (Montrelay, *On Folding and Unfolding*, p. 209). Despite the toll on the analyst, periods of stagnation and blockage, the feeling is often that "the **drawers** that could be opened are infinite" (ibid.). This evocation of the infinite, not less that of drawers, immediately makes us think of feminine *jouissance* in the work of analysis. Inhibition, which for Montrelay is keeping the patient's desire in check unnecessarily, is what analysis always seeks to unlock. She has faith in a ground of differentiation within the unconscious that allows her to work at the limit, not only of the patient's reason, but her own – to begin to touch this infinite, where, she says, "energy is to be found" (Montrelay, *On Folding and Unfolding*, p. 216).

This place is localised more and more by the work of analysis until it is 'pushed out' – a bodily and hysterical metaphoric work, to be sure. It is not the analyst's mind that is in danger of being ejected, nor is it even aspects of a patient's life that are in danger of being annihilated (that already happened), but a method that breaks apart psychical formations so that new material surges forth, the neurosis pushing itself out, externalising itself in the process, and unlocking what was caught in the crossfires of familial desire. This happens as patient and analyst dream together, regress, suspend life; all without too many ideas or arguments, and certainly without judgment. The method, indeed, feels Freudian to us too, but also, quite hysterical. It is a work of close, delicate, empathic reading and listening, done almost blind. Her work with patients pushes towards a construction, wrapped in the poetics of language, at the place it can touch something infinite – painfully so, and undo itself. After Lacan dissolved his school, Montrelay never belonged to a psychoanalytic institute again.

The Analysand of a Hysteric

Let me end with a story quite apart from the scene of the French intelligentsia. The analyst Francis Tustin became famous for her work with autistic children where she goes into exquisite detail about the failures of separation between these children and their parents. For Tustin, autistic children are different from more disorganised or schizophrenic children in their experience of separation, where the latter have to dilute their recognition of separation through confusion and fragmentation, while the autist is locked in a kind of encapsulation which denotes an intactness and a sharper split:

they think the shizophrenicky ones will be treatable because they're sort of outgoing and they're warm and they're cuddly. But, in fact, they're much more difficult to treat... because they are all over the place, a bit of them is in the table, a bit of them is in the chair, a bit of them is flying about on the ceiling. To get all these scattered bits together is very difficult.

(Hunter, Francis Tustin Interview, p. 83)

She is one of the few analysts that has said that psychoanalytic treatment can *sometimes* cure autism.

The autistic child, she says, experienced a pathological form of fusion where the other is something like a limb, part of their own body, which is then too painfully and abruptly lost when separateness inevitably dawns on them – "they feel skinned alive, shorn of their skin, or they feel they've lost a supporting limb... they were one skin and one body. Yes, then they felt wrenched apart and felt wounded" and the parent couldn't help them because they were wounded too. The autism then emerges as a protection from this wounding – "And they are always trying to get that back. They take your hand to open the door. They're always trying to get extra bits of their bodies that they feel they've lost" (ibid, p. 85). Tustin notes the survival strategies of autistic children and their parents, wrapping themselves in sensations like objects, or, for adults, joining an endless series of committees that are like a protective shell. Many, she notes, when they emerge from autism, become artists. "They are the artists of our generation", she says with pride.

What fascinates me isn't just Tustin's work on autism in an age where millennials predict that we will all become autists sooner or later, wrapping ourselves in the separation-less sensations of our iphones, but what Tustin says, or rather doesn't say, about how she came to do this work in relation to her psychoanalysis with Wilfred Bion. She says right off the bat that she must have been a bit autistic herself, something that may be behind her not knowing he was a distinguished analyst until close to the end of her 14 years with him. In fact, for quite a long time, five–six years maybe, she thought of him as a nuisance and an obligation with respect to her training, until one day she realised there was something very special about him. The interviewer, surprised, asks if she remembers what he said that changed her mind, but Tustin can't remember. I only remember thinking, "I have something very special here".

She also remembers that Bion never spoke to her about her childhood, not once in 14 years, and stuck close to the present. He also called her "impenetrable" one day, which she said "hurt" and "cut to the quick"; but she knows he was right. This work, she surmises, was helping her realise she was protecting a very deep depression. However, reading this interview, a lot of what she puts together feels decidedly like a retrospective reconstruction. This wasn't anything they talked about, as if they never shifted to a meta-level and discussed what they were working on, her problems, her history.

80 Philosophy After Lacan

This is what makes the interview begin to seem so extraordinary, not only what took place, but the fact that she seems to be putting it together right then and there, as she speaks to her interviewer.

She moves quickly from speaking about how Bion handled her losing a child during childbirth, breaking some of the orthodox rules of contact with a patient in writing not only to her but also to her husband, to her sudden departure from analysis, saying to him, "Thank you very much, goodbye". She says she realised now that this repeated the abrupt departure of her and her mother from her father one day – her mother packing her up and leaving, Tustin only meeting her father again as a young adult. But, saying this now, she had no idea at the time she left Bion of anything except that she wanted to leave. The interviewer, herself a psychoanalyst, seems flabbergasted, "you stopped abruptly?....Weren't you afraid of the grief you would feel losing him?" She replies, "I've no idea". "But you were analysed!", she exclaims.

Tustin, while speaking, makes a slip of the tongue and catches herself, as she meanders through this territory of losing a child, losing her analyst, losing her father, her mother's loneliness, suddenly saying:

> My mother, poor thing, was extremely lonely, and she used me to block up the hole of her loneliness. But I wasn't a very good subject for it in a way. So I think when Dr. Bion left – I mean when I stopped with Dr. Bion, you heard what I just said! I think I must have sensed that he was going abroad or something, and that the ending was coming because I know I suddenly said, "I want to stop – I don't want to come anymore." And he sighed and I remember hearing a tiny little voice, "Well I don't know if that's a very good idea." I was so set on it I hardly heard him. So I stopped. And he went to America
>
> (Hunter, Francis Tustin Interview, p. 98).

The interviewer more-or-less ignores both her slip, and her sudden interpretation that somewhere, she clairvoyantly knew he was leaving. The interviewing analyst still can't get over the idea that Tustin leaving must mean the 14 year analysis was a failure, insisting on Bion's not being able to get to her depression if she did not expect any grief. Tustin suddenly interrupts her, saying she has a "bit of an idea": "it's only when you finish that you really feel the depression about separation. The analysis is preparing you and strengthening you, but you can only experience this bodily separateness and the pain of it when you actually experience it, when you are alone. "After all, we die alone in the final moments".

She also notes importantly, that two years after she left her analysis she experienced a new symptom, a phobic reaction to people and groups that made public speaking – something she saw both her parents do when they were still together at the Church of England and before they became disillusioned with the Church and one another – completely anguishing. As well, she was learning from the treatment of an autistic child about depressive experiences of terror, a kind of black hole that you felt could swallow you up. At first she thought the child was being so silly, until she began to see it herself, everywhere – something she describes as quite dreadful, even if at times amusing. Look at both of us! She then speaks about how wonderful being so naïve and bewildered was since everything was so new and fresh when it emerged. Bion, she notes, was also good in this way, since he never relied on textbook interpretations.

Importantly, Bion, she says, was patient with her. There wasn't the sense of expectation that she should be doing anything except what she was doing in analysis. The work happened, it seems, quite without her knowing much about it – at least at the time. But she is one of the few child analysts that I have read (especially who works with severely "disturbed" children) who refuses to blame the parents. She realises as she is speaking to the interviewer, that like these autistic children, she didn't let anyone look after her, something that definitely must have happened with Dr. Bion. And the failure to understand how hard this is for the other is the only way you could blame these parents who she sees as longing to find warmth with their children who reject them so abruptly, and are quite cruel in a quiet, underhanded way. It's a beautiful admission of her cruelty, along with, a demonstration of her unique capacity for empathy.

One reads this interview wondering – did Bion know? Or, what did Bion know when she left her 14 year analysis without a word, after which he would leave for America and never see her again? The question, rather than searching for an answer, is the answer itself: the end of analysis is a moment of absolute separation that no understanding should cover over. Should. Plenty of analyses are put into the throws of explication, but it is my contention that this is something many hysterical analysts will not tolerate – depending of course, on their taste for the Other. The way disjunction and differentiation makes itself felt over and over, throughout the course of the interview, like an analytic session itself, and quite to the chagrin of the psychoanalyst-interviewer, is one of the best testaments to analytic experience that remains to be read.

Conclusion

The diagnosis of hysteria is a problem that seems to bring a great deal of trouble in its wake, rather than clarifying the mechanism of transformation, the moments of invention in a treatment at the hinge between the kernel of trauma, the real of the body and the mechanism of transference. The problem is certainly one of precocious knowing as we have seen, something that is true to hysteria a la Kristeva, especially as way of keeping something at bay. But from the place of the analyst, the scales should be tipped in the direction of what this not-knowing, not-separating out too early makes possible, in the model of Montrelay and Tustin − bringing the patient and analyst to the edge of a hole. Both attest to what this makes possible, all the eventual pain, mourning and separation, even the acceptance of being cut to quick, the transformation of the complaint, the overturning of a question about dissatisfaction in a new form of pleasure, and a solution to the disjunction around desire and love and enjoyment. They find out what one can do in speech... as well as, in silence. I believe this. And I believe that this is also why the best psychoanalysis takes root there, as it did for Freud and Lacan, close to their hysteria and its untangling. If this isn't a model of what listening to hysteria, hysterical listening can do, then perhaps we do need to find another name. Perhaps, I even did that, without knowing that was what I was doing, when I moved from hysteria to conversion, and then had to plead with everyone not to kill hysterics. How hysterical!

Bibliography

Appignanesi, L. and Forrester, J. (1992) *Freud's Women*. New York: Other Books.

Dachy, V. (2016) *Necessity and Seduction: A Section of Hysteria in Hysteria Today* (ed. A. Grose). London: Karnac.

Hunter, V. (1994) Frances Tustin Interview. In *Psychoanalysts Talk*. New York: Guilford Press.

Kernberg, O. (1996) Thirty methods to destroy the creativity of psychoanalytic candidates. *International Journal of Psychoanalysis*, 77, 1031–1040.

Kristeva, J. (1995) *New Maladies of the Soul* (trans. R. Guberman). New York: Columbia University Press.

Leader, D. (2016) Hysteria Today. In *Hysteria Today* (ed. A. Grose). London: Karnac.

Montrelay, M. (1978) Inquiry into Femininity. *m/f*, 1, 91–95.

Montrelay, M. (1984) On folding and unfolding: An example of dream interpretation in analysis. *Psychoanalytic Inquiry*, 4(2), 193–219.

Chapter 5

Feed My Desire

Occupy Wall Street and the Prospect of a Lacanian Gay Science

Daniel Adleman

Occupying the Antisocial

Political theorist Lee Edelman has long singled himself out for his psycho-analytic approach to the idea of queerness as an uncanny social force. In *No Future: Queer Theory and the Death Drive*, Edelman brings Lacanian theoretical architecture to bear on queerness in order to articulate an altogether other queer theoretical scene, that of an unsymbolisable opacity on the side of the death drive. On account of his privileging of Lacanian theoretical optics, his work is largely unpopular with mainstream queer theorists, most of whom systematically privilege Derridean discourses of difference and Butlerian emphases on performance and performativity. Nonetheless, Edelman's erudite constellation of queer theory, Lacanian psychoanalysis, and broad political analyses of American cultural currents (and the fantasmatic textures they condense) must not be dismissed outright.

In "Occupy Wall Street: 'Bartleby' Against the Humanities", Edelman, improbably, brings this Lacanian theoretical architecture into conversation with discussions of the political efficacy of the 2011 Occupy Wall Street encampment. Describing Occupy Wall Street as a social rupture whose potency, he believes, emerged out of its "queer" refusal to resolve into a pellucid political program, he compares the movement to the eponymous legal clerk of Herman Melville's "Bartleby, the Scrivener". Against the grain of valorisations of OWS as an experiment in radical democracy and sociability, Edelman alleges that the opaque, antisocial dimension of Occupy was, in fact, the mainspring of its political efficacy. According to his reading, the "negativity that prefers not to pledge itself to the goal of a new community and declines its positivization in a recognizably political agenda remain[s] faithful, by that very refusal, to what vitalises politics as such" (Edelman, 2013, p. 116). If Occupy were absorbed into the dominant order of things and translated into an intelligible campaign to improve humanity's lot, the movement would, he believes, lose its potency in the process of assimilating into the homogenising network it was meant to short circuit.

DOI: 10.4324/9781003425953-6

In this essay, I will argue that, in mapping his model of antisocial queerness onto a far-reaching social movement, Edelman overhastily dichotomises Occupy's itinerary as either potently disruptive (yet without an agenda) or counterproductively oriented towards a future that reproduces the neoliberal conditions its progenitors revile. This essay will look to the work of Jodi Dean, Slavoj Žižek, Glen Coulthard, and others to conjure divergent psychoanalytic visions of efficacious twenty-first century activism. While Edelman's breathtaking critique of shallow neoliberal discourse cuts deep, his prescriptions would leave the spirit of Occupy with no recourse but to congeal into an atomised posture of what I refer to as *misanthropocentrism*, an ironic withdrawal from the fraught, drawn-out struggle to build the coalitions required to make the world a better place. Edelman's position, I argue, neglects the manifold ways that the Occupy movement has already, in spite of his predilections, metamorphosed into a project oriented towards a better future for the 99% in a fashion that is by no means reducible to the odious fantasies of reproductive futurism that he places in the crosshairs.

Strange Bedfellows

The genesis of the antisocial psychoanalytic vision that recrudesces through Edelman's writing can be located in the pioneering work of Leo Bersani. In *Homos*, Bersani takes up the thorny contradictions that inhere to the impetus for queers to integrate into the mainstream of American culture. Interrogating "the rage for respectability so visible in gay life" (Bersani, 1995, p. 114), he situates an anti-assimilationist model of "homo-ness" as more meaningfully disruptive of normative frameworks of sociability. Influencing subsequent generations of queer scholarship, what has come to be known as the "antisocial thesis" has sent ripples through most every sphere of humanistic thought on account of its investment in a *"massive redefin[ition] of relationality"* (p. 76; Bersani's emphasis).

In *No Future: Queer Theory and the Death Drive*, Edelman conducts Bersani's already psychoanalytically-informed conception of "homo-ness" through a Lacanian prism. He then deploys his version of the antisocial hypothesis to launch an erudite onslaught on the pervasive fantasy of "reproductive futurism", the ideological apparatus that justifies all social and political calculations with the (blithely heteronormative) injunction to prioritise the well-being of children and lay the foundation for a better future. Reproductive futurism, the prevailing diachronic investment in the indefinitely postponed future of humanity, privileges the sacrosanct figure of the innocent child as humanity's telos and only worthwhile organising principle. Aligning antisocial queerness with the Lacanian death drive, Edelman characterises queer negativity as an irruption of ironic *jouissance* that refuses to give way to the doe-eyed fantasy of a better future for generations to come.

Eight years later, in the wake of Occupy Wall Street, Edelman applied his antisocial conception of queerness to OWS. Examining the movement's disruption of a moribund political status quo, he writes,

> [O]n September 17, [2011] the Occupy Wall Street protests began. With the encampments in Egypt's Tahrir Square as their model, hundreds, later thousands, of people showed up to represent "the 99 percent," those whose needs, as the protestors saw it, had been sacrificed for the sake of big banks, mortgage lenders, and other corporations whose campaign contributions bought all-important influence with elected officials in both major political parties.
>
> (Edelman, 2013, p. 99)

Citing critical accounts of Bartleby's "radical refusal" and his story's "resistance to singular interpretation", he then takes up fiction writer and cultural commentator Hannah Gersen's proposal that Occupy's dissident potency should be thought through in the context of Melville's most famous and cryptic *thantagonist*; Bartleby's queerness, avers Edelman, derives not just from his refusal of patriarchal norms, family, and community, but, perhaps more importantly, from "the dignity of his resistance to power, his refusal of specific demands or requests and his poignant lack of connection to the world that would make him comprehensible" (p. 103). "From his first appearance", writes Edelman, the seemingly inhuman Bartleby "seems, to the narrator who will soon employ him, an image of life's withdrawal into a stillness beyond itself" (p. 103). In Edelman's nimble hands, Bartleby figures as a sort of queer(er) Antigone; and "I would prefer not to" figures as a *jouissensual* rallying cry against the hegemony of Wall Street.

Nonetheless, the fact that, just a few years earlier, in *No Future*, Edelman just as readily tacked queer negativity to the obstreperous, misanthropic figure of Ebeneezer Scrooge (Edelman, 2004, p. 44) should give us pause about the intrinsic compatibility of his misanthropocentric conception of queerness with the communal spirit of Occupy. Anyone who has spent time at an Occupy site (from Wall Street to the Vancouver Art Gallery grounds to the encampment outside London's St. Paul's Cathedral) will testify to the groundswell of experiments not just in dissidence but *in community* that occupiers undertook. The experience was overwhelmingly jubilant (we might even say "gay"); over the course of several months, there were public lectures and debates, free public meals, ballooning donation libraries, study groups, poetry readings, and even concerts; people from every walk of life inserted themselves into the fray and formed relationships with neighbours whom they would never have otherwise had the occasion to meet. The milieu, though antipathetic to the smooth functioning of business as usual, was intensely communitarian and sociable – very far removed from Bartleby's solitary repetition compulsion or Scrooge's resentful parsimony.

86 Philosophy After Lacan

The Message is the Medium of Change

Edelman's insistence on Occupy's *a priori* negativity stems not just from his reading of Melville and Bersani but also from his uptake of Slavoj Žižek's expositions on Occupy. After participating in OWS, Žižek wrote feverishly about the protest's significance. Just one year before Edelman's article was published, Žižek, in *The Year of Dreaming Dangerously*, claimed that Occupy's poignancy emerged out of its negation of prevailing language games:

> The Wall Street protests were thus a beginning, and no doubt one always has to begin this way, with a formal gesture of rejection that is initially more important than any positive content – only such a gesture opens up the space for a new content. In the psychoanalytic sense, the protesters are indeed hysterical actors, provoking the master, undermining his authority; and the question with which they were constantly bombarded, "But what do you want?" aims precisely at precluding the true answer – its point is: "Say it in my terms or shut up!" In this way, the process of translating an inchoate protest into a concrete project is blocked.
>
> (Žižek, 2012, pp. 83–84)

Žižek argues persuasively that the genius of the dissident occupation of Wall Street resided in its status as an open wound on the ideological milieu of "friction-free capitalism" that had reshaped so much of the world in its own image. When the only choices one is offered are Coke or Pepsi, "I would prefer not to" resonates as a powerful clarion call to reject the ruling class's mendacious alignment of "free markets" with free speech, democracy, and the well-being of the body politic.

But Žižek's account of Occupy is not altogether reducible to Edelman's ironic silo. In contradistinction to Edelman's idealisation of Bartleby as the *Real* be-all-and-end-all of OWS, the Slovenian philosopher articulates the need for a supplementary program to the traumatic Bartleby function. This parallel *Symbolic* tributary, Žižek claims, must flood neoliberalism's circuitry with a goal-oriented activist message, or concatenation of messages: "The art of politics", he writes, "is also to insist on a particular demand that, while thoroughly 'realistic', disturbs the very core of the hegemonic ideology" (Žižek, 2012, p. 84). Such a demand, "while in principle feasible and legitimate, is de facto impossible (universal healthcare for example)" (p. 84). Quick on the heels of Occupy Wall Street's initial salvo, argues Žižek, "we should indeed endeavor to mobilise people around such demands – however, it is no less important to remain simultaneously subtracted from the pragmatic field of negotiations and 'concrete' proposals" (p. 84).

Žižek's reasoning here operates along several pathways. In addition to the inaugural act of negation (which Edelman takes up and celebrates as taking place in a vacuum), he posits that "concrete proposals" like the demand for universal healthcare can serve as utopian acts of radical affirmation. America's decadent two-party consensus has long been unified around (among other issues) refusing to grant Americans the right to free or universal healthcare of the sort enjoyed by citizens of forty-three other developed and developing nations. But Occupy Wall Street, Žižek argues, was a Big Bang moment for communal interrogations of the twenty-first century American economic status quo, as evidenced by the popularity of the Bernie Sanders campaign. Žižek artfully anticipates Edelman's concerns about domesticating measures that, by divesting negativity of its uncanny power, reduce a potentially revolutionary Event to a mundane liberal democratic platform. However, he also argues for a different manner of discourse about the future. Far from writing off utopian imaginings as mere fodder for liberalism, Žižek insists that when activists dare to "dream dangerously" by voicing hitherto unthinkable demands, they subtract their utterances "from the pragmatic field of negotiations and 'concrete' proposals", thereby avoiding the pitfalls of reproductive futurism.

Desiring Dangerously

Both Žižek's and Edelman's Lacanian moorings lead them to favor Occupy's repetitive "drive" dimension, its inward-turning negativity. Also drawing on Lacanian psychoanalytic optics, political theorist Jodi Dean diverges from her colleagues by privileging revolutionary *desire* over the self-preoccupied drive. She distinguishes what she refers to as a "collective desire for collectivity" from the kind of centripetal drive-based orientation favoured by Edelman. Desire, Dean avers, "doesn't turn inward; it looks outward, toward the horizon". Dean's outward-turning politics of desire "break[s] out of the trap of reflexivity, [by] installing a gap ... a rupture of the circuit that lets us look outwards" (Dean, 2013a). According to Dean, this shattering of impotent narcissisms can arise only in a political nexus organised by competent leaders and solidary political collectives that "bring together people with different skills, experience, and knowledge" (Dean, 2013a) with a view to engineering new modes of resistance and effecting meaningful political transformations.

In *Cruising Utopia*, queer theorist José Esteban Muñoz, who is much more ambivalent about psychoanalysis, nonetheless operates on a similar wavelength to Dean: "The here and now is a prison house" (p. 1), writes Muñoz. In contrast to Edelman's formulation of a drive-based queerness that refuses to address the future (on account of the idea of the future's entanglement in reproductive futurism), Muñoz insists that a queerness that is concerned about the future may, accordingly, be more aligned with desire than the death drive. "Queerness", he writes, "is a desire for another way of being in both the world and time" (p. 96). Commenting on Muñoz's utopian desire-bound formulation, philosopher Robert Loss adds, "Utopia is never a place we really arrive at ... . Utopia is an always-forwardness" (Loss, 2017, p. 131), a

88 Philosophy After Lacan

locus of pure potentiality. In spite of his antipathy to psychoanalysis, Muñoz's utopian orientation is, like Žižek's, predicated on "dreaming dangerously" without any guarantee of awakening along the path to a righteous destination.

In tandem with Muñoz and Dean, gender scholar Jack Halberstam underscores the importance of solidarity, courage, and community over formalism, irony, and authenticity. Objecting to Edelman's conveniently narrow conception of negativity in *No Future*, Halberstam suggests that Edelman's preferences betray a decadent aestheticism masquerading as political radicalism. "While the Sex Pistols used the refrain 'no future' to reject a formulaic union of nation, monarchy, and fantasy", he writes, "Edelman tends to cast material political concerns as crude and pedestrian, as already a part of the conjuring of futurity that his project must foreclose" (Halberstam, 2006, p. 824). Edelman's mis-labelling of all orientations towards the future as "reproductive futurism" allows him to disavow political discourse that operates outside of his well-curated *misanthropocentric* comfort zone. He is, of course, welcome to adopt any disposition he chooses. But his seamless shift from the descriptive to the prescriptive register smacks of rationalisation and unnecessarily obviates new architectures of solidarity.

Inveighing against Edelman's brand of antisocial formalism, Halberstam calls for a "truly political negativity", one that feeds off of "[d]yke anger, anticolonial despair, racial rage, counterhegemonic violence, [and] punk pugilism" (Halberstam, p. 824). Marked by the "loss of mastery and meaning, unregulated speech, and [unloosed] desire", Antisocial 2.0 would seek "this time, to fail, to make a mess, to fuck shit up, to be loud, unruly, impolite, to breed resentment, to bash back, to speak up and out, to disrupt, assassinate, shock, and annihilate" (p. 824). He adds, in a jab to Edelman's formalism, the updated antisocial thesis would also need to "abandon the neat, clever, chiasmic, punning emphasis on style and stylistic order that characterises both the gay male archive and the theoretical writing about it" (p. 824).

None of this is to say that either Halberstam or Edelman necessarily wins the day when it comes to prescribing a thoughtful, courageous way forward. The partisan hostility that they demonstrate towards each other might bespeak their antinomic tension as mimetic rivals. While Edelman's eloquent *misanthropocentrism* is meant to serve as a corrective to mainstream queer theory's excessive prioritisation of individual identity and autonomy, the model of utopian desire articulated in the work of Halberstam and Muñoz productively countervails Edelman's recalcitrant rejection of future-oriented projects.

The Beginning of the Beginning of a Gay Science

In 2012, as Occupy began to unravel under the weight of increasingly vehement governmental pressure as well as its own structural impasses,

Feed My Desire 89

sympathetic activist thinkers began to reflect on the movement's deadlocks. Criticising the invidious cult of individualism and the resistance to long-term organising she found at Occupy, Jodi Dean takes umbrage with both the pervasive fetishisation of social media (i.e. praising the so-called "Twitter Revolutions") and the parasitic emphasis on individual entitlements; she views both currents as marking the beginning of the end of Occupy's political efficacy. Just as describing revolutions "in terms of their platforms" mistakes the digital capitalist tool for its hijacking, prioritising individual autonomy over solidarity confuses indulging personal preferences for creating a better world. In both cases, the long, arduous, often frustrating work of organising is displaced by ephemeral measures that inevitably fizzle out and give way to malaise.

In this regard, both the anti-futurism avowed by Edelman and the atomising emphasis on identity favoured by mainstream queer theory may be much less antithetical to the neoliberal order than their respective adherents would have it. "[E]mphases on individual autonomy", Dean writes, "appealed to people who had grown up under neoliberalism, who had been taught to celebrate their own uniqueness and who had found themselves stuck, losing and increasingly desperate" (Dean, 2013b, p. 55). Just as clicktivism seduces digital subjects into treacherous simulacra of solidarity, frameworks that hypercathect in subject positions (i.e. Halberstam's camp) and ironic *jouissance* (i.e. Edelman's) are too readily confused with the more laborious work of political organising and solidarity building.

Reoccupying the Occupiers

If the pitfalls of atomisation, irony, and impotent hashtags seemed to mark the beginning of the end of Occupy Wall Street proper, sociologist Todd Gitlin nonetheless highlights Occupy's status as "the beginning of the beginning" of a new political moment. Writing for the *New York Times* a decade after the occupation, Gitlin takes up journalist Michael Levitin's argument that Occupy inaugurated a new political subjectivity and mode of American political engagement. Looking back at the arc of the movement, its decomposition, and its recomposition in vibrant new forms, he makes the case that Occupy was a sort of "sandbox" for twenty-first century left activism:

> Over the next years, waves of activists discovered, or rediscovered, a taste for civil disobedience and other direct actions. Occupy activists went to the aid of victims of Hurricane Sandy; helped block the Keystone XL pipeline; joined the Lakota Sioux to resist another oil pipeline at Standing Rock; and threw themselves into all manner of climate-change campaigns ... . Occupy veterans joined union organizers in a "Fight for $15"

90 Philosophy After Lacan

campaign that swept the fast-food industry and inspired minimum wage referendums and laws throughout the country, even in red states.

(Gitlin, 2021)

For Levitin and Gitlin, the Bernie Sanders campaign took up the mantle of Occupy and ran with it in directions that might have seemed ridiculously utopian in 2011. "For example, Occupy's Strike Debt spinoff became the template for Sanders's 2017 proposal to make public universities free, which in turn evolved into Biden's more modest but still significant proposal for community colleges" (Gitlin, 2021).

Viewing the ramification and metamorphoses of the Occupy movement into a multitude of unfolding adjacent struggles, Levitin writes:

Some of the most skilled Zuccotti Park organizers also later founded the organization Momentum to train activists such as Weber to develop tangible policy goals and create a road map for enacting long-term, structural change. As a result, Sunrise helped marshal the youth vote in the 2018 midterms to elect a slate of House progressives including Alexandria Ocasio-Cortez, who would elevate the group's climate-jobs plan – which came to be known as the Green New Deal – to the top of the Democratic Party platform.

(Levitin, 2021)

Rather than resonating as by-products of "reproductive futurity", new manifestations of the spirit of Occupy have operated in accordance with a principle that we might call *transductive maturity*; that is to say, as these irreducible emanations and offshoots of OWS converge with other currents, adapt to the vicissitudes of the moment, change shape, and branch off into new political formations, they are still recognisably taking part in the *reoccupation*. Identifying the toolbox and subjectivity inaugurated at Occupy and the Arab Spring in #MeToo, BlackLivesMatter, and the Women's March, Levitin adds, "In the years since, a cascade of social movements influenced by Occupy have altered the national conversation ... . And in a sense, the protesters have never gone home" (Levitin, 2021).

Levelling his gaze on contemporary Indigenous and environmental struggles, Levitin adds:

The six-year battle that defeated the Keystone XL pipeline and the 10-month defense of the Standing Rock Sioux tribe in its challenge against the now-illegal Dakota Access Pipeline are two other examples of Occupy galvanizing the U.S. environmental movement as activists recommitted themselves to halting oil, gas, and coal infrastructure projects nationwide. From the fossil-fuel-divestment campaign to the 2014 People's Climate March, which preceded the Paris Accord, and from

Extinction Rebellion's militant direct actions to the global climate strikes that brought millions of young people into the streets in 2019, Occupy's groundbreaking message and tactics set the modern climate movement on its course.

(Levitin, 2021)

Arguably some of the most significant currents to coalesce with the ongoing Occupy moment have involved the increased cross-pollination between Indigenous sovereignty and (heretofore predominantly white and middle class) environmental movements. Inasmuch as Levitin's account of the itinerary of OWS holds water, one of the most vibrant and sustaining new configurations of this alliance has been the Idle No More movement.

Anishinaabe political scholar Glen Coulthard points to the North American Idle No More movement's indebtedness to and escape velocity out of Occupy Wall Street. Apropos of Edelman's emphasis on the power of anti-social negativity, Coulthard situates Idle No More against the "civilised" colonial state politics of recognition. While colonial Canadian accounts of the nation state's relationship with Indigenous civilisations has long been predicated on a quasi-Hegelian master–slave dialectic of recognition, Coulthard mobilises the psychoanalytic political work of Frantz Fanon to reject reciprocal recognition in favour of the lambent power of negativity. If Occupy was an "hysterical" rejection of the master's mandate to "say it in my terms or shut up", Coulthard frames Idle No More as a sovereign rejection of the nation state's supposedly self-evident dominion: the movement "prefers not to" acknowledge the colonial master's legitimacy or any obligation to co-operate (politely or otherwise) on his terms.

However, in contrast to Edelman's ahistorical, atomised posture, Coulthard's historically grounded, forward-looking social vision preserves a necessary place for affirmation, community, and communion with nature. Elaborating on the panoply of tools at the disposal of Indigenous peoples who refuse to forget the harms of colonialism (or allow corporate-governmental petrochemical partnerships from running roughshod over their territories), Coulthard includes roadblocks and other unfriendly direct actions as necessary strategic measures to obstruct incursions on Indigenous territories:

> Through these actions we physically say "no" to the degradation of our communities and to exploitation of the lands upon which we depend. But they also have ingrained within them a resounding "yes": they are the affirmative enactment of another modality of being, a different way of relating to and with the world.
>
> (Coulthard, 2014, p. 169)

Occupying a political posture commingling affirmation and negation, as well as historic-rootedness and utopian striving, Idle No More has been one of

92 Philosophy After Lacan

the most successful expressions of a "collective desire for collectivity" beyond the ambit of the hegemonic corporate order of things. Transcending the bounds of Occupy Wall Street, Idle No More has activated "another modality of being, a different way of relating to and with the world" in a courageous, unoverdetermined manner that opens onto a number of different possible political terrains. "As for the future?" writes Levitin, "[I]t lies ahead. Anyone looking for assurances of where our national upheavals are heading will need a clearer crystal ball than [his]." He continues, "But it is no exaggeration to say that Occupy Wall Street and its offshoots changed a good deal more of the landscape than Zuccotti Park's three-quarters of an acre in New York's financial district" (Levitin, 2021).

Picking up Dead Letters

Edelman concludes his eloquent but overly constrained vision of Occupy by equating the movement not just with the inhuman figure of Bartleby but also with his putative philosophical forebear Socrates. Counterpoising Socrates' gadfly negativity against the practical humanistic wisdom of Cicero, he launches into a virtuosic meditation on the godfather of philosophy's inherent superiority to the great Roman orator:

> Against that Socratic irony, Cicero, the Roman, despite his admiration for the Greek, affirmed the role of 'positive judgment' and with it the centrality of philosophy to public life and to the state … . Humanism, Arendt reminds us, "like culture, is … Roman in origin; there is no word in the Greek language corresponding to the Latin humanitas." In its Roman origin, however, that concept already opposes the queerness, the irony, of relentless negativity in order to identify culture with the conservation of human community. Cicero himself declares, after all, "One thing, therefore, ought to be aimed at by all men; that the interest of each individually, and of all collectively, should be the same; for if each should grasp at his individual interest, all human society will be dissolved".
>
> (Edelman, 2013, p. 115)

Audaciously situating the rhetorician Cicero, "the father of the humanities", on the side of Wall Street's economic hegemony, Edelman positions Socrates, the ironic apostate, alongside OWS. He observes that Bartleby's gaze remains transfixed on the bust of Cicero while his disconsolate Wall Street employer browbeats him on account of his occupational malfeasance.

Lionising the scrivener's refusal to give way on his preference, Edelman asks, "Does Bartleby know that the lawyer is to him what Cicero was to Socrates and will similarly eradicate his queerness through the very humanity that claims to embrace it?" (Edelman, 2013, pp. 115–16). We'll never know.

Feed My Desire 93

But Edelman seems to engage in a form of inverted Platonism in his coupling of Bartleby and Occupy. While Plato believed that art's sole value emerged out of its faithful imitation of the world, Edelman endeavours (mistakenly, I believe) to reduce Occupy's value to its fidelity to an exquisite – but, ultimately, incommensurable – work of literary art.

I like to think that Bartleby is caught up in a different slipstream of ruminations from those proposed by Edelman. While it is true that Cicero admonishes his Greek predecessor, in effigy, for his over-reliance on "negative dialectics", he also takes Socrates to task for brutally missing the mark on of some of his more myopic political recommendations. The philosophically astute "man of sharpness", writes Cicero, must be immersed in the messy throng of humanity and put himself in the position to "feel the pulses of every class, time of life, and degree, and to taste the thoughts and feelings of those before whom he is pleading or intending to plead any cause; but his philosophical books he should keep back for a restful holiday" (Cicero, 1967, p. 159). Even though Cicero exhumed his Greek predecessors from obscurity and revered them as mainsprings of wisdom and critical thinking, he also observed that Socrates' ideas about public life betoken an undue measure of estrangement from the experiences and needs of the citizenry; so much so that Socrates' philosophical prescriptions seemed to Cicero to have originated out of an absurdly hallucinatory vacuum.

As I imagine the scene playing out, the archaic visage of Cicero induces Bartleby to recall the Roman orator's sharp criticism of Socrates' maladroit ideas about Athenian politics: "Plato, when he thought fit to put these things into writing, depicted in his pages an unknown sort of republic, so completely in contrast with everyday life and the customs of human communities were his considered statements concerning justice" (Cicero, 1967, p. 159). Suddenly, it occurs to the solitary scrivener that, under different circumstances, he might have adopted a more agile political strategy, echolocated kindred spirits, and participated in engineering a world-rattling, desire-based kinetic movement. But now, locked into a tailspin of self-regarding negation, he realises that his precarious occupation of Wall Street has been for naught. His dead letter will not arrive at its destination – unless (as Cicero did with Socrates) more strategic and communitarian occupiers bravely resurrect it, reshape it, and carry it forward into the uncertain future.

References

Bersani, L. (1995) *Homos*. Harvard University Press.
Cicero. (1967) *De Oratore*. Trans. E.W. Sutton. Harvard University Press.
Coulthard, Glen. (2014) *Red Skin, White Masks: Rejecting the Colonial Politics of Recognition*. University of Minnesota Press.

Dean, Jodi. (2013a) "Admitting the Communist Desire." Interview by Joseph G. Ramsay. *Counterpunch*, July 11, 2013, www.counterpunch.org/2013/07/11/admitting-the-communist-desire.

Dean, Jodi. (2013b) Occupy Wall Street: After the Anarchist Moment. *Socialist Register*, 49(1), 52–62.

Edelman, Lee. (2004) *No Future: Queer Theory and the Death Drive*. Duke University Press.

Edelman, Lee. (2013) Occupy Wall Street: 'Bartleby' Against the Humanities. *History of the Present*, 3(1), 99–118.

Gitlin, Todd. (2021) "Was Occupy Wall Street the 'Beginning of the Beginning?'": A Review of Michael Levitin's Generation Occupy: Reawakening American Democracy. September 18, 2021.

Halberstam, Jack. (2006) *PMLA*, 121(3) , 823–824.

Levitin, Michael. (2021) Occupy Wall Street Did More Than You Think. *The Guardian*, September 14, 2021.

Loss, Robert. (2017) *Nothing has been Done Before: Seeking the New in 21st Century American Popular Music*. Bloomsbury.

Muñoz, José Esteban. (2009) *Cruising Utopia: The Then and There of Queer Theory*. New York University Press,.

Žižek, Slavoj. (2012) *The Year of Dreaming Dangerously*. Verso.

Chapter 6

Doomsday Fantasy
The Logic of Logistical Blocking of the Left

Arian Behzadi

Introduction

What can we say about our current post-political position (Žižek, 2018) of passively accepting the catastrophes of our time? While the "objective" crises, such as climate change, are worsening day by day and have already exceeded previous scientific predictions, the "subjective crisis", as Badiou terms it (Badiou, 2002) is showing itself, on the one hand, in passivity, hopelessness, survivalism, and "capitalist realism" (Fisher, 2009), and on the other hand, in the abhorrent rise of global fascism and a perverted denial of the catastrophe. Can we see a secret and complicit acting out of these trends?

While phobic objects such as COVID, artificial intelligence (AI), unidentified anomalous phenomena and the Anthropocene, without any prior significations, continue to administer traumatic blows to the collective psyche on a daily basis, the title of the still-relevant film *Dr. Strangelove or How I Learned to Stop Worrying and Love the Bomb* continues to capture the dominant and perverse logic of our time. This logic has been extensively analysed by Žižek (1989) and, recently, by Zupančič (2022), and its roots in psychoanalytic literature have been addressed. The truth of desires for these phobic objects is common knowledge in the field of psychoanalysis.

In a recent paper, Zupančič (2022) shows how radical politics is forgotten or disavowed for the sake of a form of pure adaptation to dramatic changes imposed from the outside. She argues that acceptance, knowledge and appreciation themselves act as the fetishist object of the disavowal. However, we can also see avoidance of "worry" in a secret love for the "end". The "worry" is strongly connected to agitation, aggression, revolution and, especially, to hysteria and fight or flight survival defences, behaviours that are abandoned in favour of a perverse "collapse". The logic of perversion is the following: the superego mandates enjoyment; it disavows limitations and symptoms by briefly acknowledging the limitations and catastrophes of the system, and this recognition enables the subject to continue its enjoyment. The new, strange circumstances mentioned above (AI, COVID etc.) are met with extreme fear, but the fear is defended against with appreciation,

DOI: 10.4324/9781003425953-7

recognition and knowledge. However, could it be that, on another level, in many situations, these apocalyptic situations are actually purely desired? Žižek (2023) states: "Only a catastrophe can save us". He argues that with the COVID pandemic, we have witnessed a push toward a political economy in which the ideological claims of neoliberalism and economism have been debunked. This logic is close to Freud's idea that, during times of war, the unconscious denial of death vanishes. However, during the post-COVID period, we are learning that there is something even more catastrophic than the pandemic: that the hope for a new form of global political economy, induced by the urgency of the virus, is rapidly fading after confrontation with the concrete logic of the status quo and capital.

So where is the hope for a catastrophe as a "wakeup call" situated in this logic? On the darker side, is anything more horrifying or more complicit with the perverse logic of the reassertion of the status quo than its appearance at a subjective level within leftist movements themselves? Is it possible that something that has not yet been signified, something that is "blocking" the total entrance of its significance in the political field, is connected to the repetitive puritanism of the Left − and that this "something" is a very private state of essential hopelessness, a secret delusional and melancholic state, one that we are urged to call a fantasy − that is, the "doomsday fantasy" − just so that we are able to talk about it. This is the melancholic belief that not only will everything end but that "things are already over". The extreme self-reproach and unconscious guilt about the destructiveness of contemporary life that is reflected in lifestyle movements, extreme identity politics and woke culture are structurally different from a common, perverse ideological denial and are based on a different logic: the logic of foreclosure rather than that of disavowal.

In reaction to our objective crisis, the old hegemonic question of "Why do the proletariat continue to vote for the fascists?" remains as valid as when Gramsci was imprisoned, but what is most disturbing, as Lacan observes, is why "the structural introduction of the discourse of the hysteric by means of artificial conditions" (Lacan, 2007) by the Left is so suppressed on an ethical level. The famous unattributed statement that "it is easier to imagine a total catastrophe that ends all life on earth than it is to imagine a real change in capitalist relations" (Žižek, 2008), in fact shows the avoidance of imagining real change in capitalist relations. We can all agree that this imagined future is hated in both liberal and conservative circles, but why is it fundamentally banned in some leftist circles as well? Why is the politics of hysteria (of a militant imagining of the end of capitalism) and revolution so unimaginable in the Left, and is there a secret complicit agreement between this unimaginability and the perverse and hyperactive neoliberalism?

On the hyperactive, manic, a "hyper-objective" narcissism (Britton, 1998) and omnipotent version of the perverse logic is obvious. This is the version that is focused on seeking a technological fix. In a recent survey of AI specialists (Grace, 2023), nearly half of the AI researchers who responded stated that, although there was a 10%+ chance that their work would lead to human extinction, their work in AI might be able to avert the climate crisis. This type of justification is something we have seen echoed by many progressive parties in the form of complicit agreements with neoliberal ideology once they get into office. There are many examples of political parties – from the Green Party in Germany to Syriza in Greece – that won elections only to turn their backs on their previously expressed radical values and that, upon gaining political power, allied themselves with fascists and conservatives, claiming that "when we have power, we will fix it" and "we need 'their' vote". Thus, the vote became fetishised. This is the most striking version of a late, universal representative politics that is trying its best all the time to target the crisis but remains oblivious to the core of the crisis: absolute capitalism (Balibar, 2019)as the complete financialisation of everything.

Another version of the subjective crisis, but with the same logic, is observable in the paradoxical position of status quo liberal politicians. While apparently advocating that the globalist universal political hegemony combat climate change and fight against the terrifying waves of nationalist right movements, in reality, their local ecological policies (not politics) pursue "resiliency strategies" against the Anthropocene, with faith that the current universal treaties (Paris and so on) will not result in any meaningful result. The nationalist interests of democracy are considered untouchable, almost holy; these resiliency policies work in the interests of nations, creating new markets for a form of the Keynesian nation–state model.

It seems that a major trend among the intellectual left, at least in the West, is to accept that there is no future beyond capitalism (referring to Fisher's notion of "capitalist realism"). At best, in the most desperate gesture, they would advocate that people vote for the bad against the worst (referring to "resistance in surrender" [Žižek, 2007]) or what has been described as infinite demands, a constant moral attack on the state, and as Žižek, argues, the perfect merging of a superego left and an executive manager state/status quo. It is as if there can be no vision of politics beyond the current voting rituals. The total ideological denial of the already existing ways of life in other parts of the world is deafening, and the silence in the face of demands (e.g. riots) for total change from the subaltern mass is ignored in favour of a comfortable, numb cancelled future (Fisher, 2014). Although there has been a novel revitalisation of some central but overlooked Marxian ideas about nature and even some utopian visions (such as degrowth communism [Saito, 2023]), organised political activism is absent. In fact, while the future might be imagined in many different ways, the question of strategy remains vague. It is as if, at a time when the "total agency for change" is needed more than ever, the praxis has "cancelled itself", and no actual universal organising politics can be imagined, while visions of post-capitalism, both utopian and dystopian, are represented as totally possible. Fisher's (2014) claim that "the future is cancelled" acts as an ideological veil that obscures the actual cancellation of activism in the present. The subjective crisis can be crudely summarised by noting that it is characterised by either a paranoid/persecutory fear or by the Right's mania for nostalgia, which we see, for example, in some radical libertinism, such as the Dark Enlightenment (Dark Enlightenment) and the self-indulgent, guilty and passive paralysis of the left. In both cases, the subject is "haunted" by impossibilities (Fisher, 2014).

Let us return to the idea that imagining the end of the world is easier than imagining the end of capitalism (Žižek, 2008). The word "imagine" is central here and is an implicit reference to the "subjective crisis". But what is a crisis? Usually, the word "crisis" denotes a rupture, a sudden and recent malfunctioning of a previously harmonious relationship. On this topic, Badiou engages with Fukuyama as follows: "Fukuyama was not wrong: the modern world [has] arrived at its complete development and [is] conscious that it is bound to die – if only (which is plausible, alas) in suicidal violence" (Badiou, 2012). Suicide is the ultimate end of the subjective crisis. Suicide is clinically known as the rejection of impossibilities (for example, the impossibilities of being; death anxiety). In omnipotent postmodern theory, the symptoms and the crisis are not only denied but, to some extent, are accepted as just a blip in the routine. We can imagine that this denial/acceptance might be working secretly with a sense of total melancholic and catatonic paralysis. This might be why the accelerationist movement, which originated in the radical Left, is connected to alt-right or libertarian technophilic movements at one extreme and, at the other extreme, continues to inspire despotic Marxist thinkers such as Mark Fisher (Beckett, 2017). The fixation on the word "imagine" or the impossibilities of the imaginary could be the commonality between these two.

I argue that the unseen melancholic aspect of leftist ideology functions in secret complicity with the more obvious part of the ideology. The doomsday fantasy includes a merging of "the end of history" with "the end of nature", which makes the ideological assumption that these are two separate entities, which is in opposition to Marx's assertion that nature has always been a condition of human labour. In this logic, there are traces of the deterministic and linear reading of history that has recently been criticised in the logic behind the melancholy of the Left (Traverso, 2017).

The Doomsday Fantasy

The doomsday fantasy, or the fantasy of the end of the world, is well-known in psychoanalysis and psychiatry. The term "doomsday fantasy" is somewhat misleading, as in the clinical sense, it does not reflect a wish for or vision of doom. Instead, it articulates the nihilistic delusion of existing in a plane of non-existence, or living in the afterlife. In psychiatric semiotics, it was first described by Cotard in 1880 as a delusion of "negation" in which patients believe that "they are dead or that the world no longer exists" (Casas López,

2021). The patient confuses the subjective change in their own attitude toward external things: the real world seems to have completely disappeared for the patient or appears to be dead.

Freud, in his pivotal paper on Schreber (Freud, 1958), describes the phenomenon. Schreber believed that the world had already ended. At the peak of his illness, influenced by visions that were "partly terrifying, but partly of indescribable grandeur" (p. 68), Schreber became convinced of an impending great catastrophe, the end of the world. Voices told him that the efforts of the past 14,000 years had come to naught and that Earth's existence was limited to another 212 years; during the final part of his stay in his psychiatrist's clinic (for whom he had eroticised a delusional transference), he believed this period had already arrived. He saw himself as "the only real man left alive", explaining the few human figures he saw – the doctor, attendants and other patients – as "miraculously created, hastily improvised men". Occasionally, contrary delusions emerged: he believed that he had been given a newspaper with a report of his own death or that he existed in a second, inferior form, and that one day, he had quietly passed away in this second form.

Freud distinguished between neurosis and psychosis as follows: "Neurosis results from the ego's conflict with the id, while psychosis stems from a similar disturbance in the ego's relationship with the external world" (Freud, 1961, p. 148). In Schreber's case, the delusion persisted despite functional improvements in the patient. This could be interpreted as the patient's attempt to return to functioning only after retaining the core node of the delusion. His new world was entirely different after the old world ended, and his return to function was linked to the remnants of that delusion. Reality remained distorted, albeit with a better organised ego. Freud interpreted this presentation as follows:

> In any case, the world's end was a consequence of the conflict between Schreber and Flechsig, or according to the etiology in the second phase of his delusion, the indissoluble bond between him and 'God.' Schreber's paranoia towards Flechsig was explained as a substitution for a homosexual love towards his father and brother. Thus, the doomsday fantasy essentially provided a resolution to a highly distressing psychic reality.
>
> (Freud, 1961, p. 69)

In this manner, the end of the world served as a way to create a new space between Schreber and God (the Other in the Lacanian sense), a space that had been structurally and developmentally rejected (foreclosed) initially and was subsequently reinvented to restore the minimal functioning of the ego. We will return to this later. This phenomenon was elucidated by Lacan in the structural topology of the sinthome, in which a new circle is necessary to maintain the connections between the "untied" circles of the Imaginary and the Real. Lacan introduced numerous innovations in psychoanalysis, but what set him apart clinically throughout his career was his clear distinction between neurotic, psychotic and perverse structures, each arising as a way of dealing with the Oedipal trauma. This clinical discovery would play a significant role in distinguishing between a melancholic and a perverse dilemma.

One can draw parallels between the logic of certain tendencies on the Left (such as accelerationism) and the doomsday fantasy of Schreber. In Zupančič's (2022) elaboration of "crazy heroism", it appears that individuals would rather die than be terrified to death by the impending future if threatening events are allowed to follow their natural course. This is especially evident in the context of climate change: the fear of being frightened to death outweighs the fear of actual death. In this manner, psychotic anxiety is defended by the delusion of "being dead".

However, we need to critically ask if this situation necessarily results in a different emotional state, a complete emotional collapse, or psychotic anxiety compared with the "passionate and superficially elated state" of perversion, as Zupančič suggests. Furthermore, the melancholic reaction lacks any fetishistic "object". In the extreme case of Cotard syndrome (total denial of symptoms), one can observe a form of zombification, in which the patient appears to be stoic, relatively calm and numb. Cotard originally described this syndrome as follows:

> If the patient would be asked their name or age, they have neither – where were they born? They were not born. Who were their father and mother? They have no father, mother, wife, or children. Do they have a headache or stomach pain? They have no head or stomach, and some even lack a body. When shown an object like a rose or flower, they respond, 'that is not a rose, not a flower at all.' In some cases, negation is total. Nothing exists anymore, not even themselves.
>
> (as cited in Casas López, 2021)

As is evident, this symptom no longer pertains to the future; there is no notion of the world ending. The tense is present and complete. This position appears to be perfectly stoic (akin to radical acceptance in contemporary psychotherapeutic terms) from an external standpoint.

This reaction goes beyond mere extreme denial; it represents something even more fundamental – a melancholic foreclosure.

Lacan described foreclosure as being in a mutually exclusive relationship with disavowal. As Grigg (2015) explains, Freud's failure to acknowledge this mutual exclusivity led to significant confusion in differentiating between mourning and melancholia and also gave rise to faulty clinical techniques, in which analysts' desire to see mourning in melancholic patients who fundamentally could not achieve it can result in worse therapeutic reactions. These shortcomings in orthodox Freudian methods later led to historical divergences in psychoanalysis, such as self-psychology.

In perversion, the unconscious fantasy remains active as a truth, with the fetish object serving as a witness to it. This is what captures the essence of perversion in object relations theory. However, another element in this dialectic is often overlooked. Many psychoanalytic texts suggest that perversion is considered unanalysable because accepting the objective reality might lead to a psychotic breakdown. Some even propose that perversion is unconsciously chosen over psychosis. Therefore, when encountering a perverse fantasy, one should also look for a corresponding psychotic fantasy (delusion).

In the psychotic structure, continued fusion is ontologically impossible. In many psychoanalytic situations, the reinvention of space with "imaginary objects" can be observed. This represents a form of castration that creates a new lack, reducing anxiety by addressing the lack of lack as the root cause. This reaction is observable in certain responses toward the "end of the world". The unconscious belief that "we are already dead" – noticeable in some left-leaning circles – can be interpreted as a response to a deeper layer of anxiety, an impasse that the Left has been grappling with at the level of strategy and organisation, encapsulated by the term "left-wing melancholia". The doomsday fantasy is more than just a denial of a partially conscious reality; it represents a foreclosure of reality itself. It negates the reality that we still exist and are, in fact, fully capable and responsible for preventing our own extinction. Viewing the world as already deceased is distinctly evident in fantasies centred on surviving post-extinction, such as fantasies of acquiring shelters and retreats, which imply not just a sense of helplessness but also a belief in immortality and omnipotence.

Freud vs. Lacan: Perspectives on Human Extinction

For Lacan, the desired subject could be understood as the surplus of need and the substance of demand, only as signifiers in the symbolic order. In this way, the psychoanalytic study of the subject is feasible only through structuralist investigations, which eventually allowed for the integration of linguistics into the analysis of the unconscious. From this perspective, Lacan suggests that post-Freudian analyses of psychosis based solely on an imaginary investment fall short in effectively situating their own discourse beyond the initial entry point. Such an approach would appropriate psychoanalysis as an ideological tool for constructing a false imaginary sense of wholeness/normalcy. Lacan suggests that there is ontological relevance in the margins between psychosis and neurosis. This distinction highlights how the subject differs from personality and psyche, aiming to avoid essentialist traps when exploring destructiveness. The introduction of the symbolic realm as a space to recognise the imaginary represents a pivotal structural shift in Lacan's thinking, allowing for the split of the "ego" from a symbolic rather than an imaginary perspective. However, when confronted with the collective crisis on a profound level, this approach falls short in explaining why the boundaries between human life and animal life are so fragile, which becomes crucial.

This might explain why psychosis is central rather than peripheral in Lacan's framework. This shift allows for a revaluation of neurosis itself, problematizing it as a "not normal" position that, in fact, stems from a fundamental universal psychotic position. The problematisation of neurosis, akin to hysteria, becomes an essential aspect of practical theory, often overlooked in contemporary left literature.

In the Lacanian context, the boundary between nature and nurture (the symbolic) becomes blurred, complicating nature itself as a signifier, a construct. Before entering the symbolic realm, the "natural state of the subject" can be signified only in retrospect. This parallels Marx's concept of nature in his German manuscripts, in which nature is constructed through human labour. Nature becomes a construct of labour relationships. Marx's fundamental assertion, relevant once again, is that "nature" has always been a constructed concept, accessible only through human labour (Marx, 1932). Thus, the Anthropocene emerges as a potential epoch imprinted with a "human condition".

It is widely recognised that Freud's political views were paradoxically conservative. He has been characterised as politically rationalist and elitist. Despite his rationalism, he remained pessimistic about communism and the idea of an enlightened mass. He envisioned a society led by a group of enlightened elites who would guide the public toward a peaceful civilisation in which aggressive drives would be sublimated. Paradoxically, Freud displayed a blend of liberal idealism and pessimism, a juxtaposition that has been extensively discussed (see Roazen, 2017). This paradox becomes especially evident when Freud's psychoanalytic thinking is examined in the context of real-world crises.

A historical perspective reveals that Freud's psychoanalytic theories confronted the existential realities of his time, particularly the two world wars and the rise of fascism. His reflections on these events are significant but expose the limitations of essentialist theories focused on studying "human essence" rather than the "subject". As noted by Gifford (1988), Freud's fixation on a purely libidinal/economic theory to explain aggression has contributed to the ongoing confusion in post-Freudian psychoanalysis. The constant oscillation between the death instinct and eros and the various interpretations of the death instinct as aggression, self-preservation or an attempt to recover from early traumas underscore the complex interplay between human nature and nurture (civilisation). This conundrum mirrors the debates of essentialist philosophy, which sought to pinpoint the origin of aggression either in biological instincts or within civilisation as a whole. However, these essentialist or humanistic explanations fall short when addressing the perplexing phenomenon of aggression.

Freud's statement that "Men have gained control over the forces of nature to such an extent that with their help they would have no difficulty in exterminating one another to the last man" (Freud, 1961, p. 92)) reflects his paradoxical stance when responding to the questions posed by Einstein. This statement sheds light on Freud's complex position regarding the potential for human extinction and the role of aggressive instincts. As Zupančič (2022) elaborates, Freud stated that the unconscious remains entirely oblivious to death and remains speculative even during experiences of death anxiety or experiences disavowal when faced with imminent death. Zupančič's critique of Freud revolves around the question: If the unconscious remains oblivious to death, how does it initiate disavowal?

For Lacan, anxiety does not arise solely from a lack but rather from the lack of lack itself. This existential crisis, which I interpret as an understanding of the libidinal/economic issue through the lens of structure, is not objectless; it centres around object A, the cause of desire. In a neurotic society, this would generate significant anxiety and terror. Lacan's innovation lies in his integration of economic and structural positions, embodied in the concept of object A, which functions as a structural element, representing both economic and structural aspects. It marks a departure from previous psychoanalytic attempts to understand the subject, moving beyond psychology, personality and individuality. This shift leads to the exploration of a subject that goes beyond mere imaginary objects.

Lacan's return to Freud can be seen as a radical revitalisation of psychoanalysis, shifting the focus from an obsession with ego strengthening and essentialist approaches to psyche assessment. Instead, it engages in an ontological movement that situates the subject in a split between various aspects of language, need, demand and the cause of desire (object A). Clinically, this split subject embraces its symptom as the core of collective bonding, a universal human condition. Lacan's main contribution, object A, pertains to the study of how objects differentiate from their background and from each other (objectality). It also serves as a residue of the alienating function of the Name of the Father. The ego, initially an imaginary object, undergoes a process of alienation through symbolic function (language) to become contained, neurotic, future-oriented, politicised (becoming a subject) and even recognisable as an ego. Lacan proposes psychosis as a pure possibility of human subjectivity when this fundamental alienation is foreclosed.

Lacan describes psychosis as a private matter that essentially presents itself as the sign of an impasse (Lacan, 2006). This reference to freedom pertains to the realm of "sets of signifiers", the symbolic, where desire, anxiety and drive are ultimately experienced and signified as possibilities − references to freedom − that can unfold. The emphasis here is on possibilities, the creation of a neurotic situation. The analyst's role is essentially to assign meaning to a sign, or as Lacan stated elsewhere, to hystericise the subject within the neurotic structure. This hystericisation takes a different form within the psychotic structure.

In this context, the doomsday fantasy is not just a signifier; it is a sign indicating an impasse − an impasse of possibilities and politics. The

104 Philosophy After Lacan

doomsday fantasy does not conform to the object-relational definition of a "fantasy"; rather, it manifests as pure acting out. However, before delving into the state of impasse present in melancholia and the doomsday fantasy, it is crucial to understand why Lacan's position, which challenges and problematises neurosis, is necessary to comprehend this ideological reaction (referred to as the doomsday fantasy) to the current crisis.

In essence, Lacan's theoretical framework provides a fresh perspective by emphasising the role of structure, desire and the symbolic realm in shaping human subjectivity. While Freud's focus on the economic aspects of aggression has its merits, Lacan's approach adds depth by incorporating structural and symbolic dimensions, thus shedding light on the intricacies of human existence and its vulnerabilities in the face of crisis.

Melancholia

An essential aspect of foreclosure is the impossibility of the "object", as is evident in the description of Cotard syndrome. Unlike perversion, where the fetish object serves as a residue or witness of the perverse fantasy and is crucial for the libidinal economy, psychosis is characterised by a problem of space (objectality in Lacanian terms) rather than the object itself. This is why, in the melancholic state, the lost object becomes so intertwined with the ego (incorporated rather than interjected) that self-defeating guilt tends to be acted out rather than passionately felt with depression, as is typically the case with a known sense of "anger".

At the level of melancholia, the concept of the doomsday fantasy as a psychotic state is not metaphorised. However, at the level of perversion, as Zupančič (2022) states in his elaboration of the logic that "the world is ending, but this is not the end of the world", a hyper-metaphorizing occurs in a way that the second statement completely negates the first one. The idea that imagining the end of the world is easier than imagining the end of capitalism exposes the issues of impoverished metaphorisation. While the end of the world serves as a metaphor for the end of humanity, the end of everything is literalised into the idea that the world is tightly bound to the logic of modernism/enlightenment, where the foreclosure of natural history is akin to the foreclosure of the "big Other". This radical problem is connected to an individual's direct connection with the "end of nature", not as a species, but as a psychotic melancholic subject assumed to be all-encompassing and central. As Leader formulates it (2012), while the mourning subject asks "why is that object lost?", the melancholic subject remains fixated on asking "what is lost?" The identification with the lack and the similarities between melancholic and paranoid reactions has been known since the early years of psychoanalysis.

In the "progressive" reactions to the Anthropocene, the melancholic subject perceives that the world has already ended. The subject experiences a degree of the same feeling experienced after a loss. Essentially, in the melancholic reaction, the entire world ends with the demise of the lost object.

Something positive projected from the subject onto the lost object cannot be retrieved or mourned. The narcissistic world of the melancholic subject is skewed in two phases: first, their world becomes highly subjective, and then the entire world is projected onto the lost object, which also carries the projected negative aspects of the melancholic subject. This is similar to the idea that imagining the end of the world is easier than imagining the end of capitalism. If the loss is not symbolised adequately by a deficient Name of the Father (modernism/enlightenment, perhaps?) and, instead, remains a lack rather than a loss, it remains unachieved internally.

The phenomenon of left-wing melancholia is well-known in Marxist literature. Žižek astutely observes that left-wing melancholia involves identification with a lack rather than a loss, where communism is seen as it was dreamt and expected, not as it was realised (i.e. the state socialism of the former USSR) (Žižek, 2000). This concept has been coined "left-wing melancholia". Traverso (2017) describes the traces of this phenomenon becoming more mainstream in the Frankfurt School. Following the disappointments of Stalinism and the rise of fascism, left-wing melancholia was extensively explored in the works of Adorno and was recognised by Benjamin, as well. In their exchanges, as Traverso describes them, Adorno takes a different position concerning the real politics of his time, showing scepticism towards any form of practice. The general disappointment with the situation in Russia, Stalinism and the sabotage against Trotsky might have led Adorno to seek reasons for violence in concepts like "enlightenment". The totalising view of history in Adorno's works conveys a sense of complete melancholic collapse. Adorno's pessimism about practical solutions could lead to practical alignment with the capitalist state apparatus (as seen in the events of 1969, when he called on the police to suppress the radical student movement). However, identifying (incorporating the lack) with the lack itself is almost a psychotic position – a true melancholic state. This idealised loss-object represents the lack of the lack. Lacanian psychoanalysis addresses this problem. The structural Lacanian view is essential here to move beyond the lack and respond to the "no-answer" of determinism in the Frankfurt School. There are many unspoken similarities between Freudian essentialist views of the double drive and the historical materialism of certain aspects of the Frankfurt School (such as Adorno).

The "I give-up" attitude towards radical/global politics can be seen as a logic of psychosis. While the certainty of reality (i.e. climate change) is still being questioned by some, the dire effects on individuals are becoming more evident on the left. At a hyper-subjective level, identity politics take precedence over organised collective politics. Subjects feel psychotically responsible, believing themselves to be the sole origin of doom rather than realistically positioning themselves within their class and means of living. This guilt-driven society produces possible solutions only through other disastrous measures, such as AI (Klein, 2023).

Leader (2012) outlines two main forms of psychosis: hypersubjective and hyperobjective. In hypersubjective psychosis, the locus of projection is one's self-image, while in hyperobjective psychosis, it is an imaginary Other. In the context of melancholia, the neurotic question of "why I lost" transforms into a psychotic question of "what I lost". The certainty of loss itself becomes questionable, and the lost object is perceived as uncomfortably close.

Cotard syndrome, often associated with melancholia, involves feeling like a "walking dead" person, with a lack of internal organs. It serves as an extreme defence against the anxiety of melancholia, leading to a sense of being immortal and having lost one's soul or blood. Cotard syndrome is linked to the idea that "what is lost is unknown" or that the object of loss is too present, causing significant anxiety and a tendency to withdraw. In this context, the syndrome provides a solution through the belief that "I am already dead", which aligns with the concept of societal "zombification" described by Žižek – a hyper-subjective state characteristic of melancholia.

Didi-Huberman (2016) demonstrates how the dialectical revisiting of emotions and psychoanalytic readings of history are essential to avoid an ideological closure. The doomsday fantasy, or left-wing melancholia, acting as a screen memory, conceals a dangerous emotional reality – a collective disavowal of responsibility for waste, destruction and failed revolts. This screen memory reinforces a perverse law that promotes passivity and fruitless, repetitive individual efforts, contributing to a sense of impossibility. This concept parallels Badiou's (2022) idea of modern constructivism and highlights the paradoxical nature of endless technological possibilities coupled with total political impasses within a linear version of history.

Brown describes the Left as follows:

> What emerges is a Left that operates without either a substantive critique of the status quo or a substantive alternative to it. But perhaps even more troubling, it is a Left that has become more attached to its impossibility than to its potential fruitfulness, a Left that is most at home dwelling not in hopefulness but in its own marginality and failure, a Left that is thus caught in a structure of melancholic attachment to a certain strain of its own dead past, whose spirit is deathly, whose structure of desire is backward-looking and punishing.
>
> (Brown, 2000)

This passage describes the fixations and fetishism that the Left displays toward some of its obsolete concepts while it continues to project its failure onto identity politics or postmodernism. We can observe that the repetitive focus on the perverse aspects of the subjective crisis has the same role as the object of projection.

The melancholic fantasy that is not being talked about (and is unmentionable) but, in fact, is acted upon can be seen in the following: political detachment (pacifism); bureaucratic passivism; the search for retreats and new, progressive "urban designs"; and career survivalism in academia. The complicit and secret interaction between the perverse and melancholic forms of subjective crisis will end up avoiding the symptomatic and hysterical reactions that would be present in militant and organised political engagement. Thus, there is a lack of any meaningful organised political engagement.

In the most recent social upheaval in Iran, known as the Women, Life, Freedom movement, which has been described as a cultural revolution, a T-shirt slogan captures a poignant sentiment: "They make us afraid of dying, as if we are now alive!" Embracing the apocalypse becomes a means of staying alive, offering a unique articulation of the perceived deadness of the current state of affairs. This reflects the profound impact of existential anxieties and the search for meaningful activism in the moment of collapse.

References

Badiou, A. (2002) *Ethics: An essay on the understanding of evil.* Verso Books.

Badiou, A. (2012) *The Rebirth of History: Times of riots and uprisings.* Translated by G. Elliott. Verso Books.

Badiou, A. (2022) *The Immanence of Truths: Being and event* III. Bloomsbury Academic.

Balibar, E. (2019) Absolute capitalism. In W. Callison and Z. Manfredi (Eds), *Mutant neoliberalism* (pp. 269–290). Fordham University Press.

Beckett, A. (2017, May 11) Accelerationism: How a fringe philosophy predicted the future we live in. *The Guardian.* www.theguardian.com/world/2017/may/11/accelerationism-how-a-fringe-philosophy-predicted-the-future-we-live-in.

Britton, R. (1998) *Belief and Imagination: Explorations in psychoanalysis.* Routledge.

Brown, W. (2000) *Resisting Left Melancholia.* Verso Books.

Casas López, A. C. (2021) "Cotard's Syndrome," a description of two cases. Delusion of negation in melancholia versus delusion of negation in paranoia. *Revista Colombiana De Psiquiatria*, 51(2), 158–162. doi:10.1016/j.rcp.2020.10.012.

Dark Enlightenment. (2023, August 28) *Wikipedia.* Retrieved August 29, 2023. https://en.wikipedia.org/wiki/Dark_Enlightenment.

Didi-Huberman, S. (2016) To render sensible. In A. Badiou, P. Bourdieu, J. Butler, G. Didi-Huberman, S. Khiari and J. Rancière (Eds), *What is a People?* Translated by J. Gladding (pp. 65–86). Columbia University Press.

Fisher, M. (2009) *Capitalist Realism: Is there no alternative?* Zero Books.

Fisher, M. (2014) *Ghosts of my Life: Writings on depression, hauntology and lost futures.* Zero Books. http://search.ebscohost.com/login.aspx?direct=true&scope=site&db=nlebk&db=nlabk&AN=760896.

Freud, S. (1958) *The Standard Edition of the Complete Psychological Works of Sigmund Freud* (Vol. 12, 1911–1913), (J. Strachey, Ed.). The Hogarth Press and The Institute of Psychoanalysis.

Freud, S. (1961) *The Standard Edition of the Complete Psychological Works of Sigmund Freud* (Vol. 19: The ego and the id and other works), (J. Strachey, Ed.). The Hogarth Press and The Institute of Psychoanalysis.

Freud, S. (1961b) *The Standard Edition of the Complete Psychological Works of Sigmund Freud Vol. 21*, 192–1931: The Future of an illusion, civilization and its discontents and other works (J. Strachey, Ed.). The Hogarth Press and The Institute of Psychoanalysis.

Gifford, S. (1988) *Freud's Fearful Symmetry: Further reflections on the life and death instincts.* In H.B. Levine, D. Jacobs and L.J. Rubin (Eds), *Psychoanalysis and the Nuclear Threat: Clinical and theoretical studies.* Routledge. doi:10.4324/9780203778357.

Grace, K. (August 3, 2023) 2022 expert survey on progress in AI. AI Impacts. https://aiimpacts.org/2022-expert-survey-on-progress-in-ai.

Grigg, R. (2015) Melancholia and the unabandoned object. In P. Gherovici and M. Steinkoler (Eds), *Lacan on Madness: Madness, yes you can't.* Routledge. doi:10.4324/9781315742755.

Klein, N. (2023, May 8) AI machines aren't 'hallucinating'. But their makers are. *The Guardian.* www.theguardian.com/commentisfree/2023/may/08/ai-machines-hallucinating-naomi-klein.

Lacan, J. (2007) *Seminar of Jacques Lacan Book XVII: The other side of psychoanalysis.* Translated by R. Grigg; illustrated edition. W.W. Norton & Co.

Lacan, J. (2006) *Ecrits: The first complete edition in English.* Translated by B. Fink. W.W. Norton & Co.

Leader, D. (2012) *What is Madness?* Penguin Random House UK. www.penguin.co.uk/books/177519/what-is-madness-by-leader-darian/9780141047355.

Marx, K. (1932) Economic and philosophic manuscripts of 1844. Retrieved July 17, 2023, from www.marxists.org/archive/marx/works/1844/manuscripts/preface.htm.

Roazen, P. (2017) *Freud: Political and social thought* (3rd ed.). Routledge. doi:10.4324/9781351310802.

Saito, K. (2023) *Marx in the Anthropocene: Towards the idea of degrowth communism.* Cambridge University Press. doi:10.1017/9781108933544.

Traverso, E. (2017) *Left-wing Melancholia: Marxism, history, and memory.* Columbia University Press.

Žižek, S. (1989). *The Sublime Object of Ideology.* Verso Books.

Žižek, S. (2000) Melancholy and the Act. *Critical Inquiry*, 26(4), 657–681.

Žižek, S. (2008) *In Defense of Lost Causes.*

Žižek, S. (2018) *Living in the End Times.* Verso Books.

Žižek, S. (2023, March 4) "Only a catastrophe can save us" Slavoj Žižek – Elevate Festival 2023. www.youtube.com/watch?v=UsNBv3noSG8.

Zupančič, A. (2022) Perverse Disavowal and the Rhetoric of the End. *Filozofski Vestnik*, 43(2). doi:10.3986/fv.43.2.04.

Chapter 7

Real Ethics and the "Ethics of the Real" after Lacan and Wittgenstein

Paul M. Livingston

In this paper, I will try to articulate in a preliminary way what I will call *real ethics* and can be indicated by two features, one negative and one positive. The first (negative) feature is that it does not take the individual agency or action of a self-conscious subject as the primary locus of ethically relevant philosophical considerations, or seek to determine a positive conception of ethics primarily from out of this locus. The second (positive) one is that it finds terms to respond in a relevant way to the most characteristic and pervasive problems of global life today. These include, for example, the massiveness of the anthropogenic violence of the human against the non-human beings of the earth in general, and the capitalist form of consumption and destruction marked by consequences such as the climate crisis, deforestation, despeciesisation, etc. My suggestion will be that the negative and the positive features are linked, and that thinking about the ethical implications of Lacan's psychoanalytic and Wittgenstein's philosophical methods can help us understand how. In this, they contrast with typical positions of contemporary academic ethics and meta-ethics, whose palpable failure in the second respect (i.e., as a real response to today's global ethical problems) can be seen (I will suggest) as an outcome of their failure to contemplate an alternative of the type suggested under the first.[1] The key to this contrast in both cases, I will argue, is a more thoroughgoing understanding of the significance of setting the problems of ethics (or of geopolitical organisation) as problems, not of subjective choice or action, but rather of the relationship of life and language: thus, as problems to be treated from within the "linguistic turn", which allows them to be formulated as problems about linguistic sense and our everyday life with it. This connection and the set of implications of it I will discuss here, however, have not featured prominently in the secondary literature on either Wittgenstein's or Lacan's "ethical views" or "positions". And they are both obscured by attempts to ally these views with projects for which the problems of ethics are, rather, problems about the subject, its freedom or responsibility, or the determination of its will: for instance those of German Idealism in its Kantian or post-Kantian forms.

DOI: 10.4324/9781003425953-8

110 Philosophy After Lacan

As I shall argue here, by contrast, the drive to the kind of *real ethics* that can arise from both Lacan's and Wittgenstein's projects emerges clearly only if we consider how both thinkers consider *critically* the underlying *symbolic* conditions for what is, for both, only the *imaginary* unity of a "self" or "subject's" thinking and agency. On the level of these conditions, the unity of any possible "subject" of ethical action or behavior is never simply given, but is rather conditioned by its prior dissimulation of the constitutive illusion involved in its relationship to the language it speaks. This unity is, then, an imaginary construction that serves to cover the really empty, and even (ultimately) nonsensical, form of the totality of the symbolic, in relation to which it tries to situate itself. But positively speaking, at the same time, the articulation that both Lacan and Wittgenstein give to the aporetic limit of the symbolic allows their respective analytic projects to evince the terms in which a real ethics might begin to respond to the systematic real and symbolic violence that dominates collective planetary life today.

I

In his 1930 *Civilization and its Discontents*, right at the beginning of his speculative analysis of the structure of civilisation [*Kultur*] and of the particular frustrations and forms of suffering to which its social structure irrevocably consigns the human quest for action directed toward happiness,[2] Freud considers the psychogenetic origins of what Romain Rolland had characterised as the "oceanic feeling", of the individual's unity with the whole of the universe, which appeared to him to be one characteristic source of religious feeling:

> The idea of men's receiving an intimation of their connection with the world around them through an immediate feeling which is from the outset directed to that purpose sounds so strange and fits in so badly with the fabric of our psychology that one is justified in attempting to discover a psycho-analytic – that is, a genetic – explanation of such a feeling. The following line of thought suggests itself. Normally, there is nothing of which we are more certain than the feeling of our self, of our own ego. The ego appears to us as something autonomous and unitary, marked off distinctly from everything else. That such an appearance is deceptive, and that on the contrary the ego is continued inwards, without any sharp delimitation, into an unconscious mental entity which we designate as the id and for which it serves as a kind of façade – this was the discovery first made by psycho-analytic research, which should still have much more to tell us about the relation of the ego to the id.[3]
>
> (p. 12)

Thus, the response suggested by psychoanalysis's decisive discovery of the unconscious to the "feeling" of the individual's unity with the cosmic whole is to suggest that its content is an imaginary, and essentially illusory, production on the basis of the correspondent fiction of the ego's own unity, which itself bears a complex and indirect history of development in each case. As Freud goes on to suggest, this development can be understood only by way of the complex of processes by which an originally undifferentiated and all-encompassing field of organic sensation becomes differentiated in such a way as to be able to "[separate] off an external world from itself".[4] The crucial impetus to this process is the developing infant's progressive differentiation of the sources of stimulus that can provide sensation at any moment from those that only reappear as the result of its expression of need: "In this way there is for the first time set over against the ego an 'object', in the form of something which exists 'outside' and which is only forced to appear by a special action".[5] Over the course of the infant's development, the slow differentiation of the intrinsic and organic sources of pleasure from those dominated by the reality principle allows for the practical purpose of defending oneself against the painful sources of unpleasure and frustration arising from what thereby comes to be defined as the reality of the external world.[6]

In just these terms of the psychogenetic formation of the specific structure of agency on the basis of the speaking being's fraught and constitutively disharmonious relationship to reality, and drawing on his own characteristic triad of the real, imaginary and symbolic, Lacan notably defines in his 1959–60 seminar *The Ethics of Psychoanalysis* the psychoanalytic perspective as one on which "the question of ethics is to be articulated from the point of view of the location of man in relation to the real".[7] Lacan suggests that it is in relation to just this possibility of articulation that Freud's position constitutes a decisive advance over previous ethical positions, including most characteristically all those that, like Aristotle's, orient the questions of ethics around the ideality of a unitary and sovereign Good. For Lacan, by contrast, the progress in ethics that is possible on the basis of the psychoanalytic position does not consist in concerning itself with the ethically ideal, but rather, quite to the contrary, with "going more deeply into the notion of the real" as it is situated specifically in its complex and dissymmetric interactions with the other two registers of the symbolic and the imaginary.[8] In particular (and characteristically for Lacan) any possible progress of psychoanalysis in the ethical domain rests on its insight into the unconscious and into its specific structure as a "function of the symbolic:" namely that the "unconscious itself has no other structure than the structure of a language".[9] In relation to a speaking being's desire, this function means specifically that its operation in what Freud called the "pleasure principle" is irreducibly and structurally consigned to the demand of making itself articulate in language and always able to miss, and sometimes find again, what has the specifically symbolic structure of a *sign*. It is through this articulation alone, Lacan suggests, that the relationship of the function of desire to its object itself becomes available to consciousness. And so it is in the difficult articulation between this function and the constraint of reality that, alone, it becomes possible for something like a subject to articulate this desire or, inversely but symmetrically, to experience the demand of what it thereby imagines as a superior and absolutely enjoining set of commandments or moral law, which it thereby comes to locate in imaginary terms as coming from the locus of what is other than itself.[10]

From the beginning of its appurtenance to consciousness, however, this symbolic articulation of desire is in a fraught relationship with the constitution of reality, one marked by the basically "antinomic" structure of the speaking being's relationship to the totality of the symbolic itself. It is this structure in which Lacan, without providing a definition, repeatedly suggests may be understood as that in which the dimension of the "real" uniquely appears. More specifically, he suggests an essential relationship between this antinomic dimension of the speaker's lived relationship to language and what Freud introduces, in the "second topography", as the "death instinct" together with its closely associated "compulsion to repeat", something that, Lacan suggests, thereby, "beyond" the pleasure principle and situated exactly within the constitutive gap between it and reality, "controls in the broadest of senses the whole of our relationship to the world".[11] The psychoanalytic investigation of the implications of this instinct for this relationship – that is, for the reality that we inhabit and act in everyday – will lead us, Lacan says, to the "special area" of "psychic reality, which presents itself to us with the problematic character of a previously unequaled order", leading us "a long way from something that can be expressed under the category of wholeness".[12]

In later texts, Lacan confirms and develops this understanding of the specific dimension of the real as essentially structured by the antinomic or paradoxical structure at the limits of the totality of the symbolic. In seminar XX, in connection with the appeal he develops here to a specifically mathematical formalisation of writing that serves the analytic process "in that what invisibly holds bodies is designated therein", Lacan famously describes the real as that which "can be inscribed only on the basis of an impasse of formalization:" this real cannot be directly represented or designated by any significant sign endowed with sense, but appears only in the impasse of the formalisation that attempts to designate the individual's relationship to the totality of the order of signifiers itself.[13] This (failed) inscription of the subject's relationship, at the limit, to the totality of signification is not the designation of a substantial being or significant function of symbolic articulation of a possible sense of the subject's life or experience, but rather a senselessly mute indication (Lacan says "contrary to meaning" and "almost 'à contre-sens'") of 'signifierness' itself – that is, as we have seen, of that medium within which any possible articulation of the individual or collective life or action of a subject or subjects is alone possible.[14]

In the 1960s and early 1970s Lacan often develops the relationship of this impassive and aporetic indication of the real to the imaginary positioning whereby a "subject" constitutes itself in relation to the (itself antinomic) totality of signifiers itself. For example, in the 1966 article "Science and Truth", Lacan describes the subject in terms of the constitutive structure of its "splitting" [*Spaltung*] between its knowledge and the truth of its origin.[15] Indeed, Lacan suggests that the positional and indexical place of the "I" as signifier is produced only on the basis of the dissimulation of this more fundamental splitting between its knowledge and the truth of its constitution. In seminar XVII (1969–70), Lacan suggests both that the imaginary construction of the transcendental and self-identical "I" – what he calls the "I-cracy" of philosophy – can only be the outcome of the *suppression* of the total battery of signifiers in the context of the "university" discourse and that, from the position of the liberation of this field of signifiers in the "analyst's" discourse, its production can only correspond to the operation of a specifically *linguistic* desire.[16] This is the operation of attempting to occupy the position of a *metalanguage* with respect to (what is thereby pictured) as the totality of signifiers itself – or, in equivalently Lacanian terms – the desire to be someone's (big-O) "Other". But in the terms in which it is possible, with Lacan, to recognise that the Other does not exist, it is thereby possible to see this operation as radically illusory, and the operation of desire that it represents as basically incapable of any possible satisfaction.[17]

Returning to "ethics", then, what can we say about the implications of this aporetic and specifically symbolic topology of the real, in relation to the symbolic, for the broadest problems of individual and collective life? First, that psychoanalytic ethics is *not* primarily "about" the self-conscious determination of individual action, volition or intention but rather – insofar as it concerns itself with individual action at all – about the deeper psychogenetic conditions that determine these on the level of (individual or collective) "psychic reality" and as a matter of our lived relationship to the real proper to it. In this sense, Lacan's psychoanalytic ethics is not a matter of telling us "what to do" or "how to live", but rather about (as Freud's own multiple interventions into the development of psychoanalytic research as a fundamental "work of culture" already make clear) the more basic structures and relationships of the symbolic and imaginary that first make any such articulation possible at all. But second, and more importantly, this ethics offers us the structures from the position of which we can see how the determination of individual action – as of all action or of the "meaning" of lives and practices themselves – is possible only on the basis of an essentially *imaginary* operation that constitutes this meaning in the form of an projected unity, while *covering over* the real disunity of the underlying situation – namely, that of aporia, antinomy and impasse – of the symbolic in relation to this real. In these terms, the real problems of "civilization" or culture – those that find their most painful evidence, as Freud suggests, in our discontent with the political or social arrangements that we, ourselves, have made – are evidently just those of the real conditions of our relationship to the symbolic reality that we build and inhabit, as well as to our imaginary or ideological mystification of its real structure. "The real", in the sense in which the impasses of our lived attempts to accommodate ourselves to it matter to ethics, is not some chimerical transcendent object situated beyond the bounds of possible knowledge or description; nor is it some impossible, hyperbolic *jouissance* defined or made possible by its own prohibition. Rather, it is the limit of our symbolic reality itself – the reality of the symbolic that is the structural precondition of our using language to "mean" anything at all – as we find our individual and collective lives taken up within its own immanent aporias.

II

It is from this perspective that I believe we can now usefully turn to the much-discussed "ethical" register of Wittgenstein's early work, in the *Tractatus Logico-Philosophicus* and in the "Lecture on Ethics" that he gave soon after his return to Cambridge in 1929. Somewhat famously, whereas the *Tractatus* itself contains only four remarks explicitly about ethics and declares that "…it is impossible for there to be propositions of ethics", Wittgenstein wrote in a letter to the publisher Ludwig von Ficker soon after completing it that the "book's point is ethical".[18] According to the letter, the "ethical" part of the *Tractatus*, in particular, is not contained in what the *Tractatus* says but in what it does *not* say: as it were, the "other" part of the book is, according to Wittgenstein, the actually important part. In this way, the book allows the limit of the ethical to be drawn "from the inside:" the only (Wittgenstein says) "*rigorous* way" in which that limit *can* be drawn at all. Here, Wittgenstein refers specifically to the preface of the *Tractatus* as well as to its "conclusion", the famous remark 7 enjoining or prescribing that we keep silent [*schweigen*] whereof we cannot speak.[19]

Reading this together with the explicitly "ethical" remarks of the *Tractatus* that declare ethics "transcendental" in the sense that it "cannot be put into words" and that there cannot be "ethical propositions", we may begin to see (as Cora Diamond suggests in Diamond (2000), p. 152), at least in negative terms, *how* the *Tractatus* indicates the ethical by delimiting it "from inside". It does so by clarifying the form of all that can be said and showing that there can be no "ethical" remark or statement that fits within this form. This form is given, in the *Tractatus*, as the general form of a proposition in remark 6, and the remarks explicitly on ethics (i.e., 6.42–6.423) directly follow from this, by way of the remark (6.4) that "all propositions are of equal value". Given that there is no proposition having any greater value than any other, no propositions can express what we are (imagining this sphere as "higher") imagining the sphere of the ethical to be. The main methodological suggestion of the "Preface" then may be read as specifying more fully *how* the delimitation of the ethical "from the inside" actually works. The aim of the book as a whole is not to draw a limit to thought, but rather "to the expression of thoughts... It will therefore only be in language that the limit can be drawn, and what lies on the other side of the limit will simply be nonsense".[20]

What kind of "ethics", though, is it that is thus "delimited"? To begin with, it is clear that the philosophical ethics of the *Tractatus* is no ethics of the *subject* or of its volitional choice, action, or freedom. Explicitly, at 5.631, "There is no such thing as the subject that thinks or entertains ideas". [*Das denkende, vorstellende, Subjekt gibt es nicht*]. A bit earlier, at 5.5421: "...there is no such thing as the soul – the subject, etc. – as it is conceived in the superficial psychology of the present day". [...*dass die Seele – das Subjekt etc. ... ein Unding ist.*] In both of these cases, the considerations that show this themselves follow from considerations about the general form of propositions and facts, and about the limits these imply of the totality of the world, the totality of all that is the case. At 6.423, underscoring again the implications of the nonexistence of ethical propositions, Wittgenstein writes "It is impossible to speak about the will in so far as it is the subject of ethical attributes. And the will as a phenomenon is of interest only to psychology". This does not mean that there is no "philosophically" or ethically relevant self at all, but that self ['das Ich'] that is thus relevant is "not the human being, not the human body, or the human soul" but rather "the metaphysical subject", i.e. "the limit of the world – not a part of it". But such a subject – i.e. one that is no human being, nothing in the world, but *only* its limit – is not in any clear sense *even possibly* an agent or subject of self-conscious volition. Its reality, within the world, is to vanish to a pure point, leaving nothing behind whereby desire or determine things to be any way rather than another.

> Here it can be seen that solipsism, when its implications are followed out strictly, coincides with pure realism. The self of solipsism [das Ich des Solipsismus] shrinks to a point without extension, and there remains the reality coordinated with it.
>
> (5.641)

If, then, there is no ethics of the subject's agency in the *Tractatus*, nevertheless its reflection on the linguistic form of the proposition and the limits of the world, and the articulation this gives to the limits of language as the boundary between sense and nonsense, nevertheless offers to show in a different way the sources of our inclinations to articulate (what we imagine to be) a substantive "philosophical ethics". In the 1929 "Lecture", Wittgenstein further clarifies the linguistic form of the desire which yields the tendency to "write or talk Ethics or Religion" and its internal relationship to the nonsensicality which is, as he argues, "the very essence" of the propositions (or seeming propositions) with which we try to express our sense of the ethical as something absolute. For if someone were to object that a statement literally asserting the absolute value of some fact or experience is simply one, perhaps, whose correct logical analysis we have not yet found – Wittgenstein responds that:

> ... when this is urged against me, I at once see clearly, as it were in a flash of light, not only that no description that I can think of would do to describe what I mean by absolute value, but that I would reject every significant description that anybody could possibly suggest, *ab initio*, on the ground of its very essence. That is to say: I see now that these non-sensical expressions were not nonsensical because I had not yet found the correct expressions, but that their nonsensicality was their very essence. For all I wanted to do with them was just *to go beyond* the world and that is to say beyond significant language.[21]

The underlying form of the "ethical" drive, as Wittgenstein clarifies it, is thus the desire to "go beyond the world" and thereby, and in this sense, to go beyond significance itself. The desire is thus coeval with, and specifically implicated in, the structure of propositional language that also serves to articulate the limits of possible meaning in the sense of what can possibly be said. In fact, as Wittgenstein argues earlier in the lecture, this conclusion about the actual form of our "ethical" desire is vindicated in detail by the reflective analysis of those expressions by which we attempt to put into words the "absolute" sense of the various experiences which we are inclined to characterise as ethical or religious. These include, for example, the experiences of "wondering at the existence of the world"; the experience of feeling "absolutely safe" in the hands of God, or that which we would be tempted to express by claiming that a particular man's life was "valuable" (that is, in an "absolute" rather than "relative" sense of "value"), or the experience of being guilty in an absolute sense. About all of these, Wittgenstein says that their associated expressions appear to amount to similes. But whereas, in the usual case when one describes a fact by means of a simile, one can also drop the simile and just describe the fact directly, in these cases of religious or absolute-ethical expression "as soon as we try to drop the simile and simply to state the facts which stand behind it, we find that there are no such facts" and our attempt to characterise our experience in those terms now is seen to be "mere nonsense".[22]

With this, Wittgenstein clarifies not only how the drive to expression which yields the ultimately nonsensical "ethical" expressions of the absolute is grounded in the specifically human tendency or inclination to attempt to go beyond the bounds of significant meaning, but *also* – and in the same movement – how a clarification of the form of this inclination can itself operate as an "ethically" relevant form of self-clarification itself. The clarity that is involved in this, and thus in the positive claim of Wittgenstein's method to contribute in an ethically relevant sense to the clarification of life itself, is a kind of self-clarification of the relationship of this life to its language, marked in the recognition of some of our own inclinations as inclinations that cannot be satisfied on the level of the satisfactions that they seem to demand. The point is not only that these satisfactions are merely imagined, that they are mere chimeras having, in themselves, no grounding in experience or empirical reality, but (more profoundly) that they witness the dissymmetrical and irreconcilable movement by which the linguistic imagination attempts to cover over the actually irreducible impasse of its own encounter with the limits of language, with its own inclination to go beyond the world and produce its own position as one of absolute fusion with it.

This has evident significance, not only to the question of the psychogenesis of the ideational content associated by an individual with her own "religious" or "moral" feelings but equally, and in a sense more deeply, to the imaginary structure of the metaphors that are most conspicuous and regular in the social or social-political justification of widespread practices of culture, and by means of which the social or collective imaginary of our language routinely attempts to inscribe or produce a(n actually impossible) totalising unity there. With respect to these metaphors, as we have seen, Wittgenstein's critical analysis our spontaneous attempts to express what is involved in "absolute" expression of our feelings of wonder or of guilt directly mirrors the psychoanalytic one: here, for example with respect to the characteristic "feeling of wonder at the existence of the world" that Wittgenstein considers, the parallel to Freud's deflationary analysis of the ideational content associated with the "oceanic feeling" of unity should be obvious. As in that case, the deflation of the ideational content is sufficiently achieved by the consideration of the actual sources of the tendency to produce that content in ideological fashion; and by the description of the underlying situation of the production of that illusion from the dissimulation of the linguistic-relational structure actually underlying it. The aim of this ethics is not any kind of *moralism*: not, that is, the inscription of a moral law or the development of any positive claim or demand of philosophically explicable 'normativity' upon the facts or occasions of our lives. It is, rather the attainment of a clarity, the kind of clarity that the later Wittgenstein also marks as that of our acceptance of what has to be accepted on the level of the agreement that structures a collective or individual "form of life".[23]

III

In a series of texts, Cora Diamond has discussed the ethical sense of Wittgenstein's early thinking, in continuity with her development of what has come to be called the "resolute" interpretation of the *Tracatatus*. The signature of this interpretation is an "austere" view of the nonsense that Wittgenstein characterises his own propositions as being, in the penultimate remark of the *Tractatus* which says that the reader will understand him – Wittgenstein – only once they recognise them as such. On this view, the nonsense of the *Tractatus* is not ultimately any kind of "significant" nonsense – not, for example, a kind of nonsense that points to or gestures at (or "shows") a substantial logical or metaphysical structure of reality, or a sublime or mystical ineffable "beyond" to the world or to significant language itself. Rather, we come to understand the text's author and accomplish the suggested task of "kicking away the ladder" only when, and insofar as, we pass from supposing these remarks to have a significant descriptive sense to seeing that they can have none: we pass, in other words, from taking ourselves – insofar as we engage in (or attempt to engage in) the kind of philosophical theorising that they (appear to) exemplify – to have given sense to our expressions used in that way, to seeing that we have not. So doing, we come to see that the "perspective" from which we thought ourselves capable of pronouncing on these (seemingly) substantive matters – among other things, the perspective from which we thought ourselves capable of taking a view of the world as a whole – was no perspective at all: that there is no position from which we can give sense to a language or a discourse that would, *per impossible*, master the world as a whole from outside.[24]

In this remainder of this paper, I will not contest the "resolute interpretation" but will take it as "read", while trying to ask what it might be like to read Lacan's ethics in line with something like it. Such a reading may illuminate differently, I will suggest, the ethical stakes of Lacan's specific understanding of the relationship of ethics to the real in its dissymmetry with the symbolic; and at any rate will articulate the positive claims that such an ethics makes on us rather differently than is usually done, including by Lacan himself. But though I take the resolute interpretation for granted, I also want to suggest that articulating some of its internally constitutive theoretical problems may lead us into a closer understanding of the field of *ethical* problems that most directly and pressingly call for response today. This is especially the case insofar as these ethical problems can be seen as arising from patterns of collective practice that might, in another kind of philosophical discourse, be called "ideological" – that is, that sustain their motivation from practical justifications and legitimations that, though pervasive in contemporary collective life, cannot stand up to real and honest ethical reflection.

As Diamond has emphasised in her work on Wittgenstein and ethics, understanding the possible ethical significance of Wittgenstein's critical methods requires that one distinguish these methods sharply from the ones characteristic of most academic treatments of ethics. For example, it requires distinguishing these methods from any that are about "ethics as branch of thought, ethics as kind of discourse, ethics as about right or wrong things to do and what things are good, and what it means to speak about such matters".[25] This need for distinction from the methods that academic ethics standardly uses and the background assumptions that it makes is related to seeing the type of their bearing on the real ethical problems of collective planetary life, as well as the failure of those usual academic methods (for example of abstract argumentation, or reasoning about how the "capacities" of ourselves and others may be thought to "ground" specific claims, on their behalf, for rights or "moral consideration" or equality or liberation) to bear on them in any real way. In "The Difficulty of Reality and the Difficulty of Philosophy", Diamond considers a series of examples of experiences which are marked by our spontaneous finding of them to, painfully or astonishingly, challenge or escape our capacities or possibilities of thinking. The second and most drawn out of these examples is taken from J. M. Coetzee's *Elizabeth Costello* and from the set of lectures given by Coetzee's character or avatar at the core of that book.[26] Elizabeth Costello is, as Diamond says and by her own self-presentation, not only a woman "haunted by the horror of what we do to animals" but herself a "wounded animal", pained at her core by this awareness, and by her awareness of others' lack of awareness of this.[27] As Diamond strikingly shows, the kinds of responses or readings that Costello's lectures may get at the hands of those who treat them as embodying (only or primarily) an "argument" for a conclusion about an "ethical issue" (for example the issue of "animal rights"). For as Diamond points out, one of the things that Costello is presented by Coetzee as pained by, indeed as wounded by, is the commonly taken-for-granted attitude that the question of "how we should treat animals" is itself just an "ethical issue" in this sense (any more than, Diamond says drawing on Costello's own suggestions, Holocaust denial is such an "issue").[28] And so any understanding of Costello's response – or of Coetzee's – as a really ethical one must be one that does not ignore this pain and woundedness, as the academic discourses of ethics standardly do.

The "treatment of (non-human) animals" thus names one area where, as Diamond shows, any possibility of something like a real ethical response depends on, as a minimal although certainly not sufficient condition, turning away from the kinds of assumptions that standardly frame these discourses. But this is also the case with respect to the ethical problems posed by other large-scale areas of global practice and organisation today. Diamond suggests, drawing on Cavell, that any real ethical engagement in these cases will also require positively that we engage with the experiences of limitation and of fragmentation that the "difficulty of reality" there presents, experiences that are marked not by their rational significance or implications but in the way they evince limits to what we know how to say (or think). Now, as I have argued above, the characteristic ethical engagements of not only Wittgenstein, but also of psychoanalysis, appear to witness a deep kind of appreciation of the ethical "difficulty of reality" in this sense, and although

Diamond does not discuss psychoanalysis (as far as I know), it seems reasonable to consider how we might understand this reckoning in these terms, and both its connection to and distance from the standard discourses of "philosophical" ethics on these topics. And as I have suggested above, it seems especially relevant here to consider, in particular, what kind of engagement or critique a "real ethics" in this sense would imply or provide with the particular cluster of claims of those discourses that surround "the subject", its will, volition, freedom and responsibility; and the structure and limits of its 'powers' or 'capacities' (of *any* 'powers' or 'capacities') for language and thought.

IV

A good opportunity for just this consideration is afforded by Alenka Zupančič's perceptive and penetrating *Ethics of the Real: Kant and Lacan.* This is so in particular insofar as Kant's ethics might, I believe, reasonably be seen as – both in its original formulation and the characteristic forms of its contemporary academicisation[29] – among the varieties of what are assuredly the discourses of academic ethics today, the one that is nevertheless in various ways situated "closest" to the kinds of critical/therapeutic engagements with the ideological bases of contemporary life that both Wittgenstein's and Lacan's projects suggest.

In the first chapters of the book, Zupančič develops a series of analogies between Kant's and Lacan's descriptions of the subject and its structure in order to underscore what she identifies as two crucially shared ways in which the ethics of both break with the characteristic of traditional philosophical ethics. First, both reject the ordinary assumption that what is *required* by ethics must be *possible*, seeing morality instead, quite by contrast, as a demand for the *impossible*: thus, Kant already discovers, according to Zupančič, the "essential" characteristic of ethics in relation to desire, in that it "circles around the real *qua* impossible".[30] Second, and relatedly, Kant is the first to reject any conception of ethics according to which it is concerned with the "distribution of the good" or (in Lacan's terms) the "service of goods".[31] Both of these rejections come together, according to Zupančič, in Kant's recognition of an ethical demand of duty – that of the moral law – that is, as Kant says and Zupančič underscores, quite alien to one's own life, and indeed essentially at odds with this life and the enjoyment intrinsic to it.[32] The excessive and hyperbolic character of this demand with respect to the motivations of pleasure and desire takes shape, for Zupančič, as a kind of essential paradox of undecidability that runs through all of our actions and motivations, according to Kant, and essentially articulates the structure of our freedom. This is the paradox that, while for Kant, the realm of causal determination is complete, so we can never be sure that any of our actions are "really" free, at the same time Kant insists that we are always responsible for *all* of our actions: we can never appeal legitimately kind of necessity or causal determination as a way of excusing our immoral actions.

It is here that Zupančič returns to Lacan, suggestively identifying the structure underlying this paradoxical undecidability of Kantian freedom in Lacan's terms of the Other as all that, on the side of structure, is distinct from the subject and its relationship to the real:

> Even in this sketchy presentation of the Kantian foundations of freedom, it is possible to detect an echo of Lacan's famous claim that 'There is no Other of the Other'. In other words, the Other itself is inconsistent, marked by a certain lack. What Kant is saying is that *there is no Cause of the cause;* this is precisely what makes for the subject's autonomy and freedom.[33]

In this sense, according to Zupančič, it is already for Kant the case that the autonomy and freedom of the subject is located, not in any kind of deter-mination that the subject is capable of that somehow escapes from the structure of ordinary causal determination (there is nothing that thus escapes), but in the overall character of the total field of structure itself, and indeed in what Zupančič characterises as its "inconsistency". This is readable in Lacanian terms as, exactly, a matter of the determinate way in which the structure of language, as total, nevertheless relates at the limit to the Real that is proper to it:

> Of course, Lacan follows structuralism in its 'de-psychologizing' of the subject. In his words, 'the unconscious is structured like a language' ... However, if structuralism ultimately identifies the subject with structure (the Other), Lacan intervenes, at this point, in a very Kantian manner: he introduces the subject as a correlative to the *lack* in the Other; that is, as correlative to the point where the structure fails fully to close in upon itself ... This amounts to saying that the depsychologizing of the subject does not imply its reducibility to a (linguistic or other) structure. The Lacanian subject is what remains after the operation of 'de-psychologiz-ing' has been completed: it is the elusive, 'palpitating' point of enunciation.[34]

In this way, Zupančič locates the 'Kantian' subject (or at least the 'Lacanian' one, thought in a "Kantian manner") in relation to the totality of structure, as well as the specific 'real' that is plausibly proper to it: this provides for, according to Zupančič's argument, a way in which one can still 'think' the structure of this subject and its paradoxical freedom, even given the radical implications of Freud's breakthrough to the unconscious as a field of scientific discovery and Lacan's recognition of its linguistic (or language-like) structure.

Now, I do not want to suggest that this is not a plausible way to read Lacan; nor do I want to contest the depth with which Zupančič's reading articulates a constitutive conception of the philosophical subject of freedom broadly in accordance with Kant's project that remains plausible – perhaps as the only possible such reading that is still plausible – today. But I do want to indicate a possible alternative, which I think can *also* be grounded and motivated from within Lacan's project and may indeed gains a certain degree of independent motivation, as well, from its apparent connection to what I have discussed as the early Wittgenstein's ethical project above.

To begin to see the alternative, let us return to the considerations about structure and the real which we saw, above, are plausibly common to both Lacan and Wittgenstein in the *Tractatus*. For both (and as Zupančič underscores in the case of Lacan), structure, in this sense, is *complete*: there is no act or event or possibility that escapes its totality or stands somehow outside of it. This totality of structure, understood as the totality of the facts of the world, is for Wittgenstein (as we saw) the basis of the claim that all facts are of equal value and thus of the possibility of articulating ethics "negatively", from the inside out, as an aspect of the project of differentiating sense from nonsense that is the boundary-drawing project of the *Tractatus* as a whole. And as we saw, for Lacan as well, it is at least possible to understand the specific Real that is relevant to ethics as uniquely marked in the impasse of sense that also appears at the limit of its total formalisation. Here, that the Real is marked or indicated *uniquely* in such an impasse of formalisation means that it does not correspond to any substantive object or definable field of meaning, but is rather itself marked only as *the nonsense of the failed formalisation of the totality of sense itself.* This means that – if we read Lacan this way – this Real is not some impossible or hyperbolic object beyond language or possible description: it is not "what cannot be symbolized" but rather what is structurally implied in the recognition that there is *nothing* that cannot be symbolised. That is (cleaving to the latter Lacanian motto according to which structure *itself* is the Real, as it appears in language), it is just what is indicated as language's own proper impasse in its own, necessarily failed, attempt at a complete and consistent self-formalisation. As indeed, for Wittgenstein (at least if we read him in the way suggested by the "resolute interpretation"), the project of the delimitation of language that operates by way of identifying the general form of the proposition does not point to some kind of transcendental being, entity or function "beyond" structure or constitutive of it: what is beyond "structure" in this sense is revealed as mere (plain) nonsense, *including the very nonsensicality of any attempted "drawing" of this line 'between' sense and nonsense as a line between thinkable contents itself.*

In these terms, the point of reflection at which any kind of ethical reflection is possible is not (as Zupančič says) "correlative to the point where the structure fails fully to close in upon itself" but rather to the point of the recognition that the structure "closes in upon itself" completely: that there is no "outside" to it or any possible position from which it is possible to "survey" it as a whole. The specific real that is invoked by the recognition of the exceptionless closure of structure is not that of some transcendence or subjective exterior to the world, but the actual impasse of any attempt to position oneself outside this closure, any attempt to occupy the position of the Other in relation to the totality of structure or to embody the totality of its structure in oneself.

I have suggested that an overriding sense of this specific real – one that is not defined as "lack", "gap" or "blind spot" but rather as the impasse proper to structure, in its totality, itself – may offer ultimately more helpful terms to situate the multiple "difficulties of the real" to which a contemporary "real ethics" – in the sense I have tried to articulate it here – must try to respond. Ethics operative in this mode works, among other things, as a clarification of the form of a collective life, a life that is in some sense shared *but without depending on* any kind of substantial being of unity or shared identity for this (in fact, empty) form. However, it remains to be said how this kind of response might actually positively operate and what kinds of suggestions it might provide in relation to these problems, given that it cannot appeal to any antecedently fixed conception of the good, and that it evidently cannot turn (as we have seen) on any kind of appeal to subjective freedom, either. I cannot here provide anything approaching even a preliminarily adequate answer to this question. But in closing, I would like to suggest that a part of the positive significance of the critical kind of operation of ethics that I am suggesting might be partially marked in its inheritance of another part of Kant's critical project: namely his development of a "logic of illusion" in connection with the rational ideas of Soul, World and God in the *Dialectic* of the first *Critique*.

For Kant, these ideas are each the products of a certain kind of projection (a "dialectical inference") of reason, inherent to its own operation in synthesising the concepts of the understanding into the form of their "highest" possible unity, but remain without objects insofar as they cannot be given in any possible experience or produced by any actually possible act of unification of which a finite subject is capable. At the same time, the idea of unity which each infers on the model of a specific kind of syllogistic inference remains active, and unavoidably so in the course of any systematic activity of the subject's understanding, in producing the *illusion* of the objective existence of these unities themselves.[35]

Now, the kind of position that I have tried to articulate here as that of "real ethics", there fairly evidently cannot be any direct passage from these (illusory) ideas to to the posits or demands of the "practical", and Kant's own attempts to trace such a route through his claims for the "merely regulative" application of the transcendental idea can only mean that the self-application of his own critical apparatus of questioning with respect to the form and origins of reason's unity here remains crucially incomplete. However, we have seen another way in which Wittgenstein and Lacan are involved in an essentially critical logic of illusion, and in which this very

124 Philosophy After Lacan

critical logic may be seen to bear ethical relevance, with respect to the "givens" of the forms of practice and shared life most characteristic of collective life today. This is the sense in which – as we saw most directly in connection with the "resolute" reading of Wittgenstein – these practices and forms may be seen as largely sustained by what we may come to see as an *illusion* of sense: an illusion, that is, that our words and intentions with respect to them can be borne, that they can be seriously or consistently or unitarily meant. If the linguistic critique of the sense of these practices is also the critique of the boundaries by which they open onto the exteriority of their force, then the "logical" or "formal" critique of these boundaries is also the "ethical" critique of their production of this exteriority as well. The study or "practical" (that is, real) application of ethics is then a recurrent and ineliminable reflection on the forms of effective unity that linguistic sense imposes, and their irreconcilable but inseparable relationship to the real operations of force and violence that they dissimulate, in the course of their maintenance of this exteriority: that is, their very effectiveness in the determination and constraint of lives, all around the planet today.

Notes

1 That is, they contrast with (for example) consequentialism, virtue ethics, care ethics, Levinasian ethics of the transcendent Other, ethical intuitionism, non-cognitivism, ethical realism and anti-realism, and deontological ethics (among others). (But I will say something more about the relationship of Lacan's and Wittgenstein's ethics to Kantian ethics in section IV, below).

2 "As regards the third source, the social source of suffering... we do not admit it at all; we cannot see why the regulations made by ourselves should not, on the contrary, be a protection and benefit for every one of us. And yet, when we consider how unsuccessful we have been in precisely this field of prevention of suffering, a suspicion dawns on us that here, too, a piece of unconquerable nature may lie behind – this time a piece of our own psychical constitution.

When we start considering this possibility, we come upon a contention which is so astonishing that we must dwell upon it. This contention holds that what we call our civilization is largely responsible for our misery, and that we should be much happier if we gave it up and returned to primitive conditions" (Freud, 1930, pp. 37–38).

3 Freud (1930), p. 12.

4 Freud (1930), p. 15.

5 Freud (1930), p. 14.

6 "Thus we are perfectly willing to acknowledge that the 'oceanic' feeling exists in many people, and we are inclined to trace it back to an early phase of ego-feeling. The further question then arises, what claim this feeling has to be regarded as the source of religious needs.

To me the claim does not seem compelling. After all, a feeling can only be a source of energy if it is itself the expression of a strong need. The derivation of religious needs from the infant's helplessness and the longing for the father aroused by it seems to me incontrovertible, especially since the feeling is not simply prolonged from childhood days, but is permanently sustained by fear of the superior power of Fate" (Freud, 1930), pp. 20–21.

Real Ethics and the "Ethics of the Real" after Lacan and Wittgenstein 125

7 Lacan (1960), p. 12.
8 Lacan (1960), p. 11.
9 Lacan (1960), p.12; p. 32.
10 "The reality principle dominates that which, whether conscious or preconscious, is in any case present in the order of reasoned discourse, articulable, accessible and emerging from the preconscious. I pointed out that to the extent that they are dominated by the pleasure principle, the thought processes are unconscious, as Freud emphasizes. They are only available to consciousness to the extent that they can be verbalized, that a reasoned account brings them within range of the reality principle, within range of a consciousness that is perpetually alert, interested through the investment of its attention in discovering something that may happen, so as to allow it to find its bearings in the real world". (Lacan 1960), p. 48.
11 Lacan (1960), p. 21.
12 Lacan (1960), p. 21.
13 Lacan (1973), p. 93.
14 Lacan (1973), p. 93.
15 Lacan (1966), pp. 726–727.
16 Lacan (1970), pp. 62–63.
17 Lacan (1970), p. 61; p. 66.
18 Lacan (1921), 6.42; letter to Ficker quoted in Diamond (2000), p. 152.
19 Quoted in Diamond (2000), p. 152.
20 Wittgenstein (1921), p. 3.
21 Wittgenstein (1929), p. 49.
22 Wittgenstein (1929), pp. 42–43.
23 Compare here Cavell (1979), pp. 175–76: "If philosophy is the criticism a culture produces of itself, and proceeds essentially by criticizing past efforts at this criticism, then Wittgenstein's originality lies in having developed modes of criticism that are not moralistic, that is, that do not leave the critic imagining himself free of the faults he sees around him, and which proceed not by trying to argue a given statement false or wrong, but by showing that the person making an assertion does not really know what he means, has not really said what he wished. But since self-scrutiny, the full examination and defense of one's own position, has always been part of the impulse to philosophy, Wittgenstein's originality lies not in the creation of the impulse, but in finding ways to prevent it from defeating itself so easily, ways to make it methodical. That is Freud's advance over the insights of his predecessors at self-knowledge, e.g., Kierkegaard, Nietzsche, and the poets and novelists he said anticipated him".
24 Diamond (2000), pp. 154–55; pp. 163–64.
25 Diamond (1995), p. 10.
26 And earlier published separately as part of the book *The Lives of Animals* along with responses by several prominent philosophers and critics.
27 Diamond (2008), pp. 46–47.
28 Diamond (2008), pp. 48–52.
29 Including, I think, not only the standard forms of this academicisation in "analytic" philosophy but also those characteristic of Zupančič's own Ljubljana school.
30 Zupančič (2000), p. 3.
31 Zupančič (2000), p. 3.
32 Zupančič, (2000), pp. 7–8.
33 Zupančič (2000), pp. 28–29.
34 Zupančič (2000), pp. 29–30.
35 A 296–298/B353–354.

References

Cavell, Stanley. (1979) *The Claim of Reason: Wittgenstein, Skepticism, Morality, and Tragedy.* New York: Oxford University Press.

Diamond, Cora. (1995) *The Realistic Spirit: Wittgenstein, Philosophy, and the Mind.* Cambridge, MA: MIT Press.

Diamond, Cora. (2000) Ethics, Imagination, and the Method of Wittgenstein's *Tractatus.* In *The New Wittgenstein*, ed. by Alice Crary and Rupert Read. London: Routledge.

Diamond, Cora. (2008) The Difficulty of Reality and the Difficulty of Philosophy. In *Philosophy and Animal Life.* Ed., with introduction, by Cary Wolfe. New York: Columbia University Press.

Freud, Sigmund. (1989) *Civilization and its Discontents.* Translated and edited by James Strachey. New York: W.W. Norton and Co.

Lacan, Jacques. (1998) *Encore: The Seminar of Jacques Lacan, Book* XX. Translated by Bruce Fink. New York: W.W. Norton and Co.

Lacan, Jacques. (1999) *The Ethics of Psychoanalysis 1959–1960: The Seminar of Jacques Lacan, Book VII.* Translated by Dennis Porter. Routledge.

Lacan, Jacques (2002) Science and Truth. In *Ecrits: The First Complete Edition in English.* Translated by Bruce Fink. New York: Norton.

Lacan, Jacques. (2007) *The Other Side of Psychoanalysis: The Seminar of Jacques Lacan, Book XVII.* Translated by Russell Grigg. London: W.W. Norton and Co.

Wittgenstein, Ludwig (1974) *Tractatus Logico-Philosophicus.* Translated by D. F. Pears and B. F. McGuinness. London: Routledge.

Wittgenstein, Ludwig. (1993) A Lecture on Ethics. In *Philosophical Occasions 1912–1951.* Ed. by James Klagge and Alfred Nordmann. Indianapolis, IN: Hackett.

Zupančič, Alenka. (2000) *Ethics of the Real: Kant and Lacan.* London: Verso.

Chapter 8

Lacan with Derrida

Chris Vanderwees

> We are two ships, each of which has its goal and its course...the almighty force of our projects drove us apart....That we had to become estranged is the law *above* us; through it we should come to have more respect for each other.... There is probably a tremendous invisible curve and stellar orbit in which our different ways and goals may be *included* as small stretches – let us rise to this thought!
>
> Friedrich Nietzsche, *The Gay Science*

With and After

How might we read Jacques Lacan's archive *with* philosophy? If we wish to explore philosophy *after* Lacan, we ought to look no further than one of his philosopher contemporaries, Derrida, another Jacques whose commensurately prolific *oeuvre* also revolved around a fierce interest in language, linguistics, philosophy, ethics and psychoanalysis. Nearly a decade *after* Lacan's death, Derrida gave a presentation at the symposium, "Lacan with the philosophers", which was held in Paris at the International College of Philosophy in 1990.[1] In this presentation, "For the Love of Lacan", Derrida spoke about his personal encounters with the psychoanalyst, reiterated some of their theoretical differences and reflected on the question of what it might mean to consider Lacan's relationship *with* philosophy. Although Derrida emphasised the *with* in this context of the symposium as his translators deliver this weight in italics, he uncharacteristically forwent the opportunity to examine the etymology of this versatile word.

For the purposes of thinking Lacan *with* Derrida as the theme of this chapter, let us take a Derridean detour and account for the fact that the English "with" and the French "*avec*" similarly originate as replacements for the Latin "*cum*", which literally means "together with" and later evolved as a prefix to allow us words such as "company" and "communication". Beginning in the ninth century, however, long *before* its function as a denotation of "accompaniment", "association", "proximity", "responsibility" or "exchange" in senses of

DOI: 10.4324/9781003425953-9

movement "alongside" or "towards", among two objects or amidst two parties, *with* has a prevailing sense in English that denotes a position that is "face *with* face" – close to the French *vis-à-vis* – a phrase used to "compare" or juxtapose two things "against" or in "opposition" to one another. In this respect, we could consider the implications of bringing psychoanalysis face to face *with* deconstruction.

When exploring Lacan *with* Derrida, we might also look to the earliest sense of the word "with" where we find notions of "adversity", "distance" or "separation" especially in forms that employ the prefix to convey being "away" or "back" as in *withhold, withstand, without, withdrawal*, or *withsaying*. We also have the word *wither*, which conveys death and decay and obsolete forms that once referred to what was "contrary" "hostile" or even "violent" (OED). The polyvalence of this etymology is particularly important to take into consideration when thinking Jacques *with* Jacques. Frequently characterised as two of the most important figures involved with the poststructuralist movement, Lacan and Derrida are less commonly acknowledged for their strained personal relationship or their significantly different approaches to philosophy and usually without mentioning the ambivalence that each had in regards to what we define as "poststructuralist".[2]

It is then not only *with* in the context of Derrida's "love" for Lacan that I will draw attention towards but also *with* in the earliest sense of the word relating to "conflict, antagonism, dispute, injury, reproof, competition, rivalry, and the like" (OED). I provide an overview of Derrida's complicated personal encounters with Lacan before positing some questions concerning how we might read Lacan's archive in light of Derrida's important critical commentary, which seems to have garnered little response from those who identify as Lacanians. In his presentation from 1990, Derrida suggested that there was a "history to come of the *being-with* of Lacan and the philosophers" (p. 53). This chapter is a minor contribution to that history where I outline the philosopher's personal encounters *with* the psychoanalyst prior to gesturing what might come *after* Lacan through Derrida's critiques.

Encounters in Baltimore

Published in two parts in the December 1965 and January 1966 issues of *Critique*, Derrida's essay *"De la grammatologie"* quickly became a topic for conversation in French intellectual circles.[3] According to Elisabeth Roudinesco, "Lacan devoured [the essay] as soon as it appeared in *Critique* and let the philosopher know, through [Jacques-Alain] Miller and Francois Wahl, how highly he thought of the text" (p. 409). Nevertheless, Lacan did not meet *with* Derrida at the *École Normale Supérieure* in Paris where they both taught, Lacan as a professor of psychoanalysis in the Department of Philosophy, Derrida as a professor of French Literature in the Department of Humanities. The two Jacques would not meet for the first time in France, but rather in the in the United States at a conference on structuralist theory,

"The Languages of Criticism and the Science of Man", which took place in Baltimore at Johns Hopkins University from October 18 to 21, 1966.

The conference was a major event. Wanting to introduce structuralist ideas to the American academic scene, humanities professors René Girard, Richard Macksey and Eugenio Donato, organised the meeting in Baltimore and invited not only Lacan and Derrida, but also esteemed intellectuals across disciplines including Hans-Georg Gadamer, Georges Poulet, Lucien Goldmann, Tzvetan Todorov, Roland Barthes, Jean Hyppolite, Guy Rosolato, Nicolas Ruwet and Jean-Pierre Vernant. Well-known literary theorists Northrop Frye, Paul de Man and Joseph Hillis Miller also attended the conference. The same year would see the publication of *The Order of Things*, a seminal text of the structuralist movement that proposed the idea that every historical era exists with its own underlying epistemic postulations, determining the consensus on what can be considered true in academic discourses on any subject. The author of this text, Michel Foucault, was notably one of the most prominent thinkers who did not attend the gathering.[4] The event was a watershed for the exchange of ideas between European and American philosophers and opened the path for a reassessment and ultimate upheaval of structuralism's tenets. It was a landmark occasion in the evolution of thought towards poststructuralist theory and critical theory in the United States and beyond.[5]

Upon arriving in Baltimore, Girard introduced Derrida to Lacan, the former surprised to learn that the latter had requested a deluxe hotel room be reserved for him. Lacan's words, "uttered in a friendly sigh", Derrida remembered, were an acknowledgement of the absurdity of encountering each other for the first time so far from home: "So we had to wait to come here, and abroad, in order to meet each other!" ("For the Love", p. 50). The thirty-six-year-old philosopher had a chance to speak at more length with the psychoanalyst during a dinner held by the conference organisers. Their conversation revolved around ideas on the Cartesian subject, the notion of substance and the linguistic signifier. In her history of the French psychoanalytic movement, *Jacques Lacan & Co.*, Roudinesco recounts what became a confrontation:

> Standing as he sampled a plate of cole slaw, Lacan replied that *his* subject was the same as the one his interlocutor had opposed to the theory of the subject. In itself, the remark was not false. But Lacan then added, 'You can't bear my having already said what you want to say.'....It proved too much. Derrida refused to go along, and retorted sharply, '*That* is not my problem.' Lacan was being made to pay for his remark. Later in the evening, he approached the philosopher and placed his hand gently on his shoulder, "Ah! Derrida, we must speak together, we must speak." They would not speak.

> (p. 410)

Derrida disclosed more about this encounter during his presentation given in 1990.[6] He reflected with the hindsight of many years the realisation that Baltimore is the place where Edgar Allan Poe was buried. Of course, Poe's story of "The Purloined Letter" became a significant work for both Lacan and Derrida, the former opening his *Écrits* with a psychoanalytic interpretation of the text and the latter responding to this interpretation with a critical essay, "The Purveyor of Truth", published nine years later in *Poetique* and then reprinted later in *The Postcard* in 1980.[7]

During the presentation, Derrida played upon what he called "Baltimore's mortal name" given that in French the phonetics of the city's name could suggest a homophonous phrase, *bal / de / mort*, conjuring the Medieval notion of the dance of the dead, referring to the equalising power of mortality. "I remark that the only two times we met and spoke briefly one *with* the other", said Derrida: "it was a question of death between us, and first of all from Lacan's mouth. In Baltimore, for example, he spoke to me of the way in which he thought he would be read, in particular by me, after his death" (pp. 50–51). Lacan was thinking of death in Baltimore while in his late sixties and on the verge of publishing *Écrits*, which compiled the majority of his life's work in writing up until that moment. He confided in Derrida that his publisher, Le Seuil, convinced him to assemble all of his papers into a single nine-hundred-page monograph and worried that the book's binding would not be able to support the weight of so many pages and would fall apart.[8] "[H]e told me as he made a gesture with his hands", Derrida recounted, "You'll see…it's not going to hold up" (p. 52). Lacan was concerned about what might happen to his archive *after* his death. He worried about how his work would be read and interpreted afterwards or if it would be read at all.

At the Baltimore conference, Derrida presented his paper, "Structure, Sign, and Play in the Discourse of the Human Sciences", where he outlined some of the main ideas regarding deconstructionist theory. If the centre of each structure is what organises the limits surrounding what types of discourse can be considered truth, Derrida proposed that the stability of the centre remains open to the possibility for linguistic play and difference. Each centre establishes a set, but does not have a fixed place or natural grounding and so must continually establish and rewrite itself through a process that entails the infinite substitution of signs. We could call this a process of continual resignification. Derrida rejected notions of centrism (for instance, logocentrism and phonocentrism) and suggested there is really no fixed centre point to any structure except for the one that is assumed, which always yields to another that arrives and may be replaced in the traces of the previous one. Although the centre might appear to be relatively stable and tend toward coherence and consistency, it will contain inconsistencies or contradictions that allow for the structure to be modified or challenged over time in response to various discursive shifts. For Derrida, the task of deconstruction is to question dominant discourse, hierarchies, power relations, binary oppositions and the organising principles responsible for what is considered institutional truth within a given structure. According to Derrida, the meaning of every text possesses an inherent instability. Deconstructionist work questions the pretensions surrounding what is understood to be "normal" or "natural", which allow a given structure to persist. Derrida's proposal is that one can begin to account for possible areas of rupture within dominant discourses and to allow for the emergence of counternarratives that might undermine established orders. In short, deconstruction seeks to upend everything we assume or take for granted as an established state of affairs.

Whereas Derrida's paper was received as a highlight of the conference, Peter Salmon has written that Lacan's insistence to present in English despite his lack of fluency led to a somewhat confusing and haphazard presentation that was "baffling to most concerned" and made "his abstruse theories just that little bit more abstruse" (p. 114).[9] Following the conference, Derrida received a signed copy of Lacan's *Écrits* with a dedication from the author: "To Jacques Derrida, this homage, which he can take however he pleases" (Peeters, 2010, p. 168). Derrida wrote in the only letter he would send to Lacan that he was thankful to receive the *Écrits* and would look forward to reading it, but not without addressing the surprising dedication: "An impregnable text, I thought at first. On second thoughts, adding, as your overture invites us to, my own ideas, I changed my mind: this dedication is true and I should receive it as such. 'True' is a word about which I know that you have your own ideas"(quoted in Peeters, 2010, p. 168). It is perhaps this questioning of truth that could be said to generate the most significant contention between these two thinkers.

Encounters in Paris

One year after the conference in 1967, the two Jacques met again for the second and last time at the home of Jean Piel for a dinner party in Paris.[10] During that same year, Derrida published three major works including *Of Grammatology, Writing and Difference*, and *Speech and Phenomena*. According to Roudinesco, "Lacan clasped Derrida's hand warmly in his oily palms and asked him what he was working on" and, after listening to Derrida's thoughts, suggested how "curious it was" that they had been working on and thinking about "the same themes" (pp. 410–411). Over the course of this conversation, Derrida told the psychoanalyst about a startling occurrence involving his own young son, Pierre:

> One evening, as his son Pierre was beginning to fall asleep in his mother's presence, he asked his father why he was looking at him. 'Because you're handsome.' The child reacted immediately by saying that the compliment made him want to die. Somewhat troubled, Derrida

132 Philosophy After Lacan

tried to figure out what the story meant. 'I don't like myself,' the child said. 'And since when?' 'Since I've known how to talk.' Marguerite took him in her arms, 'Don't worry, we love you.' Then Pierre broke out laughing, 'No, all that isn't true; I'm a cheater for life'.

(Roudinesco, p. 411)

In recounting this story to Lacan, Derrida was most likely seeking some expert guidance or reassurance, but the psychoanalyst apparently did not offer any. Following the dinner party in December of the same year, Derrida was shocked to learn that Lacan betrayed his confidence and retold the story about his son to demonstrate a point to an audience during a lecture at the French Institute in Naples.[11] Although he did not comment on this incident during Lacan's lifetime, years later during his presentation at the conference in 1990, *Lacan with the Philosophers*, Derrida reflected on what Lacan's motivations might have been for retelling and interpreting this story about the father and son. He mused about the possible transference at stake in Lacan's interpretation of the story, but also about Lacan's anxiety about the question of his own death in regards to the psychoanalytic archetypes of father and son:

Lacan's phrase speaks of a 'father,' and that's me, a father who 'does not recognize...the way he himself disregarded the Other [big O] by playing dead.' I am still not sure I have fully understood the ventured interpretation....but I have always wondered whether by making me out to be the father in this story, by naming me 'the father,' he was not taking aim at the son; I have always wondered whether he didn't mean to say the son, if he didn't want to play the son, to make me or himself into the son, to make of me the son who disregards the Other by playing dead, as he put it, or make himself into the son.

(p. 51)

Derrida wondered if Lacan's anxiety about how his work could be read after his death was not manifesting in the retelling of this personal story told to him in confidence. Lacan also must have assumed that this retelling of the story would reach Derrida at some point, given that following his interpretation, he added: "It is up to the father who told me from here to hear me or not" (Lacan, 1968, "La méprise", p. 35).[12] During his presentation in 1990, Derrida took liberty to muse about the dynamics at stake between the senior psychoanalyst and himself as the much younger philosopher, the dynamics perhaps between a father and a son in regards to the question of mortality:

[I]t was especially a question of death...even only of the death of one of us, as it is *with* or *chez* all those who love each other...[H]e spoke about it, he alone, since for my part I never breathed a word about it. He spoke...about our death, about his death that would not fail to arrive, and about the death or rather the dead one that, according to him, I was playing.

(p. 52)

Whatever Lacan's motivations for retelling Derrida's story, this incident ultimately resulted in the philosopher keeping a distance from the psychoanalyst. Despite diligently reading the *Écrits*, Derrida never sought any personal relationship with Lacan.

In 1970, when Le Seuil decided to publish a two-volume mass-market paperback edition of *Écrits*, Lacan made another nod to Derrida in the introduction to the first volume when referring to signifiers that appear in dreams as "what I properly call the instance of the letter before any grammatology" (p. 11).[13] In an interview with Jean-Louis Houdebine and Guy Scarpetta published in 1972 as "Positions", Derrida included an endnote that spans over several pages where he outlined some of his main points of contention with Lacan's system of thought.[14] In this endnote, Derrida accused Lacan of making "lighthanded reference to the authority of phonology" and for giving attention to writing and the notion of the letter through Freud, but without any serious investigation into concerns of the actual process of writing (*Positions*, pp. 108–109n44). He also highlighted motifs in Lacan's work that may be particularly vulnerable to critique including the idea of "a return to Freud" as well as the telos of "full speech" and its relation to truth (*Positions*, pp. 108–109n44).

The motif of truth as a kind of veiling and unveiling in Lacan's work is something that Derrida returned to three years later in the essay, "The Purveyor of Truth", an assessment and critical response to Lacan's commentary on Edgar Allen Poe's "The Purloined Letter". In the essay, Derrida challenged Lacan's formulation that the letter always arrives at its destination in psychoanalysis, arguing that if the possibility exists that the letter or signifier may not always arrive at its destination, this uncertainty is already part of its structure and therefore the letter is then fallible, unreliable and predisposed to get lost. This difference between Lacan and Derrida in terms of their understanding of the letter and the signifier has already been the preoccupation of many commentaries and even a book (Muller and Richardson, 1988). Suffice to say that Derrida and Lacan have different understandings of truth as a concept, understandings that are grounded respectively in their commitments to distinct philosophical and psychoanalytic projects.

For Derrida, truth is not a stable or fixed concept and cannot ever be fully grasped or defined. Rather, truth is always in a state of flux, constantly shifting, evolving and reconstructed. He wrote that every text contains internal contradictions and opposing meanings and so truth cannot be identified or achieved definitively, but rather it is the result of a complex

134 Philosophy After Lacan

interplay of multiple interpretations and perspectives. Lacan's idea of truth is rooted in the practice of psychoanalysis, which focuses on the subjective experience and unconscious mind of the analysand. Here, truth becomes what may emerge through the analysand's speech when the barriers of repression are momentarily lifted. For Lacan, truth is also not something that can be easily defined or captured, but his emphasis is more on what is being repressed and distorted by the unconscious desire of the analysand. While both Derrida and Lacan trouble traditional conceptualisations of truth, Derrida's emphasis is the instability of language. By contrast, Lacan's emphasis is on the role of unconscious desire as it is connected to the symbolic. Derrida's deconstruction undermines fixed meanings and posits truth as a complex interplay of multiple interpretations, while Lacan's psychoanalysis portrays truth as that which is shaped by the subject's desires and linguistic structures within the unconscious. If Lacan argued that the letter, for instance, is an important element in psychoanalytic practice, as it signifies both the materiality and the linguistic nature of language, Derrida challenged this claim, suggesting that the letter is always already determined by the signifier and it cannot hold a stable meaning. For Derrida, the signifier is always in a process of infinite deferral, that is, it never fully refers to a fixed and stable presence or thing, but rather operates through an overdetermined web of signification. Derrida argues that Lacan's reliance on the letter reflects a metaphysical understanding of language, which overlooks the inherent instability and playfulness of signification.

For all of the scholars who have labored and puzzled over the difficult discourses of Lacan and Derrida on their dispute in regards to this matter of the letter and its relation to truth, perhaps Barbara Johnson best underscored the absurdity of the disagreement:

> [I]n this discussion of the letter as what prevents me from knowing whether Lacan and Derrida are really saying the same thing or only enacting their own differences from themselves, my own theoretical 'frame of reference' is precisely, to a very large extent, the writings of Lacan and Derrida. The frame is thus framed again by part of its content; the sender again receives his own message backwards from the receiver. And the true otherness of the purloined letter of literature has perhaps still in no way been accounted for.
>
> (p. 505)

Suffice to say that Lacan did not ever respond to "The Purveyor of Truth" but a year later commented during a seminar with disapproval of Derrida's foreword to Nicolas Abraham and Maria Torok's book, *The Wolf Man's Magic Wand*, which he stated did not "have the right tone" (p. 47). Lacan also made a strange blunder during the same talk and disclosed to his audience that he believed Derrida to be in analysis with more than one analyst.[15]

Although he married Marguerite Aucouturier, an accomplished psycho-analyst and an important translator of Melanie Klein's works into French, Derrida maintained a distance not only from Lacan, but also from psycho-analysis as a clinical treatment. He studied Freud deeply throughout his career, studied the emerging ideas from his psychoanalyst contemporaries, but never sought a psychoanalysis for himself.

Derrida's Resistances

Let us return to Derrida's presentation "For the Love of Lacan" where he talked candidly to an audience about his exchanges with the psychoanalyst. In this lecture, Derrida spoke about the encounter in Baltimore, about receiving a copy of the *Écrits* with a dedication, about the meeting at the dinner party in Paris, about how Lacan appeared to be anxious about how others (and especially Derrida) would read his work after he was gone. Lacan would have been fearful for how his own legacy would be represented in precisely the sort of presentation that Derrida gave in 1990. From the posi-tion of deconstructionist, Derrida urged the audience of intellectuals to question what we might glean from Lacan's psychoanalytic teachings.

He posited provocative exclamations about the Lacanian archive in the future perfect tense (*futur antérieur*) including "What wouldn't Lacan have said! What will he not have said!"[16] For Derrida, these exclamations are linked with the notion of the future of the archive, the growing collection of documents about Lacan and the history of Lacanianism. In this regard, it is a question of remains after one has died, that is, the remains of what Lacan said and how those remains are now translated, interpreted and reinter-preted, given certain meanings, some aspects privileged over others that might be deemphasised for clinical, political or other rhetorical motives. Derrida's exclamations also beckon us to look towards a prospect that moves beyond knowledge that is generated under the author-function of Lacan's name and to consider all of the limitations that might come with this system of thought so as to discover innovative ways of thinking or being. He cau-tioned his audience to consider the "aporias of archivisation" that are pos-sible under the name of Lacan as it might be linked to science, to institutions and especially to psychoanalysis:

> It is always difficult to know if it is getting archived, what is getting archived, how it is getting archived – the trace that arrives only to efface itself / only by effacing itself, beyond the alternative of presence and absence. It is not merely difficult to know this; it is strictly impossible, no doubt not because there is always more to be known but because it is not of the order of knowledge....An equally keen attention is required with regard to what may be problematic in psychoanalytic discourse – for example, Lacan's – as concerns, precisely, archivization, the guard or

reserve, the economy of repression as guard, inscription, effacement, the destructibility of the letter or the name. A history that could measure up to these formidable difficulties, could be capable of taking them into account in its own historical discourse, ought to come as an addition to other readings of the archive.

(pp. 41–45)

Throughout his career, Derrida highlighted the complications with the archive, the narratives the archive produces and the ways that power becomes linked to institutionalised knowledge. Here, he imagined a form of historical or archival work that could, for instance, assess Lacanian discourse in its own historical context, but also account for the historical discourse from where one is now reading Lacan. Despite his cautions about psychoanalysis, Derrida openly admits the significance of the Lacanian movement:

Whether one is talking about philosophy, psychoanalysis, or theory in general, what the flat-footed restoration underway attempts to recover, disavow, or censor is the fact that nothing of that which managed to transform the space of thought in the last decades would have been possible without some coming to terms *with* Lacan, without the Lacanian provocation, however one receives it or discusses it – and, I will add, without some coming to terms *with* Lacan in his coming to terms *with* the philosophers.

(p. 46)

Derrida alluded to the longstanding institutional censorship surrounding Lacan's discourse within the International Psychoanalytic Association, but also to the ways his discourse conveys "a difficult form of thought...[that] does not submit easily to normalization by the media, by academics, or by publishers, one which rebels against the restoration currently underway, against the philosophical or theoretical neo-conformism in general (let us not even mention literature) that flattens and levels everything around us" (pp. 45–46). To pay homage to Lacan, Derrida suggested, would be an act of "cultural resistance" especially since what set the psychoanalyst apart from other thinkers was his radical break from traditions of analytical, rational or empirical forms of reasoning insofar as he dramatised the unfolding of the unconscious desire during his seminars. It is in this way that Lacan opened the path for a new form of philosophical culture.

For Derrida, Lacan's discourse provided his audience with philosophical interpretations of various "texts" that gave the impression of "a refinement, a scope, an unexpected illumination of the 'searchlight effect'" (p. 46). It is the searchlight effect as portion of Lacan's rhetorical prowess that gave his audiences the sense of being on the verge of discovering something covered in darkness, previously unknown, only then to have a gradual light reveal a hidden truth.[17] Although Lacan's style and surrealistic discourse may have been unprecedented, Derrida contended that the Lacanian system of thought could be subject to deconstruction through its reliance on various centrisms including "phonocentrism, logocentrism, phallogocentrism" and several apparent motifs, including: "full speech as truth, the transcendentalism of the signifier, the circular return of reappropriation toward what is most proper about the proper place, whose borders are circumscribed by lack, and so forth, through a handling of philosophical reference whose form, at least, was in the best of cases elliptical and aphoristic, in the worst, dogmatic" (p. 54). In his 1990 presentation, Derrida highlighted several theorisations of Lacanian psychoanalysis that ought to be brought under scrutiny including the notion of the proper trajectory of the letter as returning to the place that reinscribes lack, the motif of truth being formulated as an unveiling, the transcendental place assigned to the phallus, and the phono-logocentrism or *phallogocentrism* contained in Lacanian discourse.

Derrida insisted strongly that it will be most important for psychoanalysts who continue to read Lacan's work to do so in a questioning and problematising way rather than "in an apelike, orthodox, and defensive manner" (p. 60). In the wake of Lacan's death, one problem with the Lacanian archive for Derrida was that some of the keepers of this archive tended to mimic, concretise and protect their masters ideas rather than open them up for freedom of thought. A consensus around what Lacan has or has not said has now former in the decades following Lacan's death. There are numerous Lacanian groups in academic and clinic contexts all over the world, each of which emphasises certain aspects of Lacan's teachings over others to produce their own dialect or inflection of Lacanian discourse. For Derrida, the future of any archive – let alone the Lacanian archive – involves traces, forgetting, remains and absence, but the recontextualisation and rethinking of contents and materials must be an inherent part of the archive itself. We could follow Derrida's lead to raise new questions for the contemporary scene: What wouldn't we have revered most about Lacan's work? What will we have not salvaged for another generation? How will Lacan have been understood, remembered, archived?

Despite his challenging encounters with Lacan, his criticisms of his work and scepticism about his legacy, Derrida also underscored the tumultuous love for the French language that he and Lacan shared. He described the nature of this shared love in an interview with Roudinesco published only a few years before his death:

> I have for this language an anxious, jealous, and tormented love. That is one thing I have in common with Lacan, although we write in very different ways. He, too, has a way of *touching* and *mistreating* the French language, or of *letting himself be touched and mistreated* by it, which it seems to me, and if this is not too unfair, I do not sense in others. I share

with him a constant attention to a certain movement of the sentence, to a work night of the signifier, but of the letter, of rhetoric, composition, address, destinations, mise-en-scène. So in this respect I feel myself closer to Lacan than to any of the others.

(p. 14)

It is ultimately in this attentiveness to language that we can begin to read Derrida *with* Lacan. For all of their possible differences, each called us to listen to the polyvalent, libidinal, displaced and playful aspects of speech and writing. Each Jacques respectively addressed the subject's relation to *jouissance* and language. Any practitioner of philosophy or psychoanalysis that comes after Lacan (or Derrida, for that matter) must account for such phenomena.

Notes

1 Derrida and Roudinesco briefly speak about the symposium in *For What Tomorrow...* and Derrida's presentation, "Pour l'amour de Lacan", is reprinted and translated in English with two other papers on psychoanalysis in *Resistances of Psychoanalysis*. Organised by René Major, Patrick Guyomard, and Philippe Lacoue-Labarthe, the symposium took place from May 24–27, 1990, and gathered European researchers and academics together who were interested in Lacan's work. Many leading philosophers including Alain Badiou, Mikkel Borch-Jacobsen, Guy Le Gaufey, Christian Jamber, Etienne Balibar, Pierre Macherey, Jean-Luc Nancy, Elisabeth Roudinesco, Jean-Michel Vappereau, Samuel Weber, William J. Richardson, and Nicole Loraux were also in attendance at the symposium. The presentations from this symposium are also collected in *Lacan avec les philosophes*, Paris: Albin Michel, 1991.
2 Lacan is often considered a poststructuralist thinker, owing to his emphasis on language, discourse, and the role of the unconscious in shaping individual subjectivity. Some scholars, however, also identify Lacan as belonging to the tradition of structuralism, particularly in his early work on linguistics and structural anthropology. Ultimately, the question of whether Lacan was a structuralist or a poststructuralist is a matter of interpretation and may depend on the specific aspects of his work that are being emphasised. Derrida openly distinguished his theory of deconstruction from "poststructuralism" and "postmodernism" and disidentified with attempts to characterise his work as such.
3 This essay outlines the central argument of what would become Derrida's book, *Of Grammatology*, published in 1967.
4 Presentations from this conference were later published by Johns Hopkins University Press as a collection edited by Richard Macksey and Eugenio Donato in 1970, *The Structuralist Controversy: The Languages of Criticism and the Sciences of Man*.
5 Drawing upon Ferdinand Saussure's linguistics, Claude Lévi-Strauss' anthropological studies, Sigmund Freud's theories of the unconscious, and Karl Marx's political and economic treatises, structuralism called into question the fundamental notion of a human-centric philosophy. In his biography of Derrida, Peter Salmon outlines this point in plain terms: "[structuralism] proposed that all elements of human culture, and all phenomena of human life, could only be

understood as part of a 'structure,' and any explanation of motives, actions and behaviour had to overcome the illusion of a free subject. Everything could only be explained by its inter-relationship to other parts of the scheme" (2). This structuralist evolution in philosophy had a multidisciplinary impact and emerged as the dominant theoretical discourse in France, overtaking the popularity of the existentialist movement whose participants included Albert Camus, Simone de Beauvoir, and Jean-Paul Sartre.

6 At the time of the publication of *Jacques Lacan & Co.* in 1986, Roudinesco did not have more of Derrida's story about his encounters with Lacan and had not yet interviewed him for *For What Tomorrow...: A Dialogue.* The exchange excerpted from her book between the philosopher and the psychoanalyst serves as one of many examples where Roudinesco notes a reoccurring theme with Lacan who was preoccupied with the thought that his ideas would be stolen, had a fantasy that he could own concepts, and suffered from the narcissism of "priority" (410).

7 The original title of Derrida's response to Lacan about Edgar Allan Poe's "The Purloined Letter" is *"Le facteur de la verité"*, which could be translated in several ways since *le facteur* could be either be "the factor" or "the postman".

8 Lacan's concern for the binding echoed Freudian notions of bound and unbound energy, notions that have particular significance for the development of the death drive as a concept in *Beyond the Pleasure Principle.* The notion of binding initially appeared in *Studies on Hysteria* in 1895, but was further developed through Freud's letters to Wilhelm Fliess. Binding has a psychological function in Freudian theory in relation to the origin and function of the ego. Freud imagined an economics of physical and psychical energy whereby the ego is composed of a bound mass of neurons, composing a secondary process that is well connected, organised and able to have a binding effect on other processes. Perhaps most simply put, binding conveys the psychic function of signification. If energy is bound, it is linked to an object. An idea that comes to one's mind and is spoken aloud, for instance, might be understood as the free energy of the primary processes linked to the unconscious, manifesting as a bound and conscious symbolisation in the secondary processes. In other words, the drive is bound to a representative for the ego. See Vanderwees, Chris. "Freud's Beyond the Pleasure Principle and the Death Drive: A Concise Overview". *Critical Essays on the Drive: Lacanian Theory and Practice.* Edited by Dan Collins and Eve Watson. London: Routledge, 2024.

9 Lacan presented a paper called "Structure as an Inmixing of an Otherness Prerequisite to Any Subject Whatever". Derrida's paper would later by published as a chapter in *Writing and Difference.* Both Lacan and Derrida's papers are also reprinted in *The Structuralist Controversy.* Edited by Richard Macksey and Eugenio Donato.

10 Jean Piel (1902–96) was a French writer, philosopher, and editor who had deep ties to various intellectual circles in France. He became the editor of the journal *Critique* following the death of Georges Bataille who was the journal's founder. His wife was Simone Maklès who was the sister of Sylvia Bataille.

11 Lacan recounted Derrida's story in a presentation at the French Institute of Naples on 14 December 1967. The presentation is printed in Lacan, Jacques. "La méprise du sujet supposé savoir". *Scilicet,* 1 (1968): 31–41. The retelling of Derrida's story can be found on page 35 of this text. A further reprint of this same presentation can be found in *Autres Écrits* and the story about Derrida and his son appears again on page 333. See Lacan, Jacques. "La méprise du sujet supposé savoir". 14 December 1967. *Autre Écrits.* Paris: Seuil, 2001, 329–339.

140 Philosophy After Lacan

12 This is my translation of Lacan's statement in the original French, which is "*C'est au pere qui me fa dit d'ici mentendre ou non*" (35).

13 My translation from Lacan's original French: "*ce que j'appelle proprement l'instance de la letter avant toute grammatologie*" (11). Although this Points edition of the *Écrits* published in two mass market paperback volumes is documented inside the text as published in 1966, Bruce Fink confirms that this edition was not actually published until 1970 (for volume one) and 1971 (for volume two), respectively, which is where Lacan included a new introduction that gave this nod to Derrida's work while mentioning "grammatology". See Fink's "Translator's Note" for confirmation about these dates in the English edition of the *Écrits* (xi).

14 See page 107n44 in Derrida's *Positions* for his developing critique of Lacan's ideas.

15 Lacan's awkward blunder can be found on pages 46–47 of Cormac Gallagher's translation of Seminar XXIV, *L'insu que sait*, which was held during the academic year of 1976/77.

16 Derrida also intended for these exclamations to refer to the practical matter of actually sorting out what Lacan said during his seminars for a Lacanian archive: "it is inscribed there in the spoken words of a seminar that, by giving rise to numerous steno-typed or tape-recorded archivings, will have then fallen prey not only to all the problems of rights...but also to all the problems posed by the delays of publishing and of an editing – in the American sense – that was of the most active sort. Since all of these things hang by a hair, since the stakes get decided in a word, an ellipsis, a verbal modality, a conditional or a future anterior, especially when one knows Lacan's rhetoric, I say good luck to any narrator who would try to know what was said and written by whom on which date: what would Lacan have said or not have said!" (62).

17 In his classic book, *Listening with the Third Ear*, Theodor Reik described the psychoanalyst's evenly hovering attention as a kind of searchlight. Lacan dramatised this kind of attention in his seminars. This form of attention might also be considered a form of close listening, a form of attention that Lacan demanded of his audience. For more the rhetorical aspects of Lacan's discourse, the art of persuasion, and close listening see Adleman, Dan and Chris Vanderwees. *Psychoanalysis and the New Rhetoric*. New York: Routledge, 2023.

References

Abraham, N. and Torok, M. (1986) *The Wolf Man's Magic Wand*. Translated by Nicolas Rand. Minneapolis, MN: University of Minnesota

Derrida, J. (1975) *The Purveyor of Truth*. Translated by W. Domingo, and J. Hulbert.

Derrida, J. (1981) *Positions*. Translated by Alan Bass. Chicago, IL: University of Chicago Press.

Derrida, J. (1998) For the Love of Lacan. *Resistances of Psychoanalysis*. Translated by P. Kamuf, P.-A.Brault & M. Naas (pp. 39–69). Stanford, CA: Stanford University Press.

Derrida, J. and Roudinesco, E. (2004) *For What Tomorrow...: A Dialogue*. Translated by Jeff Fort. Stanford, CA: Stanford University Press.

Green, A. (2005) *Key Ideas for Contemporary Psychoanalysis: Misrecognition and Recognition of the Unconscious*. Translated by Andrew Weller. New York: Routledge.

Johnson, B. (1977) The Frame of Reference: Poe, Lacan, and Derrida. *Yale French Studies*, 55/56 (1977), 457–505.

Lacan, J. (1966) A quelqu'un, grâce à qui c'est plutôt signe...*Écrits I*. Paris: Seuil.

Lacan, J. (1968) La méprise du sujet supposé savoir. *Scilicet*, 1 (1968), 31–41.

Lacan, J. (2007) *Écrits*. Translated by Bruce Fink, W.W. Norton & Company.

Muller, J.P. and Richardson, W.J. (1988) The Challenge of Deconstruction. In J.P. Muller and W.J. Richardson (Eds), *The Purloined Poe: Lacan, Derrida, and Psychoanalytic Reading* (pp. 159–172). Baltimore, MD: The Johns Hopkins University Press.

Oxford English Dictionary. (2023) with, prep., adv., and conj. OED Online. Oxford University Press, March 2023. Retrieved May 24, 2023.

Peeters, Benoît. (2013) *Derrida: A Biography*. Translated by Andrew Brown. Malden: Polity Press.

Ron, M. and M.-R. L. (1975) *Yale French Studies*, 52 (1975), 31–113.

Roudinesco, Elisabeth. (1990) *Jacques Lacan & Co.: A History of Psychoanalysis in France, 1925–1985*. Translated by Jeffrey Mehlman. Chicago, IL: University of Chicago Press.

Salmon, Peter. (2020) *An Event, Perhaps: A Biography of Jacques Derrida*. London: Verso.

Chapter 9

"Lacan is Our Hegel"

Dialectic from Hegel to Lacan to Badiou

Reza Naderi

On two separate occasions, Badiou has attributed a unique position concerning contemporary philosophy to Lacan. His more famous account of this unique position is Lacan's anti-philosophy. His 1994–95 seminar on Lacan, recently published in English[1], the culmination of a three-year study of modern anti-philosophy, which also includes Nietzsche and Wittgenstein, is to establish Lacan's version of anti-philosophy as the one that the contemporary philosophy must be able to face off. In this relation, Badiou thinks that "Lacan appointed himself as the educator of all future philosophers. A contemporary philosopher, for me, is indeed someone who has the steadfast courage to work through Lacan's anti-philosophy".[2] In this context, Badiou treats Lacan as a "worthy adversary" that any genuine philosopher, as a friend of truths, must be able to face off. The return of truth goes through Lacan's declaration of truth being primordially a kind of powerlessness, a weakness, and if a love of truth does exist, this love is the love of that powerlessness and that weakness. Furthermore, truth itself is the concealment of this powerlessness as what affects truth in Lacan's anti-philosophy is castration, which makes truth a veil over the impossibility of saying it all. Truth is thus a mask of its own weakness.[3]

This anti-philosophy position that Badiou attributes to Lacan is distinguishable from the less-known position he attributed to Lacan in his first major philosophical book, *Theory of the Subject,*[4] where he called Lacan "our contemporary". However, here, the sense in which Lacan is our contemporary is different from the previous sense. In *Theory of the Subject,* Badiou is pursuing a materialist grounding for the theory of the subject. Badiou had to develop this theory in a philosophical and intellectual context dominated by the French structuralism of the 1950s and 1960s, critiqued and reconstructed by Althusserian and psychoanalytical revisions. The manifesto for this brand of structuralism was a short essay published in *Cahiers pour l'Analyse* called "Action of the Structure".[5] For Badiou, Lacan was the thinker who attempted to reconceive the concept of the subject not according to the essentialist and humanist notions, which Althusser had already banished from structuralism, but based on the very idea of the structure. In

DOI: 10.4324/9781003425953-10

Badiou's mind, Lacan could do that by returning to Hegelian dialectic. As such, for Badiou, if there were any hope for possible materialism of the subject, it would have been through the same line of thought as Lacan and by returning to Hegel and, ultimately, Descartes. That is why, in *Theory of the Subject*, Badiou calls Lacan "our Hegel".[6]

It is in this sense that Badiou calls Lacan our contemporary. We must go through Lacan because Lacan has worked out the dialectical thought necessary to ground a materialist theory of the subject. Lacan did that by splitting Hegel. Moreover, since Lacan is our Hegel, we must now split Lacan to reach the materialist core of the dialectic.

In this essay, we try to address three things:

What is the brand of structuralism that allows for the category of the subject, and why is it not a materialist theory?
What is the brand of dialectic that allows us to build a materialist theory of the subject from this brand of structuralism?
What splitting operation discharges the idealist commitments in Lacan (and in Hegel)?

"Action of the Structure" the Manifesto for the Theory of Discourse

The *Cahiers pour l'Analyse* aimed to develop a theory of discourse as "a process of language that truth constrains".[7] As such, epistemology, for instance, can be defined as the theory of discourse of science.

The era in which this project was announced was also distinctly charged with a new intellectual movement that we now know as post-structuralism, which brought keen attention to the theory of discourse. The French post-structuralists devised a break with modernist rationality and its latest philosophical manifestation in phenomenology and existentialism. The facets of this break are multiple and primarily unrelated concerning their genesis and progression. Still, they all agree on some crucial orientations: decentred subjectivity, deconstruction of normativity, believing in an inherent deception within the dominant narratives, and erosion of the category of Truth. Several influential philosophers contributed to French post-structuralism. Still, the ones who mattered the most to the editors of *Cahiers* were, without a doubt, Foucault, Althusser and Lacan. The shift from a dominant narrative operative in all sorts of rationalism, particularly phenomenology, was the point of departure for these great philosophers – with the concept of discourse as the central point of this departure.

Consequently, a new and independent theory of discourse was a must. It is important to note that all three philosophers were acutely aware of advances in linguistics. Still, they were determining if the theory of language would

144 Philosophy After Lacan

provide the required theoretical treatment of the concept of discourse in any of their respective fields. Orthodox linguistics is a child of modernism, and as such, it implicates a decentred rational subject that conveys meanings by using language. A decentred subject requires a decentred theory of language – this is what any tenable discourse theory should accomplish.

This finally brought a group of young philosophers together around the *Cahiers* and led to the publication of its manifesto, "Action of the Structure". *Cahiers* contained texts dealing with logic, linguistics and psychoanalysis to constitute this theory, dubbed the sciences of analysis, itself a discourse containing ideas that deal with concepts of element and combination. "Action of the Structure" is the manifesto for this theory of discourse, which in particular concerns the relations between the structure of the subject and the structure of science. Miller wrote this piece with a few other early editors of the *Cahiers* in 1964. They did not publish it until the summer of 1968, in volume 9 of the *Cahiers*. "Action of the Structure" is usually treated as a supplement to another short essay by Miller called "Suture", but neither text references the other.[8]

The theory of discourse is motivated by how psychoanalysis and Marxism provide the principle for a new organisation of the conceptual field and, for the same reason, are both misunderstood, either reduced to silence or misrepresented in theoretical terms that not only predate them but often oppose them. The theory of discourse is, therefore, an elucidation of the principles that have informed these fields – principles that, despite being operative in both, have otherwise remained unconsciously latent and, for this reason, precede these fields. Crossing the theory of discourse with these fields illuminates how this theory is unitary, and the only tribunal that summons it is that of its rigour. The theory of discourse maintains that the discourses of Marx and Freud might communicate with each other via regulated transformation and might reflect one another in a unitary theoretical discourse.[9]

Structure

The first concept reworked in the theory of discourse is structure.

According to Miller, the traditional structure concept has two crucial exclusions: experience and subject. The concept of structure operative in scientific discourse prohibits both – the definition of the model includes an irreducible distance from lived experience and, thereby, from any temporality or subjectivity.

Central to this traditional model of exteriority is the issue of causality within the structure. By rejecting temporality and subjectivity from the neutralised space of the cause, the structure, which is now exterior to what it structures, is merely obliged to preserve its already constituted objects. In this case, causality refers back to essentialist categories such as culture, biology or mind. Even in a highly "subjective" field such as linguistic structuralism, the externality of the structure, its objectivity, is preserved by a demarcation between the speech and the speaker. The trouble that motivates this separation is that the structure will not explain the dynamism of the elements it articulates; rather, it represents them as a burden to get rid of. As such, this separation convokes composition at the elemental level to do the work of explaining. That is, the theory deliberately evacuates the structure from anything pertaining to causality.

The project in the *Cahiers* aims to abolish this distance and integrate the lived into the structure. They proposed that psychoanalysis and Marxism would permit a conception of structure that goes beyond the traditional notion of a network of standalone objects. That is a conception where topological intricacies no longer contradict the dynamism articulated by the displacement of elements. In this approach, instead of excluding experience and subject, the structure embraces both – in fact, it is where both come to be. The structure is that which "puts in place an experience for the subject that it includes".[10]

What is structure, then? Miller begins with the following formulation: "Two functions qualify our concept of structure: structuration, or the action of the structure, and subjectivity, subjected".[11] The structure is generated by drawing the consequences of this hypothesis. The first function of the structure is further divided into two things: "an actual plane, in which it is given to the observer, and which constitutes its state", and the second is "a virtual dimension, through which all its states are capable of being deduced", or in other words the division can be restated as "structuring structure and a structured structure".[12]

The preceding division is hardly surprising: a structure is structured, and it structures. In other words, a structure is the outcome of previous determinations and the cause of future determinations. However, what is essential is that, in a traditional view, these features are permanently coupled together, with no fissure or delay between them. That is, between the structuring principle (determinant determination) and the structured principle (determined determination), there is no gap (the gap which, as we shall see shortly, is the subject). According to Miller and colleagues, despite being tightly conjoined, there is a subtle difference between these two orders: actual (structured) and virtual (structuring). The view offered here draws consequences from this division in the presence of another element: an element capable of turning back on reality to perceive it, to reflect on it and to signify it, an element capable of redoubling itself on its account. The claim here is that in the presence of such a reflexive element, the whole structural economy is distorted, and the division between virtuality and actuality finds a significance not formerly thinkable by traditional structuralism. The subject is born out of this fissure in the structure itself. To understand this, Miller draws our attention to two concurrent but distinct consequences, which he calls "the driving discordance".[13]

146   Philosophy After Lacan

On the one hand, we have the reduplication of reality that creates imaginary representations so that reality is a lived experience for the reflexive element. This arranges an imaginary organisation, contemporaneous with and distinct from the real order yet co-ordinated with it, and henceforth an intrinsic part of reality. A tertiary, imaginary structure constitutes itself in the real. As a result, the reduplication of the structural system, which was merely ideal at the outset, is accomplished.

On the other hand, the redoubling turns actuality into an experience, which in turn converts the virtuality of the structuring into an absence. Relating to the actuality as what the reflexive element "lives in" makes this actuality its own: the dimension of virtuality is pushed to the real. The crucial point is this: the reflexive element institutes the dimension or order of the structure but is redoubled as the structure, which is caused solely by the reflexive element itself. Hence, we get a tertiary dimension of the imaginary organisation of reality, contemporaneous but distinct from actuality. However, this reflexivity is of no consequence to the structure itself – the lived experience is comprised solely of imaginary representations resulting from the reduplication of reality – "insofar as at the structuring level there is no reflexivity".[14] The subject is born out of the reflexive element afflicted by this duality: reflexive element in the imaginary, non-reflexive in the structuring.

There is a clear torsion in a new form – reflexive and non-reflexive at the same time. However, while reflexivity, which is the ground for having an experience, is essential to the reflexive element, how can we make sense of the non-reflexive aspect? How can the reflexive element attain a non-reflexive character simultaneously under a structure's virtual order? The subject is simultaneously reflexive and non-reflexive – a gap between two signifiers as each signifier is itself the signification of the other, that is, the inclusion of the subject into the signifying chain. The reflexive element is not the author of the actuality that it lives but a mere subject to the virtual order that structures it. It merely creates imaginary representations that give it the experience of life: its own life. However, it is precisely through this activity, through the ideal representations, that it becomes a mere support for the virtual order of the structure. It becomes subject to the structuring order but misrecognises this subjection as the living experience. Thus, the subject finds a circular relation to the structure. This miscognition allows for the opposite poles to stay together. In its subjection, the subject puts into play what the subject in its reflexive mode conceals – it empowers what it hides – and the imaginary function of miscognition mediates all this internal circular relation of different modes of subjectivity. The action of the structuring works through the mode of subjection. At the same time, this work re-establishes reality in its experience of continuity through the production of imaginary representations that compensate for the absence of the structuring cause. Lack is thus never apparent since what is structured misrecognises the action that forms it.

As mentioned, the imaginary is a system of representations. It constitutes the known reality. The imaginary representations are effects of the structure-cause, but this causal relation is more complex. The imaginary can also push back and resist the causal forces of structure. Consequentially, the action of the structuring-cause on its effects is not uniform; that is, it is exercised unequally upon the imaginary depending on the resistance of representations. Overdetermination is the term Miller uses for the unequal determination that structuration has over its effects, owing to the biases that the imaginary harbours. Overdetermination signifies that the relation of structuration with its results is indirect, unequal and eccentric.[15]

The reason for overdetermination is that the cause is absent among its effects – it is a continuation of the fundamental lack and miscognition. Overdetermination is the witness to reality's declaration of independence. Two consequences follow from this.

The first is that lack shows itself under a guise somewhere in the system of representations. Later, Miller emphasises that lack is within the subject, not outside of it. It is a point within the place of representations which constitutes its weakest point.[16] The second consequence is the general deficiency that grounds overdetermination, i.e. the lack, which needs a compensating mechanism, which Miller refers to as suture. The sole advantage of such metaphors of fault points and suture is that they allude to the localisation through which it is possible to pierce beyond the imaginary organisation of reality.

Subject

All this shows that for Miller and other early editors of the *Cahiers*, the structure is only thinkable with the subject. At the same time, any theory of the subject must take structure as its ground. This axiom separates *Cahiers'* approach from any "objective" approaches that treat the human subject as an ordinary object, like those with which the sciences deal. In a broad sense, the definition of an object follows Leibniz's identity principle: every object is identical to itself. The identity principle is foundational for every structuralism in which differentiation is the basis for determination. For determination to work, we need a reliable way to differentiate elements of a structure. For any differentiation to work, we must assume every individual is identical to itself – and to itself only. However, starting from at least Hegel's time, the fundamental axiom of subjectivity is that it, unlike an object, does not simply coincide with itself – and this non-self-coincidence is interpreted as the power of negation, freedom, existence, alterity, or drive by different philosophers since.

In the case of the current theory of discourse, we should already see how this principle of non-identity frames the subject that Miller is working with:

the subject in this theory is reflexive and non-reflexive (subjected) simultaneously.

There are three possible responses to this foundational "subjective principle" concerning what science can do with such a subject – whether there is a possible discourse of science about the subject. The first response sticks to the ordinary conception of science and ignores the subjective principle. In this approach, the answer is that there is a possibility of a science of the subject, but one that treats it as any other ordinary object – this is, especially to the *Cahiers* editors, the direction taken by phenomenological psychology and, to Lacan the direction taken by ego psychology. In both cases, an object, either brain or ego, is viewed under Leibniz's principle of self-identity. The task is to apply the "normal" scientific rigour to these "objects" of study and develop a scientific definition for each. The second is the response that does admit the subjective principle but, in turn, sticks to the ordinary interpretation of science and thereby ends up banishing the subject and its treatment from the theory. To the *Cahiers* editors, this is the approach taken by Saussure, Althusser and Levi-Strauss, among many theoreticians and philosophers who essentially thought it impossible to have a theory, i.e., a science, of the subject. The third possibility questions what sort of discourse is possible that, while it theorises the subject as a non-object, is at the same time scientific. This third approach, which redefines science, is the approach taken by Miller et al., whose manifesto is "Action of the Structure", Marx and Freud are the creators of such a scientific discourse.

It is, therefore, no surprise that, to Miller, the founding axioms of Husserl concerning the immediacy of consciousness and its intentionality, or Heidegger and the immediacy of life and its worldliness, are non-starters. On the contrary, structure alone is originary, whose organisation is neither known nor experienced and it is against this structure that Miller poses the figure of the subject and the notion of subjectivity "not as regent but as subjected".[17]

Miller differentiates the notion of the subject from the human individual or the psychological subject, about which the theory of knowledge, morality, politics and law speak. No individuality or biological unity underlies the notion of the subject in the theory of discourse. In fact, to this theory, the subject is mainly understood as a gap (the non-self-identity) that "distributes its conscious being at each of the levels induced by the imaginary in structured reality". If there is a unity to the subject, "it depends on its localization, its localization in the structuring structure".[18]

However, the point is that the theory starts from an implicated subject, not its genealogy. In other words, from the fact that there is a subject, we can retroactively derive that there is a process of subjectivation. So retroactively, without assuming temporal precedence or antecedence, subjectivisation, i.e., the interaction between reflexive element and structure, coexists with the structure itself. Through this process, lack comes to take residence inside the subject. In that sense, the subject is architecturally alienated. There is no more primordial state of self-identity that the subject can return to, and there is no place to which the subject can turn to remedy this lack since it is an essential part of the subject's being. The lack the subject experiences does not pertain to its having but to its being.

The general theory of discourse must then advocate a theory of the subject whose architecture differentiates inside from outside, visible from invisible, and truth from perception, and as such, any theory that does not follow this architectural characteristic must be refuted. One such theory is phenomenology, with its "naïve or primitive state of the world through an archeological investigation of perception. Phenomenology hopes that by reducing the visible to the visible, it can secure the donation of a secret unchanging and ahistorical foundation for knowledge and history". Another such theory is psychology, which, at the end assigns "a statutorily identical position before the objects of the world".[19]

Both of these theories lack the architectural requirement laid out by the general theory of discourse. Phenomenology describes the visible by another visible, and psychology reduces the subject to an object. The refutation of these theories is the first task of the theory of the subject, whose fundamental principle is that "the subject is deceived: its misunderstanding or mistake is constitutive",[20] and as a result, although nothing will prevent the subject from registering and capitalising its experiences, and of having a system of reference in reality through which its existence adapts, this adaptation to the real is not natural or innate, and cannot be thought according to models which hold good for the animal world. Instead, the general theory proposes "the secondary intervention of a corrective system", a structure that systematises the visible and acts as the invisible law to the subject. Miller summarises refers to this effect as "miscognition".[21]

Knowledge cannot remove miscognition, as miscognition is not an operation that opposes knowledge. On the contrary, miscognition remains operative inside knowledge, as "any conceptual system, closed or as good as closed, continues the dimension of the imaginary". A case in point is psychology itself: the sphere of "volitions and appetites, in other words of motivations, is derived from the functional miscognition of the structuring, with the result that people always act in light of an end, i.e. in light of what they perceive as useful".[22] The miscognition embedded in the knowledge systems that extend and perpetuate the imaginary representations is part of the overall tertiary imaginary dimension and, therefore, subject to the same analysis.

Equally, this theory is in open conflict with Hegel and neo-Hegelianism, as the subject is reflexive and self-conscious or non-alienated only as it is effectuated as an agent in the imaginary, whereas in the real the subject, lacunar and subjected to the effects of the structuring structure, appears "only by miscognizing itself in the imaginary as an element in the structuring ... An Actor, the subject is a director in his fantasy".[23]

Science

Here, Miller immediately poses two questions: "how are we to understand the possibility of a discourse that gives itself an adequate object and develops its own norms? And first: how is a discourse of overdetermination itself even possible?"[24] Beyond the scientificity of this discourse, the question is of its possibility.

By a "field of discourse", we define any field of inquiry in which the question "Is it scientific or not?" has cardinal importance.

The field of logic governs statements. Statements are formulated according to logical codes that govern their syntax and semantics. The code is continuously present or accessible when a statement reaches a destination – the producer and the consumer share the same code. The consumer or the receiver of the statement will apply the same code to the statement. There is no ambiguity or duplication.

In contrast to logic and its statements, psychoanalysis has governance over the field of speech. The stark difference is that the code which produces speech is absent when speech is received. Miller calls this the virtuality of the code, which is a feature rather than a deficiency. Speech is only possible with the absence of the originating code. That is why speech contains messages liable to interpretation in ways other than originally intended.

However, there is another level of absence at work: the code necessary for speech production is also absent from the speaker's side. The code is in the Other, not the speech's speaker or subject-agent. So, there are two lacks operative in the field of speech: the lack of the code at the level of speech (this is what makes a speech a message, that is, its intellection is only guaranteed at the place of the recipient) and the lack of subject-agent at the level of the code (since the code is in the Other). This double split, caused by the two lacks, is the feature of speech produced by a subject, which gives rise to what is necessary for this speech to work: the Other scene – where the speech is produced/structured and consumed/decided.

The conclusion is that these two lacks are correlative with each other, and they open up the splitting of the unconscious within the interior of language. "We can now say: *the subject is capable of an unconscious*".[25]

Speech is, therefore, both produced and consumed by the Other – both what enunciates and the truth about what is enunciated take place in this Other scene, and the subject "figures in a passive function, like an element whose transitivity is ruled by a quaternary combination".[26] Psychoanalysis, made possible by this feature of speech, is the discourse that articulates this Other scene in which the subject's speech is structured (as the producer) and decided (as the consumer).

The discourse produced by psychoanalysis is neither commentary nor interpretation. It is not commentary because no meaning is missed and requires elucidation. It is not interpretation because it is not the case of transforming the enunciated speech to another speech so that it could be comprehended. Psychoanalysis is a discourse that reads the speech only for its dual lacks and thus is looking for those lacks only. "Analysis" is the name for such a "transgressive" reading that traverses the statement toward the enunciation.

The lack that produces the speech, which is the reason that speech is indeed what it is, is not in any part of the speech per se. It is not the case that because something is missing in speech, we can detect the lack. The entire speech is a sign for the lack and carries its mark: it is the hidden place that cannot be illuminated because it is based on its absence that the text was possible and that discourses were uttered: that Other scene where the eclipsed subject situates himself, from where he speaks, for which he speaks.

We should understand Miller's analysis in contrast with Saussure's linguistics. Miller appeals to the relation between structure and the subject, which, as we have seen, creates the elements of virtuality, actuality and imaginary at the level of the structure and reflexive and non-reflexive elements at the subject level. Whereas, in the case of Saussure, speech is a network of objects where meaning is acquired differentially. Saussure's analysis ignores the double lack which circles the whole text and is the "principle of the action of the structure, which thus bears the marks of the action that it accomplishes: the suture".[27] The lack is the place from where the subjected subject speaks, where subjection to the structuring structure takes place, and where the function of miscognition sutures this subject to the speaker, giving rise to both the subject of enunciation and the enunciating subject. The miscognition that sutures these two subjects also inverts the order of determination such that the speech uttered by the reflexive or enunciating subject is made in the first person but produced by the one who is not there.

What causes speech is absent; it is in no part of speech in an ordinary linguistic sense; it is not a hidden meaning that needs commentary or interpretation – indeed, the function of suture inverts the cause. Therefore, two salient features distinguish this speech analysis: the cause permeates the field of speech, and the cause is inverted and misrecognised as the effect. Here is where Lacan's account of metonymy and metaphor comes to assistance. Miller suggests that the cause operates in a metonymic fashion: metonymy is the model through which we may understand the permeation of cause through the field of speech without it being ever pinned or localised to any part of it. At the same time, "cause is metaphorised in a discourse, and in general in any structure – for the necessary condition of the function of structural causality is that the subject takes the effect for the cause. The fundamental law of the action of the structure".[28] The cause as metonymy is sutured to the metaphorised cause; the absent subject is sutured to the speaking subject in speech, which is what analysis uncovers.

It is important to notice where the focus is here: the scientificity of this discourse needs to be in its specific references to reality or in the veracity of

152 Philosophy After Lacan

its claims. This discourse does not make any claim to objectivity. It focuses instead on a singular configuration of the structure and a particular position of the subject. It refers to the statement made at the beginning: structure comprises action and subject. That is what Miller calls the closure of the scientific discourse: that it sets its laws − an autonomous, self-determining discourse without an unconscious, and what constitutes the truth in this discourse is the particular subjective position.

The closure proper to scientific discourse, Miller insists, should be distinct from the suture of non-scientific discourse. Its procedure of negation is more radical: it expels lack in the manner of foreclosure. Miller does say that the lack of the lack is a double negation, which confers positivity to this field. This conception will be taken up and put to the test by François Regnault[29] and Alain Badiou.[30] Badiou's rejoinder to this point is particularly interesting. Scientific discourses do not have utopic elements, but this particular "lack of a lack" nevertheless creates a space for ideology at the borders of scientific discourse. Badiou opposes closure in a scientific field as a fall out of its infinite interiority, not a logical consequence (lack of a lack). Therefore, the underwriter of this closure is finally ontology and not logic.[31]

It is perhaps important to mention that Miller's connection between science and foreclosure is a theme that is repeated by Lacan on several occasions, first in his class of 1966-06-01 in his Seminar XIII[32] and then in "Science and Truth"[33] where he calls the end goal of science to be a "successful paranoia":

> If one remarks, however, that a successful paranoia might just as well seem to constitute the closure of science − assuming psychoanalysis were called upon to represent this function − and if, moreover, one acknowledges that psychoanalysis is essentially what brings the Name-of-the-Father back into scientific examination, one comes upon the same apparent deadlock; but one has the feeling that this very deadlock spurs on progress, and that one can see the chiasmus that seemed to create an obstacle therein coming undone.
>
> The current state of the drama of psychoanalysis' birth, and the ruse that hides therein by beguiling writers' conscious ruses, should perhaps be taken into account here, for I was not the one who came up with the expression 'successful paranoia'.[34]

Of the two lacks, one pertains to the closure of the field of science to any external authority. The other pertains to the circumscription of the field, a foreclosure of the space from outside.

> *Foreclosure* is the other side of the closure. This term will suffice to indicate that every science is structured lie a psychosis: the foreclosed returns under the form of the impossible.[35]

So, this discourse is marked by closure and foreclosure. The closure, which defines the inside of the scientific discourse, is uncovered by the epistemological break. But overdetermination is the discourse whose privileged and novel scientific status is only recognised when one approaches it from its exterior side – "which constitutes its field at the exterior limit of all science in general".[36]

Every novel discourse emerges in a field of overdetermination at the limit of science, providing the space for the scientific subject to grasp itself anew. Althusserian Marxism and Lacanian psychoanalysis provide the two most advanced discourses of overdetermination and should join forces in a unitary theoretical discourse.

Miller metaphorised the relation between ordinary science and the theory of discourse as a topological relation between two regions of space or disjoint planes with no quilting point, wherein one slides inside the other. One of these two regions, constituting a thick circumference, termed the exterior and marked by a foreclosure, is the region belonging to the theory of discourse. This new region has only been partially developed in discourses of overdetermination – Marxism and psychoanalysis. The region interior to this thick and dense circumference is the region of (individual) science(s). This interior region is marked as a closure. This region was conceptualised by Bachelard and the French epistemology movement, which Althusser later termed the epistemological break. The relation of the exterior to science to the interior to science then is identical to the relation of meta-language to language, theory of discourse, as this dense circumference is therefore used to define what a particular science is – what is precisely operative inside it, what are its operators and internal logic, something about which an individual science is unconscious. For instance, the theory of discourse reveals that in every science, there is a "unique circuit" by which the subject of science is in a particular relation to the scene of the Other. In psychoanalysis, this pertains to the realm of speech and, in politics, the class struggle.

From Structure to Dialectic – Splitting Hegel

The theory of discourse is this unified theory of science. *Cahiers'* program strived to develop this theory, with "Action of the Structure" as the program manifesto. Their purpose was not to establish a genealogy of the subject but rather a retroactive reconciliation of the structure and the subject. In other words, it sought to answer the following question: From the existence of structure and the subject, how can we reconcile them within a single theory? Therefore, the theory of discourse aims to provide a unified theory that explains this co-existence. It sought to reconcile these elements to show how the role of the subject is to maintain the structure. Hence, in the end, the subject is this theory's principal operator of preservation.

The subject introduces the lack in the structure; paradoxically, the lack is the principle of stability in the structure, which preserves it. Unlike what structuralism had thought, the structure is not the home of stability – but precisely instability. What holds the structure together is its inherent law of exception. The central insight is this: Aside from the minute and detail-oriented effects of the algebraic operations, something stands outside. That is why, in *Cahiers'* view, Lacan was so ahead of his time. He says something that no one – in the structuralist milieu – could see at the time, which made him a leading figure of "discursive materialism". The structure – and hence the algebra – is not what maintains stability; it is the place of instability. The lack causes metonymy, and algebra stands for the mechanism of motion caused by this lack. Stability is not a consequence of structure, which the classical structuralist thought had postulated.

What did Lacan see that no one else had seen? The structure, whose grammar the logic of the signifier explains, revolves around two critical operations that not only speak to the position and formation of the unconscious but also speak, in a broader sense, to the conditions for any system of exchange (e.g. language, market, kinship structure). Lacan named these operations alienation and separation – both involving the subject. Alienation is the process through which some entity from outside (from the register of the real) comes to occupy a position within the system, during which it loses something of itself. This loss is the price that the entity must pay to partake in the structure. The loss continues to function as a mark that the entity carries with it: even if it is now integrated into and subjected to the structure, the loss will forever determine it. It is not what the subjected entity retains of itself that officiates its inscription within the structure but what it loses. The logic of the signifier is what thematises this process – the thematisation of the loss and the ensuing determination by the objectified loss. Central to this logic is the notion of the subject: the role or position within the structure that holds the structure together based on what does not exist: a primordial lack that has constituted it. Thus, the subject is the apparatus that performs two crucial roles in any structure:

1   It inscribes what does not exist as something registered within the structure.
2   It allows for what does not exist to cause the structure to function.

In short, the claim here is that any structure is built around a subjective core, and no structure exists without it. In this sense, the subject is a meta-logical apparatus and by no means refers to an experiential or substantial entity, such as human individuals.

The dynamism within a given structure is what *Cahiers* called a discourse. A simple analogy for this is a word or shape puzzle that, within its square box, contains one space that allows the other boxes to move around, one space at a time, thus solving the puzzle. The "emptiness" of the subjective position is metaphorically similar to the space within the puzzle. Similarly, an essential emptiness marks the systemisation at work in symbolic life, which elicits a subjective effect. This space allows for discourse in structure and the movement of *jouissance*, whether within language, the market, or a kinship structure.

Badiou found *Cahiers'* attempt to revive the category of the subject very valuable. However, he had issues with their approach, which we can summarise in the following two points:

1 He disagreed with the subject's derivation based on a primordial lack.
2 He disagreed with the subject as the operator of preservation.

He elaborated on the first point in his seminal essay of 1968 called "Mark and Lack"[37] and on the second point in his first major philosophical book, *Theory of the Subject*.

In his essay "Mark and Lack", Badiou criticises the view that claims every structure in its stability requires the subject as its founding elements. Badiou explains that the notion of the subject in "Action of the Structure" and "Suture" was sutured to an incoherent presupposition. The presupposition assumed the subject to stand for the principle of non-identity. Miller derived the subject from the Fregean framework. Badiou showed that the assumption of lack at the structure's foundation needs to be more coherent with the conception of science. Furthermore, Badiou argues that science does not have and does need a subject. There is no lack in science, and thereby, there is no subject of science. The dynamism within a science is due not to an emptiness but to its inherent ability to stratify itself.[38]

The remainder of this paper focuses on the second disagreement: the subject not as an operator of preservation but of novelty within a structure.

The origin and emergence of novelty within a closed system with proper interiority, such as science, politics, art and amorous relationships, is a critical philosophical issue for Badiou. Given that any structure is determined by its interiority, the question is the possibility of thinking of novelty and interiority together. It is then natural to think why Baidou turned to Hegel, as he was the philosopher of interiority and novelty. Badiou's turn to Hegel was not due to his Sartrean background. It was precisely because of his allegiance to the Bachelardian epistemological break, Althusser and French structuralism. However, this time, Badiou's dealing with Hegel is through the prism of Lacan. From *Cahiers'* revisions, Badiou wanted to preserve the subject's place in the structure but not theorise the interplay of the two under the logic of lack, which would eventually suture the subject to the

156 Philosophy After Lacan

domination of the structure. In this relation, Badiou found the answer in Hegel's *Science of Logic*.[39]

In *Theory of the Subject*, Badiou maps out the entire structuralist logic under three distinct dialectical moments. We can sketch these three moments as follows:

1 An idealist moment according to which dialectic commences based on the commitment to the One and the operations of division and circulation. The commitment to the One is two-fold: we begin with the One and divide, and we return to the One after a complete determination through the sublation of the Other.
2 The second moment after the first split of the idealist moment above. Within this moment, we forego the commitment to commence with the One and the operation of division. We replace it with two and the operation of unification.
3 The third moment after the second split of the idealist moment above. Within this moment, we forego the commitment to return to the One and the operation of sublation of the Other to the One and replace it with the operation of periodisation.

Through the materialist inversion of the first moment, we get a new logic for the structure and the subject.

The first thing we need is a conceptual apparatus with two poles: identity (represented as A) and place (represented as P).[40] A structure as a whole is a system of placement of distinct identities. Badiou proposes that this is the minimum division required to speak about something. Place constitutes the determination that an identity receives. Every identity is placed, meaning that any determinate thing is a determined identity. As such, every placed identity is a split between the pure identity or the existent (A) and the identity according to the place (A_p). Hence, we can write any determinate something as AA_p. This formula shows a scission that constitutes every determinate being: the scission between what the thing is supposed to be (A) and how it is determined by the system of placement (A_p).

In *Theory of the Subject*, Badiou identifies several metaphysical traps at the beginning of the *Science of Logic* and shows how the dialectic of identity and place can avoid them.[41] One of these traps is Hegel's attempt to show that the science of logic starts with the One, the One of Being. However, by the time we arrive at Becoming, Hegel cannot explain how Nothing comes out of Being. In Badiou's analysis, Hegel is at pains to show Becoming is a sublation of the negation of Being. A close reading of the *Science of Logic* shows, on the contrary, that the "unconscious" Hegel starts with two principles, not one. Being and Nothing are not derivable from each other, in the same way that identity and place are not derivable from each other. Hence, dialectic operation is not to start from one and divide the one into two. Instead, it is to start from two and make one out of the two. We then have two dialectical matrixes:

1   Matrix 1 for the conscious (idealist) Hegel: one principle, with the operation of division.
2   Matrix 2 for the unconscious (materialist) Hegel: two principles, with the operation of unification.

It is not hard to see the influence Lacan (directly and/or through Miller) may have had on Badiou's rereading of the *Science of Logic*. As early as 1936, in a paper Lacan wrote under the title "Beyond the 'Reality Principle,'"[42] he emphasised the role of the analysis to be the analysis of the subject's speech. Accordingly, speech is the primary datum for the analytical experience. The analysand's speech happens between the analyst and analysand, and the Other here is language itself, which, owing precisely to its exteriority, remains "other" to the speaker. The job of the analyst is to allow the analysand to speak and to prevent this otherness of language (that which in the language constraints the speech; its determining power) from being sutured in the guise of some supposition about the analyst: something is impossible to say owing to the analysand's relation to language, but it is not said, owing to what the analyst might think, for example. Therefore, the whole point is for the analyst not to allow herself to be taken for the Other of the speaker but rather to get out of the way so that this otherness can become legible. Using Badiou's terminology, the subject is the identity that seeks manifestation (A), and language is where the subject's identity is placed (P). Speech is the determined identity of the subject (A_p). The split subject, in this case, is the scission between the subject's identity (enunciation) and the situated (enunciated) subject (AA_p).

Badiou goes on to produce some of the categories of the beginning of the *Science of Logic* through the second matrix: Determination [$A_p(A)$], Relapse [$A_p(A_p(AA_p) = P$], Identity [$A(A) = A$], and limit [$A(A_p)$]. This sequence manifests that positing a scission as the beginning of logic (Badiou only commits to determination and not the prior categories, and he thus starts with the category of Something) and deriving unity through an operation manifests the materialist tenet in the *Science of Logic*. The scission is not a scission of terms but of identity and place in each term. Each *Science of Logic* category is a scission comprising an identity and the placement space. The unity of each category is a derivative of two functions that determine to what degree the identity has withstood the effects of the place and to what degree the place has determined that identity. The ingenuity of this approach is in its simplicity. Place and identity are boundaries according to which any determinate something is. A and P sketch the limitations of $A(A_p)$ and $A_p(A)$

158 Philosophy After Lacan

so that they always return to (AA_p). A classical view of a structure is an example of complete determination. In this case, structure is the place, and member is the identity placed in the structure. Therefore, a complete determination means that an identity placed within the structure will reinforce the structure itself – $A_p(A_p) = P$.

Within the third moment, the second split pertains to the circularity inherent to the first idealist moment. According to the schema we have seen, the complete return is the direct opposite of the complete determination. If the schema of complete determination is $A_p(A_p) = P$, the schema for ultimate return is $A(A_p) = A = (AA_p)$. At the pinnacle, we return to the original scission: (AAp). In Badiou's eyes, this return, as a "redemption" of the origin, manifests the overall schema of Hegel's strategy. Here, Badiou proposes to split Hegel a second time by proposing the operation of periodisation. It is essential to pay attention to how Badiou anchors the notion of periodisation – which yet again attests to Badiou's fidelity to Hegel as his master: being a true Hegelian, Badiou is forced to take a road that Hegel did not take himself. Similar to the case on the second moment, complete fidelity to the Hegelian dialectic forces us to posit two against one – even though the idea of the two was present in Hegel (unconsciously) all along – in the current case, Badiou will also go back to Hegel to split him. With two different schemas of looping around, Hegel is "standing on both edges of the knife – two dialectical matrices, as always".[43] It is interesting that – to the credit of his master – Badiou quotes Hegel three times, from three different fragments, to show that, despite the appearances – that is, despite the attempts to present the functioning of the circular schema as a smooth and flat function – Hegel was well aware of the discontinuity near the end of the loop, just before the completion of the circle and just before the return of the origin, that there is a point of singularity, a point of a qualitative shift, a jump from theory to practice and from conceptualisation to effectuation. Hegel was exactly aware that the two ends will not meet and that, in the end, the return home requires an intervention – an act – that alters the automatic and preordained succession of the circular return. What comes at the loop-back point is not what was, but something new and genuinely unforeseeable. That constitutes a passage from one stage of development to another – the schema under which dialectic does not manifest itself as a giant circle but a spiral in which every stage of development never "meets" the point of origin.

We have a point of singularity. It is the point where the place receives a new determination. At that point, the placement of the identity "forces" the place to change. Again, the *Science of Logic* has all the schemas we need. Badiou refers to the dialectic of Whole-Part and Force-Force in the category of Essence to distinguish circularity and periodisation. While circularity in moments one and two mentioned above relates to the dialectic of Whole-Part, we should understand the periodisation of moment three according to the dialectic of Force-Force. Badiou has a name for these two dialectical schemas:[44]

- Structural Dialectic (SD): The schema that follows the dialectic of Whole-Part. It is the schema for moments one and two and the operation of circularity. SD is the schema of structuralism, including *Cahiers'*.
- Historical Dialectic (HD): The schema that follows the dialectic of Force-Force. It is the schema for moment three and the operation of periodisation. HD is the schema for understanding novelty and the revolutionary subject.

HD is the name Badiou gives to the correlation under the Hegelian schema of Force-Force: HD schematises the correlation of terms when the modality of terms is strong, that is, when neither of them vanishes into the other, thus provincially qualifying HD as the foundation for theorising periodisation. Force schematises a relation between two terms, which entails a qualitative binding between them, such as bourgeoisie and proletariat classes, for example – each force is grafted onto the other. In their relationship, they condition and determine each other. In contrast, the relation of the whole to its parts is the relationship of belonging. There is no qualitative correlation between them. Under the schema of Whole-Part, each term has a fixed and irreconcilable role (whole vs part, identity vs place). The schema of Force-Force takes away the fixed roles. Under the schema of Force-Force, the terms identity and place become the terms of mutual influence and power. To emphasise the lack of fixed roles in this schema, Badiou creates neologies "outplace" and "splace" to replace identity and place, respectively.[45] The relation operative in Whole-Part is a mechanical relationship where the Whole and Part are not essentially related to each other: Part is self-subsistent on its own and ambivalent to whether it is part of a whole. Under the schema of Whole-Part, the unity of terms will eventually collapse into one: outplace always vanishes into splace. This logic, the vanishing of outplace into the splace, is the foundational logic of all forms of structuralism. Understanding structuralism under the logic of Whole-Part explains why, ultimately, structuralism calls for a strict determination of terms under the law of the structure, such that, ideally, each term repeats the structure as a whole.

Another crucial theoretical difference is that, unlike categories Whole-Part and Force-Force in the *Science of Logic*, the schemas SD and HD exist and interact with the other simultaneously, without one replacing the function of the other. For Badiou, one of these schemas cannot exist without the other. Force influences the logic of outplace-splace, while simultaneously, the relationship of outplace-splace finds distinct constructions according to the inclusion of the parts into a whole. In the same way that HD is anchored in

160 Philosophy After Lacan

SD, outplace is anchored in splace. In that sense, the terms splace and outplace have a corresponding force. Thus, while splace and outplace at the level of SD have a particular (weak) correlation and interaction, the same terms also correlate and interact (strongly) with each other as forces. In that sense, there is a force that "rules over the unity of splace (force in the position of the State, or of the symbolic)" and another that "reveals the outplace (force in the position of the revolution, or of the real)".[46]

The co-existence of these schemas and their mutual interactions is a very crucial point. An astute reader would say that following the *Science of Logic*, Force-Force should be the truth of Whole-Part. If so, shouldn't HD be the truth of SD? Badiou's answer is no. SD and HD are two distinct schematisations of terms. Badiou takes a stance here that separates him from Hegel. Badiou argues that Force-Force is not a derivation of Whole-Part. He thinks Hegel has gone too far in deriving force from the whole-part relation,[47] and in this break from Hegel, Badiou follows Lacan, his other master.

Badiou, once again, finds the more mature dialectical theorisation in Lacan. He thinks the greatest dialectician after Hegel was not Marx, Lenin, Sartre or Althusser, but Lacan. According to the late Lacan, an understanding of *jouissance* and the signifier requires a logic similar to what Badiou calls HD, in that the relation of these two is no longer that of a situation (language) and the situated (speech), which is captured through the structural logic of whole-part. Instead, language itself is situated and a source of exception. Singularity and regularity are both generated through the practice of language. Therefore, the relation between *jouissance* and signifier is better captured through the relation of forces, which is the central grammar of the historical dialectic. Lacan had explicitly theorised these two schemas. Although structural/algebraic and historical/topological schemas exist in the *Science of Logic,* they are not explicitly formalised as distinct and mutually dependent schemas. However, the early and late Lacan explicitly theorised these sequences in distinct theoretical "paradigms".[48]

In what Miller calls the fifth paradigm, Lacan realises that symbolic causality is frequently interrupted by another force beyond symbolisation. In the fifth paradigm, what was conceived as a loss of natural life as the result of alienation is interpreted as the loss of *jouissance* by the signifier: signifier comes to replace the lost *jouissance*, and that provides the inherent relation of signifier and *jouissance: objet a* becomes the signifier of the loss of *jouissance.* For the "late" Lacan, language (in Badiou's parlance, the place) is embodied; it is material and, therefore, contingent. Whatever symbolic determination we ascribe to language from the outset must be conditioned by the fact that it is in history. The relation between signifier and signified is not merely the relation between whole and parts; words are now equivocal, not transcendentally but immanently, and there is no longer a third position from where one could arbitrate and intervene in this univocity of the word. A statement can be only partially fixated on whatever is contextually decided.

However, even the contextuality is submitted to the contingency of speech being material. Lacan will say now that the Other is a reactive formation to the fact that communication is impossible; there is no pure conduit of information, and therefore, noise appears. Though noise intrinsically does not make sense, we invent the Other for whom that noise is sense. That is an inversion because there is no longer a symbolic determination. Our speech simultaneously produces both sense and the lack of sense. The lack of sense is then retroactively inscribed in the figure of the Other as an autonomous field – the figure that is instrumental to the signification itself. So, the lack of sense comes before the signification. That means that ultimately, we begin from the standpoint of embeddedness – we do not arrive at it. The Other is barred. The singularity is within the symbolic.[49]

In *Seminar XVII*, Lacan equates the effect of the signifier to the thermodynamic law as it implicates physical systems. Every physical system follows a formula that can roughly be expressed in the following way: Energy = Synergy + Exergy + Entropy. The energy that a system takes in (Energy) is always greater than the energy required to maintain the working of the system (Synergy) plus the work that the system produces (Exergy). This excess, usually produced as heat, is referred to as Entropy. Lacan's brilliance is to see the terms of this relationship in the working of the signifier.[50]

If bringing this singularity into the realm of the symbolic itself, which changes or enriches the order of the efficacious interaction between singularity and regularity – the latter being the retroactive effect of the impasse of the singularity – looks a lot like Hegelian sublation, this is no coincidence: it is the sublation of the dynamic of whole and part to the mutually efficacious dynamic of forces, what Badiou calls HD.

From Idealism to Materialism – Splitting Lacan

Badiou, following Lacan's lead as his dialectical master, came to realise that the materialist revolutionary theory of the subject must consider the advancements made by Lacan. Interestingly, Miller's understanding of Lacan's advancements was limited to the dialectic of whole and parts (SD) and not the dialectic of force and force (HD). Therefore, "Action of the Structure" is a theory according to SD, which, to recap, has the following features:

1   Two principles pertain to the origin:

    a   The primacy of process over equilibrium.
    b   The primacy of two terms over one.

2   Two principles pertain to the destination:

    a   The primacy of circularity over periodisation.
    b   The primacy of preservation over novelty.

As we saw, the first principle is a materialist principle that we obtained by splitting Hegel the first time (moment 2 above). However, the second principle is still an idealist principle. The proper materialist logic is HD, which neither in origin nor destination advocates one's primacy nor its return. So, why does Badiou call Lacan an idealist at the end?

To answer this question, we must understand the crucial relation Badiou builds between three pairs: being/thought, topology/algebra and consistency/ cause. Badiou states two fundamental postulates for materialism: the postulate of identity that states thought is the reflection of being, and the postulate of primacy that states thought always attempts to approach being but never reaches it – that there is always a remainder, in the real, that cannot be thought.[51] The remainder is the unsymbolisable residue, which reminds us of the late Lacan, to whom the signification of *jouissance* always leaves an unsignifiable residue. Similarly, the remainder is the real of knowledge or the force in the representation system that splits the place. By having a remainder, thinking (and knowledge) is historical, or as Badiou says, the remainder is thus what periodises knowledge.[52]

During his late phase, Lacan observed that any systematic representation has an unsystematic remainder, metaphorically formulated by the law of entropy: every specific order has chaotic excrements. Badiou's attempt here is analogous to Marx's inversion of Hegel. In seeing the new dynamics of order and disorder, Lacan turns inwardly towards order. Badiou's regionalisation of Lacan, which we should say is much more complex than a a simple inversion, consists of three moments. In the first moment, Badiou generalises this problem as a new orientation in thought – not just of *jouissance* and language, but of being and thinking. In the second moment, Badiou turns outwardly and towards the so-called disorder. In the third moment, Badiou relativises the relation of the system and its remainder to a localised relationship. This latter moment is akin to the character of 'unworkable' entropy, which is always relative to a given system – an aspect of this model that Lacan did not explore in his use. In this third moment, rather than having only one real, we encounter "regionalised" reals. The third moment will allow Badiou to implicitly develop the theory of discipline.[53]

The issue of cause and consistency pertains to the second moment of Badiou's regionalisation of Lacan. According to the postulate of primacy, what is at stake for the materialist theory of the subject is nothing less than the ontological rift in presentation and representation. For Lacan, this rift exists between the real and the symbolic orders, but the effect of this rift is for the symbolic order to reorganise itself constantly. The heat excrement always causes the system to work harder. A system can never fully account for the energy it receives. In other words, the real always acts as a source of causation for the symbolic. For Lacan, consistency is an imaginary construct. It neither belongs to the order of real nor symbolic. However, the appearance of consistency is maintained by the knot: the knot that holds the three registers of real, symbolic and imaginary together, while the knot itself is in the real. Maintaining that consistency is imaginary is a total relapse back to SD because the only "effective" consistency is in the symbolic – in the splace, in the whole. As the metaphor of energy and entropy suggests, we will merely obtain the reorganisation of the system to account for the lost energy. We will input more energy, making the system more efficient to lose less, for example, but we never gain anything from the lost energy. That is not what the intent of HD is: HD puts consistency not only on the side of splace but also outplace. The consistency in splace is already within the order of thought, the algebraic operation of the symbolic, and the representation. However, if we maintain that outplace is a similar pole as the splace in the dialectic of force (as HD does), a similar consistency should exist within the outplace. HD teaches us that there must be consistency in the real.

At this point, Badiou splits Lacan: Lacan of the cause and Lacan of the consistency. Lacan taught us that the real anchors causality: the real is the vanishing cause that puts the entire symbolic order in motion. To bring this novelty to a home where thoughts of change can nourish and grow, we must ensure that the real also anchors consistency as much as causality. Badiou creates two terms to refer to cause (subjectivisation) and consistency (subjective process) in the context of a new materialist theory of the subject. However, their relation is not a simple consequential relation (we first have a subjectivised mass, which must be maintained through a subjective process). The actual being of subjectivisation is only retroactively announced by the subjective process: "We must determine the subject in the subjectivizing differential and in the being of the subjective process".[54]

Lacan's proposal for where the (historical) consistency we experience comes from is thus not the symbolic but the imaginary register. As said earlier, it must have been discouraging for Badiou to witness how Lacan, after having taken us so far, just expels consistency from the symbolic in order to ascribe it to the imaginary register. Badiou proposes something different. For him, consistency is in the real itself, and the real is its guarantor.

In our view, it is relatively straightforward to see how this difference in position ties Lacan and Badiou back to their founding philosophical commitments. By finally depositing consistency in the imaginary to preserve the knot as the sole index to consistency, Lacan stands to be an idealist. Instead, Badiou takes consistency as what belongs to the real, making him a materialist. Suppose one believed (as Lacan did) that the knot is what is in the real, whose effect – the keeping of the three registers together – is what the imaginary idea (or ideal) of consistency captures. Couldn't we surmise that this strictly performs the idealist reversal to sell a capture of what there is as what is, as selling representation for presentation? The imaginary status of consistency, as a historical ideal, serves as the perfect counter-argument against the need for regulatory interventions against unfettered financial markets – it would be just the childish dream of uninformed plebs to think economy and

164 Philosophy After Lacan

consistency together, a dream whose actualisation will no doubt undo the knot that holds their contemptible lives together! In response, don't we sound much closer to the late Lacan if we assert the knot itself to stand for the retroactive capture of the impossibility of inscribing the real of consistency within our imaginary and symbolic apparatuses?

If so, couldn't we legitimately say that Badiou is more Lacanian than Lacan was?

Notes

1 Alain Badiou, Lacan, *Anti-philosophy 3*, New York: Columbia University Press, 2018.
2 Alain Badiou, "Truth, Forcing and the Unnameable" in *Conditions*, pp. 129–144. London, New York: Continuum International Publishing Group, 2008, p. 129.
3 *Ibid*, p. 130.
4 Alain Badiou, *Theory of the Subject*, London, New York: Continuum, 2009.
5 Jacques-Alain Miller, "Action of the Structure", in *Concept and Form, Volume One*, edited by Peter Hallward and Knox Peden, pp. 69–84. London, New York: Verso, 2012.
6 "Lacan, I said earlier is our Hegel, that is, he presents the (idealist) dialectic of our time". Badiou, *Theory of the Subject*, p. 132.
7 Jacques-Alain Miller, "Foreword, Volume 1: Truth", in *Concept and Form, Volume One*, p. 57.
8 Jacques-Alain Miller, "Suture (Elements of the Logic of the Signifier)", *Concept and Form, Volume One*, edited by Peter Hallward and Knox Peden, pp. 91–101. London, New York: Verso, 2012.
9 Miller, "Action of Structure", p. 80.
10 *Ibid*, p. 71.
11 *Ibid*, p. 71.
12 *Ibid*, p. 71.
13 *Ibid*. p. 72.
14 *Ibid*, p. 72.
15 *Ibid*, p. 73.
16 Using the metaphor of point to speak of lack is important. It is a way to think this lack through an architectural metaphor permeating the entire structure. As opposed to a focal place, the fault could be dissipated across the entire structure.
17 *Ibid*, p. 74.
18 *Ibid*, p. 74. There is nevertheless a link to a human like consciousness in the theory: when we speak of reflexive element we can safely assume that Miller speaks of a human individual. When Miller qualifies reflexivity as being able to go back and perceive, reflect and signify we can assume his reference is to human individuals, but he does not explicitly equate the reflexive element with what a human body circumscribes, the way for example psychoanalysis does. Despite this ambiguity, Miller is clear that subjectivisation takes place when the duplicity of imaginary and real registers afflicts the reflexive element and constitutes it as a subject. However, the challenge that remains for Miller is how he can suture Marxism with this theory of the subject, i.e. what is this reflexive element when we speak of history. As we will see Miller praises Althusser to free Marxism from history as a substantive subject. The question that remains is whether Miller is

importing back into the theory another substance under the guise of reflexive element.

19 *Ibid*, p. 75.
20 *Ibid*, p. 75.
21 Ibid, p. 75.
22 *Ibid*, p. 75.
23 *Ibid*, p. 77.
24 *Ibid*, p. 77.
25 *Ibid*, p. 78.
26 *Ibid*, p. 78.
27 *Ibid*, p. 79.
28 *Ibid*, p. 79.
29 Francois Regnault, "Dialectic of Epistemologies", in *Concept and Form, Volume One*, edited by Peter Hallward and Knox Peden, pp. 119–150. London, New York: Verso, 2012.
30 Alain Badiou, "Mark and Lack: On Zero", in *Concept and Form, Volume One*, edited by Peter Hallward and Knox Peden, pp. 159–185. London, New York: Verso, 2012.
31 Reference to the chapter on "Mark and Lack' in Reza Naderi's book.
32 Jacques Lacan, *The Object of Psychoanalysis 1965–1966*, unpublished seminar available here: www.lacaninireland.com/web/wp-content/uploads/2010/06/13-The-Object-of-Psychoanalysis1.pdf.
33 Jacques Lacan, "Science and Truth", in *Écrits, the First Complete Edition in English*, pp. 726–745. New York: W. W. Norton & Company, Inc., 1999.
34 *Ibid*, pp. 742–743.
35 Miller, "Action of the Structure", p. 80.
36 *Ibid*, p. 80.
37 Alain Badiou, "Mark and Lack: On Zero", in *Concept and Form, Volume One*, edited by Peter Hallward and Knox Peden, pp. 159–185. London, New York: Verso, 2012.
38 For a detailed analysis of Badiou's rejoinder to Miller, see Reza Naderi, "Mark and Lack: Formalism and Fidelity", in *Crisis and Critique: Philosophy and Science*, Vol. 5, No. 1, March 2018, edited by Agon Hamza and Frank Ruda.
39 George Wilhelm Friedrich Hegel, *Science of Logic*, Amhurst: Humanity Books, 1969.
40 Alain Badiou, *Theory of the Subjects*, pp. 3–12.
41 For a detailed analysis of Badiou's construction see Reza Naderi, *Badiou, Infinity and Subjectivity: Reading Hegal and Lacan After Badiou*, forthcoming by Lexington Publishing.
42 Jacques Lacan, "Beyond the 'Reality Principle" in *Écrits, the First Complete Edition in English*, New York: W.W. Norton & Company, Inc. 1999, pp. 58–74.
43 Alain Badiou, *Theory of the Subject*, p. 19.
44 *Ibid*, p. 35.
45 *Ibid*, p. 10.
46 *Ibid*, p. 37.
47 *Ibid*. p. 34.
48 The term "paradigm" is a term used by Miller to reconstruct the movement of Lacan's thought in six stages or "paradigms". See Jacques-Alain Miller, "Paradigms of Jouissance", *Lacanian Ink 17*, pp. 10–46, Wooster: The Wooster Press, 2000.
49 See Jacques-Alain Miller, "Paradigms of Jouissance", pp. 28–35.

50 Jacques Lacan, *The Other Side of Psychoanalysis, The Seminar of Jacques Lacan Book XVII*, New York: W. W. Norton & Company, Inc., 2007, p. 48.
51 Alain Badiou, *Theory of the Subject*, pp. 190–200.
52 *Ibid*, p. 202.
53 See "Thinking Discipline" in Reza Naderi, *Badiou, Infinity and Subjectivity.*
54 *Ibid*, p. 246.

Chapter 10

The Place of Mathematics

Badiou with Lacan

Jelica Šumič Riha

Can mathematics question itself? In the *Critique of Pure Reason*, Kant claims that "[m]athematics gives the most resplendent example of pure reason happily expanding itself without assistance from experience".[1] The Kantian definition of mathematics resonates with the formalism of modern mathematics, whose characteristic asceticism excludes any consideration of content. Thus, pure mathematics, according to Bertrand Russell, can be considered to be "the class of propositions asserting formal implications and containing no constants except logical constants".[2] According to Russell's definition, pure mathematics presents itself as a set of formal implications independent of any content. If one were to push the point, one could say that mathematics is "the science that coincides entirely with its writing".[3] But for today's mathematician, the issue of mathematical writing opens up another problem, that of the relationship between the mathematician and mathematics. Seen from this perspective, the mathematician is:

> someone who most completely erases the marks of the production of his text, both the marks of the subject who produces it and the marks of the society in which it is produced. It is even in the mathematical text that the erasure of marks is the most explicit. But this can only be a paradox because the explicitness of the erasure should deny it as erasure and should therefore lead to the erasure of the erasure.[4]

"Would it not be possible", asks the mathematician René Lavendhomme, "that in the very writing of the mathematical text, the relationship that this text has with the subject would come to light?"[5] By proposing another definition of mathematics according to which mathematics is a science in which one never knows what one is talking about, nor whether what one says is true,[6] Russell throws a particular light precisely on the link that the mathematician maintains with mathematics. Strictly speaking, the two Russellian definitions are not contradictory. While the first definition emphasises a formalism whose logical rigour restrains freedom in manipulating letters and symbols, the second includes an additional dimension, that of mathematical

DOI: 10.4324/9781003425953-11

168 Philosophy After Lacan

saying, which highlights the relationship of mathematicians to mathematics. The problem that arises is then: what is mathematics if the mathematician can bear to not believe in it? Does the lightness of the letter, correlative to the removal of meaning, liberate the mathematician-subject to such an extent that he or she can pride him- or herself on not knowing what mathematics talks about nor really believing in it?

To find an answer to this conundrum, we will specifically focus on Badiou's and Lacan's respective comments on the peculiar statement that, in mathematics, one never knows what one is talking about or whether what one is saying is true. Both Badiou and Lacan insist on one point, namely that the mathematician is indisputably not free to not believe in mathematics. Or, to use Badiou's own words, "the mathematician is first and foremost someone who believes in mathematics 'hard as a rock.'"[7] As to mathematical ignorance, Badiou's and Lacan's answers diverge, precisely insofar as, even if access to psychoanalysis, like access to philosophy, is a certain type of access to mathematics, it is still not the same type of access.

According to Badiou, when Russell declares that "mathematics is a discourse in which one does not know what one is talking about, nor whether what one is saying is true", he said it "without believing it, of course", and moreover "no one in truth has ever believed it, save the ignorant, and Russell certainly wasn't such".[8] If Badiou cannot believe Russell, it is because, according to him, mathematics is rather:

> the *sole* discourse which 'knows' absolutely what it is talking about: being as such, despite the fact that there is no need for this knowledge to be reflected in an intra-mathematical sense, because being is not an object, and nor does it generate objects. Mathematics is also the sole discourse, and this is well known, in which one has a complete guarantee and a criterion of the truth of what one says, to the point that this truth is unique inasmuch as it is the only one ever to have been encountered which is fully transmissible.[9]

However, Badiou seems to agree with Russell on one very precise point, namely: mathematics does not know and does not need to know that it is doing ontology. Indeed, Badiou claims that mathematics as a discourse on being can very well do without this knowledge to perpetuate itself all by itself, almost blindly. It is therefore up to philosophy to assign "ontological dignity"[10] to what mathematicians are content to put to work. But there is something more important still: this ignorance is in a certain sense constitutive of mathematics as a science of being, since, as Badiou points out:

> it is of the essence of ontology to be carried out in the reflexive foreclosure of its identity. For someone who actually *knows* that it is from being qua being that the truth of mathematics proceeds, doing

mathematics – and especially inventive mathematics – demands that this knowledge be at no point represented. Its representation, placing being in the general position of an object, would immediately corrupt the necessity, for any ontological operation, of de-objectification.[11]

After having stated that "what is sayable – and said – of being qua being does not in any manner arise from the discourse of philosophy"[12] but from set theory, the Cantorian theory of the pure multiple – after having acknowledged, like Russell, that mathematicians, caught up in the carrying out and ordeal of their practice, do not know as mathematicians that what they do is to pronounce what is sayable of being qua being – Badiou also recognises that there are "singular moments when mathematics seems to be called upon, for its own purposes, to think its thought".[13] These are the singular moments when mathematics – "under the constraint of a real stumbling block, or the inevitable emergence of a point of impossibility within its own field" – seems required if it is to achieve its own goals, to think its thought. Mathematics is only compelled to return onto itself "under the injunction of its interior stumbling block". The moment of the return of mathematics onto itself is the moment when mathematics is confronted with "its decisional dimension".[14]

On this point, Badiou is forced to distinguish two operational modes of mathematics identified with ontology: on the one hand, there is the "normal" operational mode of mathematics where mathematics thinks being without considering itself as "a thinking of the *thought* that it is",[15] and, on the other hand, there are moments of crisis[16] when "mathematics, abutting on a statement that attests in a point to the impossible to come, turns back on the decisions that orient it".[17] It is by appropriating a Kantian problematic, that of the orientation in thought, that Badiou broaches the question of whether and under what conditions mathematics is capable of becoming the thought of the thought that it is. The orientation in thought, in the case of mathematics, concerns the norm that thought gives itself to decide on existence. The orientation in thought concerns, more specifically, "what thought determines in and of itself as an access to what it declares as existing".[18] The fact that mathematics, in particular moments of crisis, encounters an impossibility, runs into a "bit of the real", and is, as a consequence, obliged to return onto its own thought according to its orientation, is something, to repeat once again, that mathematics itself cannot account for, although it manifests it, as Badiou remarks. Strictly speaking, it is to philosophy under the condition of mathematics, and more particularly, to philosophy which has put itself under the condition of mathematical eventality, since it recognises mathematics as "a singular site of thinking, the procedures the event of which must be re-traced *within* the philosophical act",[19] that falls the task of dealing with the question: What is an orientation in thought when it comes to mathematics?

170 Philosophy After Lacan

To identify and define as clearly as possible the division of tasks between mathematics and philosophy, it is necessary to specify that it is because mathematics – except in the rare moments of "crisis" – "thinks Being", but is not "a thinking of the *thought* that it is", that it is up to philosophy to "identify the ontological vocation of mathematics".[20] Now, to admit that ontology is only dealt with in mathematics by the decision of philosophy, is to delimit at the same time the space proper to philosophy, the space of that-which-is-not-being-qua-being, namely truth. How then can we understand the link between ontology and philosophy if "the sayable of being is disjunct from the sayable of truth"?[21] If "any truth is post-evental",[22] i.e. the production of a novelty that is as such unsituatable within the established system of knowledge, as Badiou maintains, and if "mathematics cannot think a procedure of truth, because mathematics eliminates the event",[23] this paradoxical multiple that escapes ontology, it is nevertheless the case that mathematics "can decide whether it is compatible with ontology that there be truths".[24] Hence, if the being of truths is conceived in the form of unconstructible or "generic" multiples, the question to be posed by Badiou is the following: "can ontology produce the concept of a generic multiple?""[25] It was the mathematician Paul Cohen who provided the answer to the question posed by philosophy by demonstrating the existence of "generic", i.e. unconstructible, multiplicities. What Badiou seeks and actually finds in mathematics is the proof of "the *compatibility* of ontology with truth". For Badiou, this compatibility implies that "the being of truth, as generic multiplicity", can and must be "ontologically thinkable, even if a truth is not".[26] It is in this sense that we propose to read Claude Imbert's particularly perspicacious remark, according to which "Badiou claims that Cantorian mathematics accords philosophy both the real of its position and the means to think it".[27]

For Lacan, by contrast, the nescience that characterises mathematics according to Russell is related to what Lacan calls "this tangible frontier between truth and knowledge".[28] In his 'improvised' dialogue with Russell, in the course of his seminar "Le savoir du psychoanalyste", Lacan clarifies Russell's definition in the following manner:

> Mr. Bertrand Russell, who moreover took the trouble to say ... explicitly, [that] mathematics is very precisely what deals with statements of which it is impossible to say whether they have any truth, or even whether they mean anything at all. This indeed is a rather extreme way of saying that all the care that he has lavished on the rigor of putting mathematical deduction into shape, is something that is assuredly addressed to something quite different than the truth, but has an aspect that is all the same not unrelated to it. Otherwise there would be no need to separate it out in such an emphatic fashion.[29]

It is in precisely this context that Lacan introduces the problem of the "incomprehension" of mathematics. Mathematical incomprehension, to use his own term, allows Lacan to ask the following question: What kind of truth can we expect from mathematics? Because mathematical incomprehension is not a simple matter of a contingent lack or deficiency but must be considered as a symptom. And Lacan puts forward a reason for this:

> The subjects who are the prey of mathematical incomprehension expect more from the truth than reduction to these values that are called, at least in the early stages of mathematics, deductive values. The so-called demonstrative articulations seem to them to lack something that is precisely at the level of a requirement of truth.[30]

According to Lacan, this requirement of truth is the cause of mathematical incomprehension, insofar as it comes from a maladjustment, a dissatisfaction with a truth value, itself reduced to the condition of demonstration. Those who do not understand mathematics would have liked it to be true, simply put, to be able to say something about something, and, as it says nothing about anything external to it, they reject it outright.[31] What is considered as proof in mathematics appears to those who do not understand mathematics to be lacking something concerning a requirement of truth. In other words, it is because we want truth that we do not understand mathematics. And, more succinctly: "[t]his confusion about mathematical incomprehension" is a symptom of "the love of truth".[32]

Thus, what appears to be the removal of the pathetic facet of the true, to borrow Lacan's formulation, leaves a void, but, to follow Lacan: "It would be quite wrong to think that mathematics is something that in effect has succeeded in emptying everything that is involved in the relationship to the truth of its pathetic dimension".[33] Far from succeeding in eliminating its "pathetic dimension", insists Lacan, the history of mathematics – through the crisis of the irrationals, the emergence of the infinitesimal calculus, the impasses of the procedures of demonstrations, but above all "the pain, the trouble generated", what Lacan calls "the Cantorian effraction",[34] resulting from an encounter with the truth that could go as far as a threat of madness in Cantor's case – testifies to "some relationship of the matheme ... with a dimension of truth".[35] It is exactly this point that Lacan was interested in: the relationship between truth and knowledge, where the author of discovery, as Cantor's case, the "tragedy of the learned",[36] shows, is him- or herself necessarily involved. The clarification of mathematical incomprehension is important for psychoanalysis insofar as understanding would imply its reduction to non-contradictory articulations that do not make space for what truth owes to desire. Indeed, for Lacan, "non-contradiction can not in any way suffice to ground truth".[37] Now, it is exactly on this question of the link between desire and truth that the joint between mathematics and

172 Philosophy After Lacan

psychoanalysis emerges. But it is no less true that, if desire supports a truth value that exceeds mathematical knowledge, the approach to it leads us back to mathematical knowledge.[38]

Hence, if Lacan insists on the issue of incomprehension, it is also because incomprehension is embarrassing for psychoanalysis insofar as the work of the analyst, unlike that of the mathematician, implies that, while knowing how to practice formalisation in analysis, the analyst has not renounced the notion of truth that the mathematician practically does without. Thus, when Lacan introduces the concept of the matheme, it is to point out that "it is absolutely not true to speak of the matheme as something that would in any way be detached from the requirement of truth".[39] But to understand both, the nature of truth that is at work in analysis and the nature of formalisation that is set to work in its literality, we must pass through the discourses that hold truth to be a value among others and which is fundamentally carried out in mathematics.

Two modes of the real: the real in mathematics, the real in psychoanalysis

In mathematics, as Lacan notes, "we begin by placing letters without saying anything about what use they can be made of"[40] because to think we must formalise, that is to say, give a literal form to thought, work on the literality of thought. If on the one hand, the very notion of mathematicity is stripped down to a strict literality to better circumscribe the real that psychoanalysis aims at, this is how we can describe the way Lacan approaches mathematics, on the other hand, however, what matters, according to Badiou, in mathematical undertakings, starting with Cantor's, is to establish "a comprehensive formalization, a general theory of the universes of pure thought ... To reduce mathematics to its *act*: the univocal power of formalism, the naked force of the letter and its codes". Thus, what the formalisation of the mathematical act aims at is nothing other than "the enunciation of the mathematical real".[41]

It is from this perspective that Badiou insists on formalisation as "a necessary requirement of thought, for mathematicians as well as philosophers" because what is important in his eyes is that "the formal presentation of mathematics envelops a founding radicality which characterises the nature of its act".[42] What lesson can be drawn from this 'passion for formalization' that characterises twentieth-century mathematics? Drawing on Gödel's demonstrations, Badiou emphasises that, even if "every formalizing stance leaves a remainder", the conclusion to be drawn from this inevitable 'failure' of formalisation is not that formalisation should be abandoned as a way of accessing the real, but, on the contrary, that the "untreated residue" by a non-completed formalisation should be taken as the starting point for a new formalisation:

This is indeed what separates formalization, as both thought and project, from a merely pragmatic employment of forms. Without ever being discouraged, one must invent other axioms, other logics, other ways of formalizing. The essence of thinking always resides in the power of forms.[43]

As for Lacan, it is quite clear that it is not so much mathematical knowledge that is important to him as the position of the mathematician subject to an unprecedented kind of desire, that of putting a symbol, a letter, where there is no meaning. Ultimately, what interests him in mathematics is not the truth, but its power of construction, even at the price of seeing truth reduced to a value among others. It is in this sense that Lacan was able to say, which at first glance may seem inconsistent: "There is only mathematical truth, that is, written truth".[44] For what is important for Lacan in mathematics, just as for Badiou incidentally, is not only its structuring power, that of giving form to its objects, but the power of wrenching away from experience and empiricity that is attributed to mathematics.[45] Thus, according to Lacan, mathematical discourse cannot be founded on anything other than "this language of pure matheme ... that alone can be taught: this without recourse to any experience, which, by always being, whatever it may be, grounded in a discourse, allows locutions that in the final resort aim at nothing other than establishing this discourse".[46]

For Badiou, too, mathematics is concerned with "the most formal, abstract, universally quasi-empty dimension of being as such".[47] What mathematics makes possible, as a "speculative resource", is what Badiou calls "absolute ontology", more precisely, "the existence of a universe of reference, of a place for the thinking of being qua being" which can only be "described, or thought, by means of axioms, or principles, to which it corresponds. There can be no experience of it, or any concept of it that is dependent on an experience. It is radically non-empirical".[48] Mathematics thus creates objects without relying upon experience. Far from positing existence as external to mathematics, Lacan and Badiou posit it as essentially determined by mathematics itself. It is in this sense that Lacan can state: "It is clear that it is only from a certain reflection on mathematics that existence has taken on its meaning".[49] Similarly, for Badiou, mathematics, considered as "absolute ontology", obeys the "principle of maximality", according to which "any intellectual entity whose existence can be inferred without contradiction from the axioms prescribing it exists by that very fact".[50]

This mathematical notion of existence is legible in the articulation of what Cantor called "the correct formation of concepts".[51] In "Foundations of a General Theory of Manifolds", Cantor explains what freedom of conception and conceptualisation in mathematics should mean:

> Mathematics is entirely free in its development, bound only by the self-evident concern that its concepts be both internally without

174 Philosophy After Lacan

contradictions and stand in definite relations, organized by means of definitions, to previously formed, already existing and proven. In particular, in introducing new numbers, mathematics is obliged only to give determinateness and, under certain circumstances, the kind of relationship to the older numbers, which in a given case will definitely permit them to be distinguished from one another. As soon as a number satisfies all these conditions, mathematics can and must regard it as existant and real.[52]

While the freedom of mathematics may well be a distinguishing feature of the Cantorian conception of mathematical existence, the difficulty that Cantor faces is that of showing that the transfinite numbers do indeed have an effective existence, in the same manner as finite numbers. By tying existence closely to non-contradiction, Cantor considers that it is sufficient for a mathematical object not to contradict any statement of the theory to which it belongs in order to exist, and therefore there is no need for an effective demonstration of its existence.

Well aware of the break with traditional mathematics, Cantor insists that his research on the transfinite numbers has "reached a point where its continuation becomes dependent upon an extension of the concept of a real whole number beyond the present boundaries; in particular, this extension goes in a direction in which, to my knowledge, no one has so far looked for it".[53] Now this new requirement to consider the new numbers, the transfinite numbers, as really existing is based on the very notion of number: "The notion of number, however developed it may be here, carries in itself the principle of an extension necessary in itself and absolutely infinite".[54] Thus, for Cantor, the transfinite numbers are as "real" as finite integers or irrationals. For the transfinite is not simply an infinitely large, "variable finite", "a magnitude that can grow beyond any finite limit".[55] Rather, if the transfinite is an actual infinite or "genuine-infinite" (*das Eigentlich-Unendliches*),[56] it is because, in Cantor's words:

> [t]he assumption that apart from the absolute – unreachable by any determination – the infinite and the finite, no modifications can exist which, though not finite, are nonetheless determinable by numbers and consequently are what I call the genuine-infinite – this assumption I do not find justified by anything ... What I maintain and believe I have proved in this paper as well as in my earlier endeavors is that after the finite there is a *transfinitum* (which also could be called *suprafinitum*), i.e., an unlimited gradation of determinate modes which in their nature are not finite but infinite, yet which, much as the finite, can be determined by determinate, well-defined and distinguishable *numbers*. I am convinced, therefore, that the domain of definable magnitudes is *not* limited to the domain of the finite magnitudes;

accordingly, the limits of our cognition may be extended further without it being necessary to do any kind of violence to our nature.[57]

Hence, the thesis traditionally advanced against actual infinity in mathematics according to which the finitude of our understanding prevents us from conceiving of the infinite that would be situated between the finite and the absolute (God) has been refuted. For the thesis put forward by Cantor is that:

> [a]s limited as human nature may in fact be, *much* of the infinite nonetheless adheres to it, and I even think that if it were not itself in many respects infinite, the strong confidence and certainty regarding the existence (*des Seins*) of the absolute, about which we are all in agreement, could not be unexplained. And in particular, it is my view that human understanding has an unlimited, inherent capacity for the step-wise formation of whole number-classes which stand in a definite relationship to the infinite modes and whose *powers* are of ascending strength.[58]

Like almost all mathematicians, Cantor adopts some form of number realism. He distinguishes between intrasubjective and transsubjective reality: the first reality, called "*intrasubjective* or *immanent*", is a matter for our understanding. But there is another reality of numbers that Cantor calls "*transsubjective* or *transcendent*", which implies that numbers have a reality outside our understanding, since they must be regarded as "an expression or image of occurrences and relationships in the external world confronting the intellect".[59] In mathematics, as Cantor conceives it, immanent reality takes precedence over transsubjective or transcendent reality, with the latter being assigned to metaphysics. Now, the fact that, in mathematics, one must "take into account *solely and uniquely* the *immanent* reality of its concepts", allows one to draw "a most important consequence for mathematics"[60]: the fact that mathematics must deal only with the immanent reality of its objects grants it a freedom that the other sciences do not have. Thus placing at the centre of his conception of mathematics its freedom of creation, Cantor upholds at the same time the idea that mathematics thinks through formalisation, but this presupposes that there is a system of axioms that does not deal with objects that exist in reality, but with objects that the axioms-prescriptions call into existence.

Badiou, likewise, subscribes to the realism of mathematicians. Indeed, if mathematics is the science of the real, it is because philosophy, which is based on the equation mathematics = ontology, starts from "the assumption ... that there is an aspect of generality or universality to what exists that is somehow immaterial. There are structures that recur in everything that exists. The study of these structures as such, of structural possibilities, is precisely the aim of mathematics".[61] In much the same way as mathematicians, Badiou believes that mathematical objects and structures "'exist' in a certain way". But, unlike mathematicians' realism, Badiou's realism is based on a certain resistance experienced in mathematicians' practice: "'something' resists when you practice mathematics... you come up against a difficult, unyielding reality".[62] Hence, it is on the basis of the resistance of "things" to thought that we must grasp the real in mathematics. The crux of the matter is to identify this "bit of the real" that manifests itself only where things get stuck, where there is an impasse, an incompatibility.

Badiou thus joins Lacan, for whom it is not only in mathematics that we best think about existence, existence is rather what mathematics thinks in its impossibility. Thus, if the notion of the impossible plays a pivotal role in establishing the relationship that psychoanalysis has with mathematics, it is because, much as psychoanalytical discourse does, mathematical discourse encounters points of impossibility. Situated at the intersection of psycho-analysis and mathematics, the notion of the impossible makes it possible for the psychoanalytical field to be organised on the one hand, and to bring to light, on the other hand, the constitutive impasses of mathematics. The impossible is therefore not entirely foreign to mathematics, since it is embodied in its history by great moments of "crisis" when mathematics hits against an enigmatic real that emerges from the encounter with an obstacle exceeding the axiomatic-deductive framework.

It is noteworthy that Lacanian realism is quite peculiar as it depends on his definition of the real as impossible. The real is not reality, but that which evades its representation. It is what makes a hole in a discourse and pushes it to renew itself. And it is precisely to better identify the impossible in psychoanalysis itself that Lacan calls upon mathematics. Because what Lacan is looking for in mathematics is a writing, given that the real at stake in psychoanalysis can only be attained through the impasses of the ways of writing. In deciding to borrow from mathematics the tools for the work to be done by the psychoanalyst, convinced of "the value of mathematical elements in making there emerge something that really concerns our experience as psychoanalysts",[63] it is not only to break with the philosophical discourse that Lacan turns to mathematics, it is principally because mathematics deals with the real. In truth, only mathematics, according to Lacan, is capable of thinking the real: "This real I am talking about is absolutely unapproachable, except by a mathematical way" and "it is precisely in this that the logical effort ought to be a model, indeed a guide for us".[64]

Like mathematics, psychoanalysis does not find its limit outside itself, but carries it within itself.[65] Approaching the real from the angle of the limit gives us, once again, the opportunity to bring to light a fundamental point in the relationship between psychoanalysis and mathematics. We propose to illustrate this paradox of the limit using the notion of infinity. If Lacan has recourse to mathematics and if he makes Cantor a privileged interlocutor, it is also in order to resolve Freud's impasse concerning the end of the analysis. As an experience of speech, psychoanalysis structurally knows no end. Now,

The Place of Mathematics   177

while for Freud analysis is "interminable", since there is nothing that can stop the deciphering of the unconscious, Lacan, by contrast, seeks to elaborate a notion of the "logical" end of analysis. It is from this perspective that the end of analysis, according to Lacan, confronts psychoanalysis with a major challenge: "What's at stake now is what will help to bring out the real-of-the-structure: what in language is not a number, but a sign to be deciphered".[66] Put simply, without the mathematical tools, the only means of localising the point of the impossible, analysis would not encounter any real.

Cantor's discovery of the transfinite will therefore allow Lacan to elaborate a theory of the end of analysis that takes account of its infinitude. And it was with this aim in mind that he proposed the famous procedure of the "pass", which marks the passage from the analysand to the analyst. Psychoanalysis, which aims at its "logical" end, seeks to identify, at the end of the analysis, what, unbeknownst to the subject, determines him or her. The rigour of this determination depends on a structure that implies the real. The isolation of the real at the end of the analysis is namely based on the construction of a framework that is supposed to encompass all the sayings of the subject's unconscious. We can see here the analogy of the act of crossing a limit that the Lacanian pass and Cantor's gesture have in common inasmuch as, in psychoanalysis, "it is a question of arriving at a formula, an $\grave{A}_0$, which is that of everyone, even if there is an $\grave{A}_0$, for all that Lacan formulated in terms of 'There is no sexual relation.'"[67]

The fact that in an analysis one can always add new statements, signals that psychoanalysis is dealing with an infinity that Cantor qualifies as an "improper infinite" (*Uneigentlich-Unendliches*). From this perspective, the cardinality of the symbolic, the proper realm of psychoanalysis, will always be finite. The properly Cantorian infinite, the actual infinite, by contrast, is only attained through a break with the notion of the infinite reduced to the inaccessible, the indefinite, or the unlimited, a break that allowed Cantor to construct a purely quantitative infinite: the transfinite numbers. In order to maintain this opposition inherent in psychoanalysis, Lacan must therefore turn to the mathematical theory of infinity. To begin with, he has to acknowledge that, in psychoanalysis, the symbolic is infinite, since it is always possible to add an additional statement to all the previous ones. Hence, if Lacan draws on Cantor's discovery of the transfinite numbers, this is because the theory of the transfinite allows him to think about the possible way of going beyond the Name-of-the-Father – the pivotal role of the castration's finitism, which for Freud presents an unsurpassable horizon for psychoanalysis – to relativise this place which until then was considered to be absolute.

The theory of transfinite numbers is important to Lacan as it offers an elaboration of a successive progression of infinite numbers that does not encounter any stopping point. Just as Cantor's problem is that of not being able to step outside the domain of the countable to reach the power of the continuum, the deciphering of the unconscious cannot reach its end. Cantor's move, which allows him to make a leap from the countable to the uncountable, the continuum, consists in understanding that one can only go beyond the countable by first imposing certain restrictions upon the otherwise absolutely infinite and untamed counting process. Hence, it is through the addition of a new signifier, aleph-zero, a number added to the infinite sequence of numbers, that the finitisation of an endless succession may be grasped. Cantorian mathematics has then the advantage of having formalised not only the notion of limit, but also that of the successive overcoming of successive limitations. Thus, in order to reach ever larger cardinals, one must apply what Cantor calls "the principle of limitation". Once the first passage to the limit has been accomplished, a transfinite number of limitations are needed to envisage the ultimate leap, which, however, is impossible to write down as it is always possible to add "one more" and thus to exceed it. One can see here how the paradox of the "greatest transfinite number" renders the place of all sets inconsistent. Now, this is precisely one of the possible ends of analysis, namely the encounter with the lack of the last signifier at the heart of the symbolic, and, thus, the incompleteness of the symbolic Other, but which, in turn, opens up the possibility for "the invention of a knowledge in the real" that, according to Lacan, by "reaching the real, it determines it just as much as the knowledge of science".[68] The challenge for psychoanalysis is thus to realise and to account for the fact that by choosing a type of the infinite, one decides what should be understood by this notion. It should be noted, however, that it is only the first type of infinity, the one that is limited to the domain of the countable, that can be used in psychoanalysis. In this respect, while Badiou criticises Lacan for not being Cantorian,[69] because the infinite for him is reduced to inaccessibility,[70] Lacan could only agree with him insofar as, like Freud, he does not admit the actual infinite in psychoanalysis; they are both essentially "finitists".

Thus, if the impossibility of writing is what mathematics and psychoanalysis have in common, we can better understand why the matheme is the pivotal point of the Lacanian undertaking. The path of the matheme, in the very form in which Lacan proposes it, is considered by Lacan to be the only possible method of producing "little bits of the real", as he himself puts it. We are confronted here with a paradox, namely, one can only produce "bits of the real" by using artifices, more exactly, by using artifices of writing. The paradox of seeing the real in writing is accompanied by the paradox of seeing the real appear only through writing. And to give an image that comes closest to this formalisation that can only be supported by writing, to this "reduction to the dimensions of the surface that writing requires", Lacan takes an image that he finds in nature:

> [t]he textual work that comes out of the spider's belly, its web. It is a truly miraculous function to see, on the very surface emerging from an

opaque point of this strange being, the trace of these writings taking form, in which one can grasp the limits, impasses, and dead-ends that show the real acceding to the symbolic.[71]

On this point, philosophy does not seem to disagree with psychoanalysis. For Badiou, mathematics is "a way of approaching the real, including the most elusive real".[72] But the real that mathematics targets according to Badiou is not quite the same as the real that mathematics aims at according to Lacan. For the latter, "[t]he real can only be inscribed on the basis of an impasse of formalization".[73] More precisely, it is only by putting formalisation to the test that we encounter a point of impossibility. However, it must also be emphasised that Lacan's formalism is quite particular in many of its aspects. Taking mathematical formalisation as a model does not amount to mixing up the two modes of the real: the real that is at stake in mathematics and the real that psychoanalysis aims at. Mathematics, and science in general, deal with a real that they transform into writing. The real that mathematics deals with is supposed to be mathematisable – without remainder. Psychoanalysis, by contrast, while being a matter of meaning, does not give meaning to the real. For psychoanalysis it is rather a question of targeting the real in meaning. For Lacan, mathematics thus represents the model of access to the real of the structure where the real is considered to be an encounter with a point of the impossible to write in the terms of that structure. In the seminar *The Other Side of Psychoanalysis,* Lacan examines a formulation of the impossible precisely as a fact of structure: "In supposing the formalization of discourse and in granting oneself some rules within this formalization that are destined to put it to the test, we encounter an element of impossibility".[74] The test is taken here in the sense that it reaches a certain real.

Cantor's Saying According to Lacan and Badiou: "a wager on the real"[75]

It is in this context that Badiou criticises certain specific aspects of Lacan's use of mathematics. We cannot enter here into a detailed discussion of Badiou's perfectly acceptable arguments, which are based on a careful reading of "L'Étourdit", and *Encore.* Before even questioning the appropriateness of his reading and/or criticism of Lacan, especially on those points where Lacan relies on mathematics, we must ask ourselves what purpose this reading of Lacan can serve in the philosophical project constructed by Badiou. Certainly, in Lacan it is the path of the matheme to deal with the question of the real, which seems important to Badiou, since he too strives to identify "what is subtracted from ontological determination", "what is not Being-*qua* Being",[76] and which is therefore not mathematisable. For the problem that Badiou seeks to address is the following: "if real ontology is set up as mathematical by evading the norm of the One, unless this norm is re-established globally there also ought to be a point wherein the ontological, hence mathematical field, is de-totalised or remains at a dead end. I have called this point the '*event*".[77] Thus, if philosophy, by assigning the task of thinking being as such to mathematics, separates itself not from just any part of itself but from what constitutes its "centre of gravity", "the ultimate refuge of [its] identity",[78] it is precisely to establish itself as "the general theory of the event... In other words, it is the theory of what is subtracted from ontological subtraction. Or the theory of the impossible proper to mathematics".[79] But in order to assign philosophy the task of determining the trans-being of the event, it is necessary to begin by admitting that "not everything is mathematizable".[80] The question that then arises is that of knowing what in the event justifies the name of the real, that is to say, the real as impossible to be written.

It is precisely on this point that Badiou cannot fail to encounter Lacan in his attempt to approach the non-inscribable real using mathematics. Thus, if it is necessary to have recourse to the matheme in psychoanalysis, this is because psychoanalysis, which like any discourse aiming at a real is articulated in mathemes, comes up against a difficulty: it deals with a peculiar knowledge that is literalisable as knowledge, but unlike other modalities of knowledge, it is not known.[81] Psychoanalysis is therefore not mathematics, even though, like mathematics, it privileges the matheme to attain the real, but, unlike mathematics, it targets the remainder of the real that escapes all formalisation. For psychoanalysis, this remainder of the real that cannot be mathematised can be summed up in the formula "there is no sexual relationship": there is only the impossibility of writing it. Yet it is precisely this point of impossibility that sustains a desire to know. It is not a desire to know despite this impossibility, but a desire based on the fact that truth, while being not all, can expand, and thus make room for new knowledge.[82] It is in this sense that Lacan attempts to write the sexual relationship, even though he posited its impossibility:

> Without attempting this relationship of writing, there is no means in effect of arriving at what I, at the same time as I posited its inex-sistence, proposed as a goal by which psychoanalysis might make itself the equal of science: namely to prove that this relationship is impossible to write, or that it is in this that it is not affirmable but moreover not refutable: under the heading of truth. With the consequence that there is no truth of which one can say all.... The truth is of no use except to create the place from which this knowledge is exposed. But his [the analyst's] knowledge is not nothing. For what is at stake is that, reaching the real, it determines it just as much as the knowledge of science.[83]

What is aimed at in Lacanian mathemes is, therefore, neither of the order of the true nor of the order of knowledge, as the matheme is situated at the junction of truth and knowledge, but the real that manifests itself in the form of the encounter, of the stuckedness, of the deadlock, of the incompatible, of the non-relation. This is why what the matheme aims at is not the real as such but the impossibility of telling the truth about the real. This is also where Lacan's use of mathematics is to be taken seriously.

As a way of circumscribing the real, the matheme goes straight to the heart of Badiou's preoccupations and, more particularly, to his self-assigned task of re-entwining philosophy and mathematics. The question to be posed is therefore that of knowing where exactly Lacan's and Badiou's paths separate, while sometimes crossing each other nevertheless. In the case of Lacan, the fact of drawing inspiration from the mathematical model does not amount to confusing two modes of the real: a real that sets mathematicians to work, the real as the cause of the work of formalisation, and a real that is generated by this formalisation or, more precisely, by its failure. First of all, it must be emphasised that the real is always related to a discourse because we only come across the real on the basis of a discourse. This can also explain why the emergence of a new real results in a fundamental reworking of mathematical discourse. This seems to contradict the spontaneous philosophy of mathematicians, the 'Platonic realism' which presupposes a pre-established mathematical universe that mathematicians have only to discover. Put otherwise, if it can be assumed that the realism of mathematicians and the production of a new real are not incompatible, it is because once produced, the new real is posited as already being there.

This is the lesson that can be drawn from the invention of transfinites: once the new numbers, the transfinites, have been constructed by Cantor and introduced into the mathematical field, it is as if he had only discovered them since they were already there, patiently waiting to be discovered. Thus, what is brought into existence through invention is considered, retroactively, as already being there, i.e. even before Cantor's creative gesture that generated it had taken place. This inversion of invention into discovery is the price to pay for the realism of mathematicians that necessitates this kind of retroaction to guarantee the "reality" of its objects which imposes itself on everyone as being necessary. This is also why, to deal with the mathematical real, it is necessary to take as a point of departure the fact that a real is produced as if outside of any jurisdiction. Hence, to produce the transfinite, it was necessary to invent the path and the steps to reach the mathematical infinite. Seen from this perspective, Cantor's diagonal method[84] was contingent, which is to say, not required by the existing mathematical discourse. It was therefore necessary to invent this procedure that was not required by mathematical knowledge at the time of its setting to work, and for good reason, since what was aimed at by the invention of this procedure was to deal with a lack within this very knowledge. However, once the invention of transfinites is accepted by mathematical discourse, this contingency turns into a necessity.

182   Philosophy After Lacan

We would therefore tend to agree with Badiou when he argues that the mathematical saying, as an event, is not based on any guarantee of necessity.[85] To understand this paradoxical articulation, already evoked by Cantor, between the freedom of creation and the constraint[86] that characterises mathematics, it is necessary to point out that, although it is produced by mathematical discourse, the real of mathematics, in order to be effective, i.e. capable of renewing mathematical knowledge, must be posited as ex-sisting in relation to mathematical discourse, and moreover as being prior to it, outside of this discourse from which it nevertheless proceeds. Concerning this issue of ex-sistence, it must be noted that only that which manifests itself as an impossibility can be considered as the real, to be taken here in the sense that it is impossible for this real to be affirmed or denied by mathematical demonstration. This amounts to saying that the status of the real of something that presents itself as an obstacle or a difficulty depends on mathematical demonstration. One could also say that the real as ex-sistence is a truth demonstrated to be impossible to demonstrate. It is precisely because it cannot be written down that we recognise this real in mathematics. The famous example which, for Lacan, illustrates the real in mathematics is the impossibility of demonstrating the validity of the continuum hypothesis. Instead of demonstrating it by the diagonal method, Cantor made the continuum hypothesis emerge as the impossible-real of mathematics. More generally, if all demonstration, once validated, implies that it is impossible to proceed otherwise, the impossibility of the demonstration, that is to say the deadlock of formalisation, the impossibility of writing or not writing a formula, by contrast, generates a real as impossible.

Badiou's critique of Lacan is situated exactly on this level. In order to tackle Lacan's particular relationship to mathematics, Badiou takes as his starting point what he calls "triangulation", which includes psychoanalysis, mathematics, and philosophy.[87] To substantiate his critical remarks, Badiou uses as a key reference a statement drawn from "L'Étourdit", where Lacan signifies the failure of philosophy to determine what is essential in mathematics: "As it is the most appropriate language for scientific discourse, mathematics is the science without conscience that our dear Rabelais promised, the science by which a philosopher can only be blocked".[88] On the other hand, what characterises the approach of psychoanalysis to mathematics hinges on the rather specific status that Lacan assigns to the matheme: the matheme ensures the integral transmission of knowledge precisely because it is being emptied of meaning. Thus, for Lacan, mathematical discourse, defined as "the language of pure matheme", is a discourse "that alone can be taught: this without recourse to any experience".[89] It is this feature that the matheme in psychoanalysis and the mathematisable have in common. But there is yet another side to the matheme that goes beyond the mathematisable: the real of "there is no sexual relationship", i.e. the non-inscribable real, around which everything in the psychoanalytic discourse is ordered. It is also this real that can only be signalled by the impasses of the mathematisable: "This is why the mathematics on the basis of which the mathematisable – itself definable as what can be taught of the real – is formulated in impasses, are likely to be coordinated with this absence from the real".[90] The "absence from the real" evoked here is nothing other than the real proper to psychoanalysis, the "there is no sexual relationship", which must be distinguished from the real that can be written and thus taught by means of mathemes. It is this real whose absence, as Badiou indicates, is to be understood as its "absence in any mathematization, or, in other words, its absence in writing".[91]

What would be the equivalent of this "absence in writing" for mathematics? As has been pointed out by Cantor, the "reality" of mathematics is grounded in the constraint of coherence. If formalisation consists in a putting in relation, the real arises as the impossibility of such putting in relation, indeed, as an impossible relation. Consequently, the real in mathematics can only emerge at those points where coherence is lacking. It is at precisely this level that Lacan seeks the real in mathematics: the real in the formalisation itself. The real we are dealing with here is the real that "can only be inscribed on the basis of an impasse of formalization". What is important to note here is that it is precisely concerning this issue that Badiou formulates his objections to Lacan. Lacan's position is, according to Badiou, an "archi-scientific"[92] one. According to Badiou's reading of Lacan's articulation of the real and the matheme, this articulation is only tenable if one does not introduce the point of "a real of the real". The formulation: the "real of the real",[93] which is nowhere to be found in Lacan's work, as Badiou readily admits, plays a strategic role in his argument, since it allows him to clarify how, according to Lacan, psychoanalysis and philosophy are respectively positioned in relation to mathematics.

Thus, to follow Badiou, in order to situate the place of psychoanalysis in relation to mathematics and science in general, the real, as Lacan conceives it, is to be doubled: the real proper to science, i.e. the real whose laws science "discovers" and then writes down in formulae, the real that can be mathematised and transmitted by way of the matheme, this real, for being writable, is also the real that can be taught, and the real proper to psychoanalysis, the non-mathematisable real that can only be written on the basis of the impasses of mathematisation. What Lacan is looking for, according to Badiou, is precisely this point of impossibility in mathematics itself that allows him to isolate the non-mathematisable real. For Badiou, the matheme, as Lacan conceives it, is archi-scientific and not scientific, because it is situated at the point of the real of mathematics. And Badiou concludes, ""it can't be mathematics, precisely because it touches the real of mathematics itself".[94] Now, it is precisely this distinction between two modes of the real that separates psychoanalysis from philosophy, which, not being able to touch the real of mathematics, remains, as Lacan emphasises, "blocked by mathematics". Hence, the fact of having granted the status of thought to mathematics,

184 Philosophy After Lacan

because only mathematics is capable of touching the real, is at the same time an opportunity for Lacan to criticise philosophy, which is incapable of recognising, in mathematics, the path of access to the real which is there, and for this very reason can only be blocked by mathematics.

If Badiou rejects outright the idea of the real thus doubled, it is because he adheres to the thesis that if there is "a locus of thought that is blocked by itself, it is surely mathematics" and the reason he puts forward is nothing other than the ignorance or unawareness of mathematics concerning "its own ontological significance".[95] This thesis allows Badiou to shed light on his main point of disagreement with Lacan by maintaining that philosophy, instead of being blocked by mathematics, is, on the contrary, that discourse that, identifying in mathematics "a blocking point when it comes to its own ontological nature", has been trying since Plato "to *unblock* it". In this respect, the philosopher "isn't someone who is blocked by mathematics", as Lacan maintains, "but someone who attempts to unblock it with regard to itself".[96]

Badiou wonders about "the real thinking dimension of mathematics"[97] that philosophy, according to Lacan, is supposed to lack or fails to grasp. He finds the answer to this query in "L'Étourdit", where Lacan maintains, precisely concerning mathematics, that "the said is constantly renewed by taking its subject from a saying rather than from any reality".[98] The neuralgic point of Lacan's argument can be found in the dialectic of the saying and the said, as has been formulated in "L'Étourdit". For Lacan, it is when "a saying [emerges] that does not always go so far as to be able to 'ex-sist' in the said", that "a certain real may be reached".[99] The occurrence of a saying on which the said depends constitutes an event in the sense that it introduces a scansion, a cut. But for a saying to take place, it must be submitted to the test of its consequences, i.e. of the said, and it is only then that a "certain real may be reached".

According to Badiou's reading of this rather singular dialectic of the saying and the said, we can agree with Lacan that the saying must occur to be able to transform, invent, or renew the said. This is because mathematics, in relating to the saying, and not to any reality, relates to a reality that is immanent to it, a point that Cantor has already insisted on. If we follow Lacan, it is precisely this point that philosophy, in its relation to mathematics, necessarily misses, namely that the renewal of the said is rooted in the saying, rather than in meaning, as philosophy generally maintains. In striving to give meaning to truth, says Lacan, philosophy fails to recognise the true nature of mathematics, which would consist, according to Lacan, but read by Badiou, in "a meaning-less saying that is realized as an absolute (integrally transmissible) said".[100] And to be even to the point, "the paradigmatic value of mathematics lies in it being the unsurpassable model of a thought that has no meaning".[101] As Badiou observes, it is curious nonetheless that on this question an anti-philosopher, Lacan, can join a philosopher, Plato, however

The Place of Mathematics   185

with one essential difference: what Lacan identifies as the paradigmatic value of mathematics is precisely what Plato criticises it for.

For Plato's objection to mathematics is that it functions based on hypotheses that it does not account for. Translated into Lacanian terms, Plato would realise, before Lacan, that mathematics is based on "a pure saying", and that "mathematics is only guaranteed by a saying", which Badiou translates as "the axiomatic dimension of mathematics".[102] Seen from this angle, the said in mathematics "stems intrinsically from a saying", since something must first be said so that there can then be "a chain of reasoning that's faithful to this constitutive original saying".[103] While criticising mathematics, Plato would thus agree with Lacan, since he too identifies "the primacy of the saying" from which the elimination of meaning follows. If philosophy is the domain where the dialectic of meaning is played out, mathematics is the domain of "the prescription of the saying" or, rather, "mathematics is governed by the prescription of the saying",[104] which is not supported by any guarantee of necessity. Drawing a lesson from Descartes, Badiou claims that the specificity of mathematical discursivity is the "event of the saying" and can therefore only be evental and contingent, but, because "it doesn't derive from reality, [it] is absolutely necessary" to be taken in the sense of being "necessary under the authority of the saying".[105] Thus, having identified "mathematics as being under the law of the saying", philosophy must recognise the constitutive paradox of mathematics, i.e. the nexus between contingency and constraint.[106]

It would thus appear that the reading Badiou proposed of the "triangulation", i.e. of philosophy, psychoanalysis, and mathematics, is perhaps not as clear as he claims. In effect, there are more points of convergence than of divergence between him and Lacan than Badiou would care to admit. Let us take a closer look at how this dialectic is played out in the case of mathematics if the place of the saying in psychoanalysis is "the analogue in mathematical discourse".[107] Indeed, mathematical discourse, if we follow Lacan, must be based on the logic of the saying and the said: "Thus the said does not go without a saying. But if the said always poses itself as truth, ... the said only couples with it by ex-sisting in it, that is, by not being of the *dit-mension* of the truth".[108] In light of this, it could then be said that if this logic of the saying presents the essence of the Lacanian conception of mathematics, this is also because, in the discourse of mathematics, "the said is constantly renewed by taking its subject from a saying rather than from any reality, even if it means summoning this saying from the properly logical sequence that it implies as a said".[109]

To take an example, incidentally, the one that Lacan himself takes: if there is a "Cantor event", a Cantorian revolution, it is because there is Cantor's saying, or rather the event of his saying. In other words, for Lacan, the mathematical invention proceeds from the saying, that of Cantor, Euclid, etc., since only a saying can renew the faulty said. But this saying occurs as a

186 Philosophy After Lacan

contingency that is not based on any reality. Strictly speaking, since the saying is at the outset nothing more than the possibility of its existence, the truth value of the said is by this very fact suspended. If the said necessarily depends on the possibility of the existence of the saying, this comes at a price: as the condition of the said, the saying ex-sists in relation to the latter. Being modal, the logic of the saying thus sheds new light on the question of existence. To clarify this point, Lacan takes two examples, that of psychoanalytic discourse and that of mathematical discourse. Concerning psychoanalytic discourse, it could thus be argued that, for this discourse and its practice, analysis, to exist, it is necessary to restore "Freud's saying" that is "inferred from the logic that takes as its source the said of the unconscious".[110] In other words, it is because Freud has discovered the unconscious that the saying of the unconscious exists. Lacan's other example, the discourse of mathematics, on the other hand, is meant to show that "the said is constantly renewed by taking its subject from a saying rather than from any reality". The mathematical saying could thus be considered to be an act due to its power to transform, more exactly, owing to its power to generate the novelty of a mathematical formula, which is to say, of a numeralisation of the real. Cantor's saying, which has already proved its power to create new mathematical knowledge, can therefore be assigned the status of the real, insofar as it ex-sists with respect to the current knowledge system. The said, on the other hand, is that which, from being posited as truth, must be put to the test by demonstration in order to validate, retroactively, the initial saying. One could also argue that the said arising from this saying is summoned – via demonstration – to ensure, after the fact, the saying of its axiomatic status.

Seen from this angle, the "mathematical saying" is "the saying" only if it engenders knowledge. But the taking place of such creative saying presupposes an unprecedented encounter, an absolute novelty, hence Lacan's idea of considering the "saying" as an event, on the condition, however, that it is an encounter with "a bit of the real". We are dealing here with the knowledge in the real, yet a knowledge that stems from a saying. Put otherwise, there is a "saying" that produces knowledge only on the condition that the introduction of new knowledge, owing to an encounter with "a bit of the real" constitutes the moment when a distinction between a before and an after is established. It is this rupture or scansion of time, then, that transforms the "saying" into an event. This also indicates why a saying is not to be confused with either mathematical discourse or demonstration. This is because mathematical discourse and demonstration are constituted on the basis of this moment of saying. It is in this sense that the "saying-event" can lead to the restructuring of the field of knowledge in its entirety.

This is where, to repeat Russell's definitions, the mathematician "never knows what he is talking about" – precisely to the extent that he confuses the event as a pure creation (in Badiousian terms, we could say: truth), with knowledge as the rational ordering of discourse – "nor whether what one is saying is true" – precisely to the extent that he does not make the difference between the registers that order saying and truth. As can be seen here, the affinity between the language of the mathematician and the unconscious is situated at the level of their relationship to the question of truth. Lacan's remark from "L'Étourdit" is most illuminating in this respect: "the mathematician has the same embarrassment with his language as we have with the unconscious, and expresses it by this thought that he does not know what he is talking about, even if it is to assure him that it is true (Russell)".[111] It is only from the perspective of this affinity that Lacan can claim that a certain real is reached when "a saying [emerges] that does not always go so far as to be able to 'ex-sist' in the said".[112]

To conclude

His attentive but critical reading of Lacan's use of mathematics allows us to see Badiou's attempt to re-entwine philosophy and mathematics from another angle. Having based his philosophical project on the thesis of the identity of mathematics and ontology, i.e. having affirmed that philosophy is under the condition of the events of mathematics, Badiou establishes a completely different relation to mathematics than Lacan with respect to psychoanalysis. Seen from this perspective, philosophy's link to mathematics consists in its acceptance of mathematics as the possible instigator of an unprecedented determination of philosophy itself. As a "condition" of philosophy, mathematics is considered here as the power of a free and secularised thought whose contribution consists in a given chance of creating a novelty. Now, in this effort to re-entwine philosophy and mathematics, a strange figure is being summoned: Lacan, who is neither a philosopher nor a mathematician, but a psychanalyst. And it is in this attempt to reconnect with mathematics that Badiou criticises Lacan's use of mathematics.

The "triangulation" (mathematics, psychoanalysis, philosophy) would thus be, according to Badiou, a singular articulation created by Lacan to demarcate his use of mathematics. Now, Badiou, too, needs such a "triangulation" to bring to light the way in which philosophy, the general theory of evental truths, approaches mathematics identified with the thought of being. And he, too, makes reference to the impasses of mathematical formalisation, which prove that mathematics, having come across an impossibility of its own, is founded on a real. The unsurpassable real of psychoanalysis: there is no sexual relation that is the real proper to psychoanalysis as such, that is to say, the real around which all the "rest" is ordered, which means all that can be inscribed, mathematised, formalised, transformed into mathemes. Now, is Badiou not also obliged to recognise that there is an unwritable real in Cantorian mathematics – namely, the idea that "there is no measurable, numerable relation" between the countable and the uncountable or continuous, between the set of elements of a set and the set of its parts – to be able to ensure the compatibility between philosophy as the thought of the eventality of truths and ontology=mathematics as the thought of the multiple being?

For in striving to re-entwine philosophy and mathematics, Badiou is compelled to fight on several fronts: against philosophers that do not recognise mathematics as creative thought (Heidegger, for example), against anti-philosophers that relegate mathematics to un-thought, and against Lacan's rather singular anti-philosophy that grants mathematics the status of thought given that only mathematics, according to Lacan, is capable of touching the real. But Lacan grants mathematics this privilege only on the condition of arrogating to himself the right to identify the point at which mathematics fails: the point of impossibility or the point of the non-mathematisable real, which cannot be written down in mathematical formulae, and which can therefore only manifest itself through the impasses of formalisation.

For what is the main objection that Badiou addresses to Lacan? That he took the position vis-à-vis mathematics that Badiou characterises as "archi-scientific" in order to identify the point of the impossible that cannot be surpassed in mathematics, the "real of the real" of mathematics, as Badiou designates it, or more precisely, to strive to pronounce "the truth of the real" of mathematics. Thus exiting the strict framework of mathematics, Lacan raises to a position that Badiou describes as "archi-scientific", a position that would allow him to circumscribe the non-mathematisable real within mathematics itself.

But regardless of the points of convergence that we have tried to mark out, Badiousian philosophy and Lacanian psychoanalysis do not and cannot have the same recourse to mathematics. For Lacan, mathematics, while occupying a privileged place among those disciplines in which psychoanalysis cannot afford not to be interested, does not constitute one of conditions of psychoanalysis, in the sense that Badiou assigns to this notion. Lacan has recourse to mathematics in view of securing psychoanalysis's orientation towards the real, of identifying more clearly the real proper to psychoanalysis, while at the same time striving to produce a knowledge that can be transmitted to all by way of mathemes. However, psychoanalysis does not depend on mathematics. Besides, Freud's invention of psychoanalysis proves it; indeed, Freud did not need mathematics to establish the theory and practice of psychoanalysis.

This, however, is not the case for Badiou. In contrast to psychoanalysis, philosophy, as Badiou conceives it, does depend on the events that have taken place and will take place in mathematics because it is only on the basis of such events that new truths are generated, those truths that it is the task of philosophy to think. In this respect, philosophy is not and cannot be indifferent to what takes place in the thought of being qua being. Consequently, as has already been noted and as Badiou himself acknowledges, not every mathematics, which for him is identified with ontology, is compatible with the philosophy of evental truths. In fact, only a mathematics capable of identifying and thinking the points of the impossible, its real, which takes the form of its impasses, aporias, difficulties – provides the necessary space for events to take place. It could then be argued that philosophy under conditions depends not only on the truths that its conditions produce, but that it depends even more on the real of its conditions, and especially on the real of the equation mathematics=ontology.

Badiou himself gives us an idea of this dependence of philosophy on the real of mathematics. Let us quote the key passage of *Being and Event*:

> Since its very origins, in anticipation of its Cantorian grounding, philosophy has interrogated the abyss which separates numerical discretion from the geometrical continuum. This abyss is none other than that which separates ω_0, infinite denumerable domain of finite numbers, from the set of its parts $p(\omega_0)$, the sole set able to fix the quantity of points in space....We can now say that it is being itself, flagrant within the impasse of ontology, which organizes the inexhaustibility of its thought; given that no measure may be taken of the quantitative bond between a situation and its state, between belonging and inclusion. Everything leads us to believe that it is *for ever* that this provocation to the concept, this un-relation between presentation and representation, will be open in being.... If the real is the impossible, the real of being – Being – will be precisely what is detained by the enigma of an anonymity of quantity.[113]

The errancy of being referred to by Badiou is intolerable for thought whose objective is, on the contrary, that "the quantitative unmooring of being" ceases and cannot therefore be satisfied with an "ontologically proven unmeasure", but aims precisely at measuring the excess, at pinpointing being where "it is no longer *exactly* sayable".[114] To clarify this rather opaque point, Badiou meticulously examines three strategies of thought, three orientations of ontological thought, as he puts it, to "remedy this excess", to say the impossible-to-say of ontology: the way of the constructible, the way of large cardinals, and the way of the generic. While the constructible path and the path of large cardinalities seek to bring the real of ontology under control, either "from below", i.e. by reducing multiplicities to the constructible, or "from above", by formulating hypotheses of the existence of gigantic cardinalities in order to prescribe "a hierarchical disposition in which nothing will be able to err",[115] the challenge of the generic path, by contrast, is not to reduce or control the excess, but to rejoin it. To ensure the compatibility of philosophy, the general theory of the eventality of truths, and ontology, the science of being, it is not enough to simply choose the generic path. It is also necessary to anticipate, as it were, that the demonstration of the continuum hypothesis, which postulates that the cardinality of R (the continuum or the set of real numbers) is the immediate successor of the cardinality of N (the countable or the set of integers), will never validate its truth.

Philosophy, as Badiou conceives it, requires an ontology capable of guaranteeing "for ever", as it were, that there would be new evental contingencies in which truths, including those of ontology, originate. *The Immanence of Truths* seems to take up and renew this questioning started in *Being and Event*, a questioning at the heart of which lies the undecidable status of the continuum hypothesis. Badiou opts, as always, for its falsity. The theory of large cardinals, located in the camp of the former adversary, with Jensen's theorem, which makes it possible to determine the power of a set, named 0#, seems to confirm the soundness of Badiou's choice.

Nevertheless, the hypothesis that Badiou himself makes about the continuum hypothesis, namely about its ultimate falsity, is based on nothing more than a wager: "a wager on the real", which, just like the real of psychoanalysis: there is no sexual relation, an unsurpassable real for psychoanalysis, constitutes the unsurpassable horizon for ontology if it is to be compatible with philosophy, the thought of the evental truths. Thus, what Badiou is looking for is an analogue of the real of psychoanalysis, and he finds it in a double form: that of the supposed falsity of the continuum hypothesis, on the one hand, and, on the other, that of the supposed existence of a 0# set.

In both cases, it is a question of a wager on the existence of unconstructible infinite sets. The problem that Jensen's "covering lemma", as Badiou calls it, solves is the following: "*There exists a set, called 0#, zero sharp, such that, if it does not exist, covering is always possible, and, if it does exist, the covering of certain large multiplicities is impossible*".[116] However, as with the continuum hypothesis, the existence of 0# is not provable in ZFC; the existence of 0# is "based on a decision", one that declares its existence "at the risk ... that the whole structure of formal ontology may collapse".[117] But then again, this risk can only be accepted by the choice that strives for creation or emancipation. Ultimately, all creative thought, Badiou writes, is compelled to take the existence of 0# as an axiom, in order to be able to go beyond the finitist framework of the given situation.

So, what is the lesson to be learned from the meticulous examination of the theory of large cardinals presented in *The Immanence of Truths*? Badiou's response is as follows: to wager on the existence of 0# should be considered to be a weapon with which to wage a successful battle in concrete situations. And to wage this battle successfully, it is necessary to:

> define the threshold, which is also the battleground. We need to think the complete infinity – which tells us that not everything is subject to finitude – but also think and practice $0_{\#}$ – which tells us where the exit from the old world occurs. And the convoluted, complex, exhausting

The Place of Mathematics 191

aspects of this *'where'*, infected as it is by the laws of the old world but also illuminated by the new infinity, cannot be avoided.[118]

Thus, if mathematics can create a new possibility for philosophy, it can only do so thanks to the contingency of what the mathematical saying produces there. So, the new possibility that mathematics creates is not just a matter of demonstration, but requires an act that is without guarantee. Here we face, once again, the dialectic of the saying and the said, or, for Badiou, the dialectic of the act and the work: just as was the case for Lacan, for whom it is through the trial of the said that the status of a true act of the creative, innovative saying is assured, for Badiou, "acts are nothing if they are not themselves also works".[119]

Notes

1 Immanuel Kant, *Critique of Pure Reason*, trans. Paul Guyer and Allen W. Wood, Cambridge University Press, Cambridge, 1998, p. 630.
2 Bertrand Russell, *The Principles of Mathematics*, University Press, Cambridge, 1903, p. 106.
3 René Lavendhomme, *Lieu du sujet. Psychanalyse et mathématique*, Seuil, Paris, 2001, p. 8.
4 *Ibid.*, p. 7.
5 *Ibid.*
6 Bertrand Russell, "Work on the principles of mathematics", *The International Monthly*, Vol. 4., No. 1, 1901, p. 43.
7 Alain Badiou, "Mathematics is a Thought", in *Briefings on Existence. A Short Treatise on Transitory Ontology*, trans. Norman Madarasz, SUNY, New York, 2006, p. 48.
8 Alain Badiou, *Being and Event*, trans. Oliver Feltham, Continuum, New York, London, 2006, p. 8.
9 *Ibid.*, pp. 8–9.
10 *Ibid.*, p. 14.
11 *Ibid.*, p. 11.
12 *Ibid.*, p. 13.
13 Badiou, "Mathematics Is a Thought", p. 51.
14 Badiou, "Mathematics Is a Thought", pp. 52–53 (translation modified).
15 Badiou, "The Event Is a Trans-Being", in *Briefings on Existence. A Short Treatise on Transitory Ontology*, p. 59.
16 Badiou discusses some examples of these moments of crisis: the crisis of irrational numbers in Pythagorean mathematics, the crisis related to the "paradoxes" of set theory, the crisis linked to the limitation theorems of formalisms, the polemics raised by the status of the axiom of choice, etc. See Badiou, "Mathematics Is a Thought", pp. 50–52.
17 *Ibid.*, p. 54.
18 *Ibid.*
19 Alain Badiou, *Conditions*, trans. Steven Corcoran, Continuum, London/New York, 2008, p. 302.
20 Badiou, "The Event Is a Trans-Being", p. 59.
21 *Badiou, Being and Event*, p. 355.

192 Philosophy After Lacan

22 *Ibid.*
23 *Ibid.*, p. 341.
24 *Ibid.*
25 *Ibid.*, p. 355.
26 *Ibid.*
27 Claude Imbert, "Où finit le platonisme?", *Alain Badiou: Penser le multiple*, Charles Ramond (ed.), L'Harmattan, Paris, 2002, p. 357.
28 Jacques Lacan, "Séminaire de Jacques Lacan, Le savoir du psychanalyste, 1971–1972" (unpublished), November 4, 1971.
29 *Ibid.*, December 2, 1971.
30 *Ibid.*
31 This is because the mathematical formalisation "runs counter to meaning – I almost said '*à contre-sens*'. In our times, philosophers of mathematics say 'it means nothing' concerning mathematics, even when they are mathematicians themselves, like Russell". Jacques Lacan, *On Feminine Sexuality. The Limits of Love and Knowledge. Book XX. Encore 1972–1973. The Seminar of Jacques Lacan*, trans. Bruce Fink, W.W. Norton & Company, New York and London, 1978, p. 93.
32 Lacan, "Le savoir du psychanalyste", December 2, 1971.
33 *Ibid.*
34 For example, when Cantor establishes a bijection between the elements of a continuous n-dimensional set and a continuous one-dimensional set, his ability to prove this theorem came as the greatest surprise to Cantor himself. Commenting on this proof in his letter to Dedekind, he writes: "*Je le vois, mais je ne le crois pas* (I see it, but do not believe it)". This peculiar confession clearly signals that in demonstrating this theorem, it is his belief system, or more precisely, his system of interpretation, his symbolic order, that is unsettled. Quoted in Nathalie Charraud, *Infini et Inconscient. Essai sur Georg Cantor*, Anthropos-Economica, Paris, 1994, p. 65.
35 Lacan, "Le savoir du psychanalyste", December 2, 1971.
36 Jacques Lacan, "Science and Truth", *Écrits*, trans. Bruce Fink, W.W. Norton & Company, New York, London, 2006, p. 738.
37 Lacan, "Le savoir du psychanalyste", December 2, 1971.
38 On this point, we refer the reader to Nathalie Charraud's book, *Infini et Inconscient. Essai sur Georg Cantor*.
39 Lacan, "Le savoir du psychanalyste", December 2, 1971.
40 *Ibid.*
41 Alain Badiou, *The Century*, trans. Alberto Toscano, Polity Press, Malden, 2007, pp. 162–163.
42 *Ibid.*, p. 163.
43 *Ibid.*, p. 164.
44 Jacques Lacan, "Séminaire de Jacques Lacan XXII, R.S.I. 1974–1975", (unpublished) December 11, 1974. And more precisely: "Mathematics refers to the written, to the written as such; and mathematical thought is the fact that one can represent for oneself a writing. "Séminaire de Jacques Lacan XXV, Le moment de conclure 1977–1978" (unpublished), January 10, 1978.
45 Thus, for Plato, mathematics is a condition of thinking because it breaks with opinion. Now, insofar as it is a "*forced* break", as Badiou points out, "involuntary, unapparent to itself, and above all lacking in freedom", mathematics, according to Plato, read by Badiou, "does not establish thought in its proper disposition of sovereign liberty". And more precisely still, defined as "*the in-between of the truth and the freedom of truth*", mathematics is "the truth as still

The Place of Mathematics 193

beholden to an unfreedom required by the violent gesture of repudiating the immediate. It belongs to truth, but in a still constrained figure of truth". To capture this oscillation between truth and freedom, Badiou proposes this striking formula: "mathematics is too violently true to be free, or it is too violently free (that is to say, discontinuous) to be absolutely true". Alain Badiou, "Philosophy and Mathematics", *Conditions*, trans. Steven Corcoran, Continuum, London, New York, 2008, pp. 103–105.

46 Jacques Lacan, "L'Étourdit", *Autres écrits*, Seuil, Paris 2001, p. 472.
47 Alain Badiou, *In Praise of Mathematics*, trans. Susan Spitzer, Polity, Cambridge, 2016, p. 34.
48 Alain Badiou, *The Immanence of Truths*, trans. Susan Spitzer and Kenneth Reinhard, Bloomsbury, London/New York, 2022, pp. 39–40.
49 Lacan, "Le savoir du psychanalyste", June 1, 1972.
50 *Ibid.*
51 Georg Cantor, "Foundations of a General Theory of Manifolds", trans. Uwe Parpart, *The Campaigner*, Vol. 9, Nos. 1–2, p. 95.
52 *Ibid.*, p. 79.
53 *Ibid.*, p. 70.
54 Georg Cantor, *Gesammelte Abhandlungen mathematischen und philosophischen Inhalts*, E. Zermelo (ed.), Springer, Berlin, 1932, p. 95.
55 *Ibid.*, p. 374.
56 Cantor, "Foundations of a General Theory of Manifolds", p. 70.
57 *Ibid.*, p. 76.
58 *Ibid.*
59 *Ibid.*
60 *Ibid.*, p. 79.
61 Badiou, *In Praise of Mathematics*, p. 63.
62 *Ibid.*, p. 63.
63 Lacan, "Le savoir du psychanalyste", June 1, 1972.
64 *Ibid.*, December 2, 1971.
65 "If the analytic inscription is indeed what I say it is, namely the beginning, the key nucleus of its mathematics, there is every chance that it serves the same purpose as mathematics. That is to say, it carries within itself its own limit". Lacan, "Seminar XXII", November 19, 1974.
66 Jacques Lacan, *Television. A Challenge to the Psychoanalytic Establishment*, trans. Denis Hollier, Rosalind Krauss, and Annette Michelson, W.W. Norton & Company, New York, London, 1990, p. 37 (translation modified).
67 Jacques-Alain Miller, "Vers un signifiant nouveau", *Revue de l'ECF*, No. 20, 1992, p. 54.
68 Jacques Lacan, "La note italienne", *Autres écrits*, Seuil, Paris, 2001, p. 310.
69 According to Badiou, the Lacanian doctrine of the subject is ultimately finite and he puts forward the following reason: "Even in the logic of enjoyment, the real existence of the actual infinite is more of a hindrance than an aid. Lacan only summons the infinite to dismiss it. The infinite must remain an operational fiction, one that points to the abyss or the crack in which the subject is constituted". Badiou, "Subject and Infinity", Condition, pp. 224–225.
70 *Ibid.*, p. 224.
71 Lacan, *Encore*, p. 93 (translation modified).
72 Badiou, *In Praise of Mathematics*, p. 49.
73 Lacan, *Encore*, p. 93.
74 Jacques Lacan, *The Other Side of Psychoanalysis. Book XVII*, trans. Russell Grigg, W.W. Norton & Company, New York, London, 2007, p. 45.

194 Philosophy After Lacan

75 Alain Badiou, *Theory of the Subject*, trans. Bruno Bosteels, Continuum, London, 2009, p. 274.
76 Badiou, "The Event as Trans-Being", p. 60.
77 *Ibid.*
78 Badiou, *Being and Event*, p. 10.
79 Badiou, "The Event as Trans-Being", p. 60 (translation modified).
80 *Ibid.* (translation modified).
81 Lacan, *Encore*, p. 88.
82 Lacan, "Note italienne", p. 310.
83 *Ibid.*
84 The Cantor diagonal method, also called the Cantor diagonal argument, is an ingenuous technique used to show that the integers and reals cannot be put into one-to-one correspondence, thus proving that the uncountably infinite set of real numbers is "larger" than the countably infinite set of integers.
85 Alain Badiou, *Lacan. Anti-philosophy* 3, trans. Kenneth Reinhard and Susan Spitzer, Columbia University Press, New York, 2013, p. 105.
86 *Ibid.*, p. 109.
87 *Ibid.*, p. 27.
88 Lacan, "L'Étourdit", *Autres écrits*, p. 453.
89 *Ibid.*, p. 472.
90 *Ibid.*, p. 479.
91 Alain Badiou, Lacan. *Anti-philosophy* 3, p. 31.
92 *Ibid.*
93 *Ibid.*
94 *Ibid.*, p. 34.
95 *Ibid.*, pp. 35–36.
96 *Ibid.*, p. 36.
97 *Ibid.*, p. 94.
98 Lacan, "L'Étourdit", p. 452.
99 Lacan, *Encore*, p. 22.
100 Badiou, *Lacan*, p. 97.
101 *Ibid.*, p. 99.
102 *Ibid.*, p. 102.
103 *Ibid.*
104 *Ibid.*, p. 104.
105 *Ibid.*, p. 106.
106 *Ibid.*, p. 109.
107 Lacan, "L'Étourdit", p. 476.
108 *Ibid.*, p. 452.
109 *Ibid.*
110 *Ibid.*, p. 454.
111 *Ibid.*, p. 452–453.
112 Lacan, *Encore*, p. 22.
113 Badiou, *Being and Event*, pp. 281–282.
114 *Ibid.*, p. 282.
115 *Ibid.*, p. 284.
116 Badiou, *The Immanence of Truths*, p. 390.
117 *Ibid.*
118 *Ibid.*, p. 403.
119 *Ibid.* (translation modified).

Bibliography

Badiou, A. (2006) *Being and Event*, trans. O. Feltham. London, New York: Continuum,.

Badiou, A. (2006) Mathematics Is a Thought. In *Briefings on Existence. A Short Treatise on Transitory Ontology*, trans. N. Madarasz (pp. 45–57). New York: SUNY Press.

Badiou, A. (2006) The Event Is a Trans-Being. In *Briefings on Existence. A Short Treatise on Transitory Ontology*, trans. N. Madarasz (pp. 59–62). New York: SUNY Press.

Badiou, A. (2007) *The Century*, trans. A. Toscano. Malden, MA: Polity Press.

Badiou, A. (2008) "Philosophy and Mathematics", *Conditions*, trans. S. Corcoran (pp. 93–112). London, New York: Continuum.

Badiou, A. (2008) "The Subject and Infinity", *Conditions*, trans. S. Corcoran (pp. 211–227). London, New York: Continuum,.

Badiou, A. (2009) *Theory of the Subject*, trans. B. Bosteels. London: Continuum.

Badiou, A. (2013) *Lacan. Anti-philosophy* 3, trans. K. Reinhard and S. Spitzer. New York: Columbia University Press.

Badiou, A. (2016) *In Praise of Mathematics*, trans. S. Spitzer. Cambridge: Polity,.

Badiou, A. (2022) *The Immanence of Truths*, trans. S. Spitzer and K. Reinhard. London, New York: Bloomsbury.

Cantor, G. (1932) *Gesammelte Abhandlungen mathematischen und philosophischen Inhalts*, E. Zermelo (Ed.). Berlin: Springer.

Cantor, G. (XXXX) Foundations of a General Theory of Manifolds. *The Campaigner*, 9(1–2),69–96.

Charraud, N. (1994) *Infini et Inconscient. Essai sur Georg Cantor*. Paris: Anthropos-Economica.

Imbert, C. (2002) Où finit le platonisme?. In C. Ramond (Ed.), *Alain Badiou: Penser le multiple* (pp. 357–373). Paris: L'Harmattan.

Kant, I. (1998) *Critique of Pure Reason*, trans. P. Guyer and A.W. Wood. Cambridge: Cambridge University Press.

Lacan, J. (2006) "Science and Truth", *Écrits*, trans. B. Fink (pp. 726–745). New York, London: W.W. Norton & Company.

Lacan, J. *Séminaire de Jacques Lacan, Le savoir du psychanalyste, 1971–1972* (unpublished).

Lacan, J. *Séminaire de Jacques Lacan XXII, R.S.I. 1974–1975* (unpublished).

Lacan, J. *Séminaire de Jacques Lacan XXV, Le moment de conclure 1977–1978* (unpublished).

Lacan, J. (2001) "L'Étourdit", *Autres écrits* (pp. 449–495). Paris: Seuil.

Lacan, J. (2001) "La note italienne", *Autres écrits* (pp. 307–311). Paris: Seuil.

Lacan, J. (2007) *The Other Side of Psychoanalysis. Book XVII*, trans. R. Grigg. New York, London: W.W. Norton & Company,.

Lacan, J. (1978) *On Feminine Sexuality. The Limits of Love and Knowledge. Book XX. Encore 1972–1973. The Seminar of Jacques Lacan*, trans. B. Fink. New York, London: W.W. Norton & Company.

Lacan, J. (1990) *Television. A Challenge to the Psychoanalytic Establishment*, trans. D. Hollier, R. Krauss and A. Michelson. New York, London: W.W. Norton & Company.

Lavendhomme, R. (2001) *Lieu du sujet. Psychanalyse et mathématique.* Paris: Seuil.

Miller, J.-A. (1992) Vers un signifiant nouveau. *Revue de l'ECF* (20), 47–54.

Russell, B. (1901) Work on the principles of mathematics. *The International Monthly,* 4(1).

Russell, B. (1903) *The Principles of Mathematics.* Cambridge: Cambridge University Press.

Chapter 11

The Logic of Institutions in Lacanian Psychoanalysis

Gabriel Tupinambá

Lacan uses the term 'institution' in many ways, without displaying a clear coherence. Sometimes he seems to refer to a more sociological concept of institution, as when he speaks of the family (Lacan, 2003), of circumcision (Lacan, 2005) or marriage (Lacan, 2007) as being institutions, that is, as social practices whose reproduction is somewhat independent of the volition of the individuals who actualise it. At other times, he uses the term to mean a recognised social entity, referring to societies and schools as "institutions" of psychoanalysis, or when he claims that the Catholic Church is a "successful institution" (Lacan, 2012). He also uses institution with some frequency as a verb, as the act of inaugurating a procedure, when speaking, for example, of the institution of the transference in the clinic (Lacan, 1979) or the institution of numbers (Lacan, 2005). The plurality of uses is not surprising: after all, there is not exactly a Lacanian concept of institution, whose theoretical stability would be similar to that of psychoanalytic concepts of "group" and "civilisation" in Freud, or of "social link" in Lacan's late work.

In fact, when Lacan had to resort to such an (absent) concept – for example, on the occasion of the dissolution of the École Freudienne de Paris (EFP) – we see that the meaning of the expression quickly slips back into familiar Freudian terrain, as when he says that the analysts who would accompany him in the process of dissolution would thus give proof that his School would not "be an institution, [that is] the effect of a consolidated group" (Lacan, 1980). Clearly the sense of institution at play here – which takes us back to the Freudian definition of the army and the church as "artificial masses" (Freud, 2010) – does not correspond to Lacan's use of the term when he speaks of the "institution, prolongation and sustaining" of the transference in the analytic process, where it is certainly not a matter of the production of a group effect through a common identification. The following question thus arises: is the absence of a Lacanian concept of institution due to the wealth of other definitions and approaches – in Weber, Durkheim, Freud, Merleau-Ponty, Foucault, etc – or does it signal a relevant deficit, an open problem, in the theoretical corpus of psychoanalysis itself?

DOI: 10.4324/9781003425953-12

It is interesting to note that, also in Marx's work, one of Lacan's preferred sources for political dialogue, we do not find a theory of institutions. In *Capital*, for example, Marx often refers to private property as a "bourgeois institution" (Marx, 2013) and makes consistent use of the term, always in relation to social practices associated to the State, but this use is not original, referring even to the way Hegel mobilises the term in his *Philosophy of Right* (2003). The writings of Marx and Engels, however, bequeathed us only a critique of Hegelian state-centrism – and therefore a critical analysis of the conditions of possibility of modern institutions – and notoriously lack their own theory of the State, a task that fell to later Marxist thinkers, such as Pachukanis, Poulantzas, among others. Analyses of capitalist institutions, such as the prison system, schools, the media, can be found in the Marxist field, but there is also no sui generis concept of institution in Marx's work.

But is it the same theoretical absence in both Marx and Lacan? It seems not. From the point of view of a political theory committed to the class struggle, the focus on institutional limits implies a *reduction* of the network of social relations under consideration: the "bourgeois institutions" of which Marx speaks *conceal* the logic of economic domination under the mask of symmetrical contracts between free private owners, restricting our understanding of the real conditions of social reproduction of the working class – which, after all, is compelled by material necessity to establish these contracts. The same is not true of psychoanalysis: the concept of institution is not located below its main object of investigation, the subject of the unconscious, but possibly *beyond* its scope, pointing to the functioning of groupings that do not depend on the logic of identification in the same way as the cases studied by Freud. The consistency and reproduction of the modern legal-penal system, for example, is not conditioned by the common introjection of an identificatory trait, that is, it is not derived from the maintenance of community ties between people, but from the maintenance of the monopoly of state violence, whose foundation is the domination of one community by another, not implying desire, belonging and mutual recognition in the same way as identificatory groups. Thus, the concept of institution poses different problems for Marx and Lacan: for the former, it is a search for a *narrower* concept of social organisation, for the latter, an *expanded* concept of group formations.

The ideological apparatus of the State

When situated within these two limits, the theory of the repressive and ideological apparatuses of the state, put forward by Louis Althusser in the 1970s (Althusser, 1998), takes on a new light. In his theory, Althusser proposes a materialist revision of the concept of ideology in Marxism through recourse to the Lacanian theory of the imaginary – which obliges him to innovate in both directions: on the one hand, he needs to demonstrate that there is a specifically Marxist sense of 'institution' and, on the other, he needs to stress the psychoanalytic conception of identification so that it is possible to think about the subjection to the particular social practices that shape the very form of individuality in capitalism.

Althusser's starting point is the investigation of the role of institutions within the mode of production, that is, the need that capitalism presents to not only produce commodities, but also to produce the conditions of its own reproduction. To this end, the capitalist system needs to rely on social means, guided by the State, that guarantee the integrity of the value of commodities, that manage social tensions, that help to form new contingents of workers, etc. It is this focus on the reproduction of the conditions of production that serves as the general orientation for the Althusserian definition of institution. From this general definition, Althusser proposes a second distinction, between *repressive* and *ideological* state apparatuses. The former are composed of the public institutions that ensure the control of social forms of reproduction through violence − direct or potential − such as the public administration, the police, the legal courts and prisons. The latter, the institutions responsible for reproducing the very form of individuality necessary for the consumption of commodity-labor in surplus value-oriented production, operating in the private sphere − such as churches, schools, the political system (parties, unions), etc. The school, for example, is not only the place where practical knowledge is taught, qualifying students for future integration into the labor market in specific capacities: it is also the place where individuals learn a certain form of ideological subjection without which it is not possible for any qualified worker to be adequately employed in the productive process.

It is up to Althusser to explain, therefore, how institutions are able to conform and reproduce behaviors that are not experienced as external impositions or laws, but as subjective dispositions − a question that Althusser himself associates with the ancient problem of voluntary servitude, which troubled La Boétie. At this point, we are no longer in the terrain of the Marxist problematic, of how we move from macroeconomic analysis to social analysis, and we approach the psychoanalytic problematic, of the need to expand, beyond the Freudian theory of identification, our understanding of coordinated collective behaviours.

Althusser's conceptual strategy is divided into two related axes. First, we have the axis that defines the function of ideology, which the theorist famously summarises as that of "representing the imaginary relation of individuals to their real conditions of existence" (1998, p. 77). Already in this first axis, we see how a concept of institution could strain the Lacanian theory of the imaginary, since ideology is not defined as a process of constitution of the "ego ideal", but as *an extension of the imaginary towards non-imaginary social conditions.* It is, after all, a matter of integrating the constitution of the I into the social world in such a way that these imaginary features are preserved or even reinforced, rather than questioned and confronted by the social forces that actually organise the limits of our actions. That is, we are not interested here in the libidinal dynamics of groups – in the way we identify with each other through a common symbolic identification, itself responding to the anxieties of lack constitutive of each other's desire. Instead, the representation at stake concerns the *harmonisation* between the libidinal economy of subjects and the conflicting and antagonistic social reality, which is why we do not analyse the functioning of ideology when we look at the way subjects identify themselves – who they consider their leaders, their peers, etc. – but at the way certain practices allow these identifications to survive in a space that constantly puts into question the power of leaders, the symmetry between equals, the scope of our freedom, etc.

This brings us to the second axis, which concerns how the ideological apparatuses of the state operate and mobilise this representation. For Althusser, the central operation of ideology is to "interpellate individuals as subjects". It is important to stress here that "subject" in Althusser's definition refers to the juridical model and not the Lacanian one (1998, p. 75). Nothing in the ISA text suggests that the divided subject of the unconscious is the product of interpellation – indeed, all of Althusser's examples go in the opposite direction, suggesting that the process of interpellation makes the imaginary ego even more compatible, more integrated, with its real conditions of social existence, in a kind of "ideological reality testing" that allows identifications not to be frustrated by the play of social forces. The ideological apparatuses of the State neither appease subjective conflicts nor encourage them – they make them *commensurable* with social reality, for example, by giving them the status of 'private matters', which is already a State characterisation of what would not fall under the rule of the State.

Interpellation thus follows the model of an empty call, coming from within the institutional apparatus, whose content is completed by the individual psyche. This is how the famous example of the policeman who questions us in the street, saying "Hey you!", works: the call itself contains nothing – and the lack of response to the call could even be replaced by violent coercion – but when we respond to this call, recognising ourselves in its emptiness, we simultaneously find a place for our identifications in a social structure indifferent to them and materially replicate a set of practices that allow the reproduction of social relations.

We thus see that the Althusserian theory of the ideological apparatuses of the state proposes theoretical innovations that respond to the two different conceptual deficits we identified earlier: it suggests that it is possible to propose a Marxist concept of institution – defined on the basis of the practices of reproduction of the conditions of production – as well as proposing a possible expansion of the psychoanalytic theory of identification – defining a new operator that manages in a practical way the tension between social

The Logic of Institutions in Lacanian Psychoanalysis 201

structure and psychic structure, a tension that is not confused with the intemperances of the subject of the unconscious.

Ideological apparatuses of psychoanalysis

We begin this chapter by stating that there is no Lacanian concept of institution – just as there is no such concept in Marx's work. We argue, however, that these are two different absences, since it is necessary to restrict the generality of the critique of political economy in order to reach the institutional field, whereas for psychoanalysis it is an exercise in expansion that is demanded. We then turned to Althusser's theory of the ideological apparatuses of the state, since it articulates these two conceptual limits in a conscious effort to supplement them with a theory of the way the institutions reproduce state structures and institute – in a different sense – social subjects through the process of interpellation.

Our choice to follow the Althusserian debate is not only conceptually justified, however. After all, Althusser played an active role in the history of Lacanian psychoanalysis and, in particular, in the history of Lacanian institutions. It is well known that it was the Marxist philosopher who mediated Lacan's welcome at the *École Normale Supérieure* on the occasion of his departure from the *International Association of Psychoanalysis* in 1962, inviting his students to attend the psychoanalyst's seminar and publishing studies in which he recognised the value of Lacan's work. But it was also Althusser who intervened, in 1980, when Lacan decided to dissolve the EFP and to found, soon afterwards, the Champ de la Cause Freudienne. This episode is of particular interest because it allows us to observe *in situ* the dissonance between the psychoanalytic theory of groups and the real movements of an analytic institution.

On January 5, 1980 Lacan sends a letter to the members of the EFP in which he announces that "there is a problem in the School (...) this problem is such because there is a solution: it is dis – dissolution". He warns that "it is high time" to dissolve the "Association which gives this School its legal status" since, otherwise, the School "would function (...) contrary to what I founded it for" (1980, p. 5). Lacan's proposal causes controversy, dividing the members of the School, and a process of persuasion begins in an effort to secure the number of votes necessary for the institution to be legally dissolved. In March, close to the time of the vote, a meeting is arranged at a hotel in Paris with Lacan and the other members of the EFP – and it is on this occasion that Althusser attends, despite not having been invited, and asks to speak.

The public record of his intervention was reduced to an anecdotal newspaper article written by Catherine Clément: *Althusser assaults the Lacan fortress*. The author, who was not present during the event, drew on notes made by Althusser himself as he prepared his intervention – notes that he

202 Philosophy After Lacan

gathered under the title *Open Letter to the Analytes and Analysts in Solidarity with Jacques Lacan*. In his article, Clément emphasises the aggressive tone of some of the philosopher's remarks and suggests that his presence at the meeting was intended to prevent the dissolution of the school. Althusser, shocked by the newspaper article, then decided to write a text – which remained incomplete – clarifying his position:

> I intervened to say that the whole question of the dissolution of the EFP was none of my business, but there is a legal procedure, which Lacan has initiated, whether he likes it or not, and he certainly knows it because he knows the law, and which simply comes down to each one knowing whether to vote yes or no tomorrow on the subject of dissolution. I have no opinion on this, but it is a political act, and a political act is not done alone, as Lacan proposes, but must be reflected upon and discussed democratically by all the interested parties – including the main one, which is 'the masses' of psychoanalysis, the analysands, the masses and your 'real teachers'. A political act cannot be carried out by a solitary individual, in secret at number 5, Rue de Lille – otherwise it is despotism, even if enlightened.

(Althusser, 1999, p. 132)

In his reply to Clemént, Althusser says that he felt the need to emphasise the political value of the dissolution because he had noticed during the meeting that the members of the EFP were treating Lacan's act as an analytic act, using the time they had to discuss the mourning they would make of the School, the unconscious reasons for the failure of the institution and the interpretative effects of Lacan's act. The reduction of the ongoing process to a gesture that would call into question the libidinal formation of a group is what motivated Althusser to take the floor and draw attention to the network of effects that such a procedure would have:

> Whatever the case, I told them, you are doing politics and nothing else; you are in the process of doing politics and nothing else. (...) And when we do politics, as Lacan and you are doing, it is never without consequences. If you think that there will be no consequences, just wait – they will fall on your heads, or actually they won't, because you are well protected and you know how to dodge. In fact, the consequences will fall on the poor bastards who come to lie on your divans, and on the people intimate with them, and the people intimate with these other people, and so on ad infinitum.

(Althusser, 1999, p. 133)

What interests us here, above all, is the contrast between two treatments of institutionality: while the members of the EFP seemed to see the legal procedure as an excrescence that pointed to inessential compromises between the School and the State, Althusser argued that, on the contrary, the legal device was *reductive*, since the real network of relations on which Lacan's school depended would extend *beyond* the limits of legal belonging, including above all the analysands, the "true teachers" of psychoanalysis. It is a concrete example of the confrontation between the two conceptual absences we have mentioned: for the Lacanian, the institution was replaced by the group, for the Marxist, it served as a point of passage to economic and social analysis, to the dependence of analysts on the work of the analysands. A historic and important confrontation – but also a monumental mismatch: Althusser's intervention was, at the time, interpreted by others present as a sign of a poorly resolved transference with Lacan... and promptly forgotten.

Institution and autonomy

Between the Marxist and the psychoanalytic, what does then it mean *to institute*? Is there a logic of institution common to both fields? Let us return, for a moment, to the definition offered by Merleau-Ponty in the course he dedicated to the concept in 1954:

> by institution we mean those events in an experience which offer the experience a durable dimension, in relation to which a series of other experiences come to make sense, forming a thinkable sequence or a history – or again, events which deposit a sense in me, not merely as a remnant or residue, but as a call to be followed, a demand for the future.
> (Merleau-Ponty, 2010, p. x)

The concept of institution is thus linked to the theme of duration – or rather, to the transformation of an event, a discontinuity, into something perennial, continuous. Something is instituted to the extent that a gesture, action or mark allows the establishment of a series, "a thinkable sequence", whose internal meaning is linked to the duration of the instituting event. Once a pact is established between two people – a friendship, for example – a certain common framework is established to which the meaning of subsequent actions refers, so that even aggressive comments or barbs exchanged between the people involved gain a new value, possibly reinforcing rather than undoing the bond between them. When Lacan comments on the 'institution of the number', it is to a similar movement that he refers: once a mark has been instituted, the following marks no longer count as singular, disconnected events, but refer back to the first, counting as units in a series.

Merleau-Ponty emphasises the temporal character of the institution, but we can also determine its spatial limit, which also demarcates a discontinuity, the beginning of a new related regime of practices, whose meaning depends on institutional boundaries. For example, just as we can analyse the school as an institution from a temporal point of view, we can focus on how certain protocols and social relations only make sense, and only find effectiveness, in the space inside the classroom, emerging as extremely unreasonable behaviors in any other social situation.

However, the dialectic of the continuous and the discontinuous, demarcating the beginning of a duration or a normative space, is not enough to qualify an institution. It is also necessary to consider the movement of *autonomisation* of the institution in relation to the event that produces it. We can understand this characteristic by contrasting the concept with that of "constitution". The legal constitution of a country, for example, remains – at least to some degree – dependent on the group of people who legitimise it, such that the citizens of a country must have the means to transform the laws that govern them if necessary. The autonomy of a legislation remains limited by the protocols established by the very body politic that constituted it. The same is not true of the institution: once created, it can acquire a greater degree of autonomy, even becoming an obstacle to those who established its initial coordinates. While citizens can vote to change legislation, police officers can arrest those who protest against the existence of the police. It is precisely autonomisation that qualifies the ideological apparatuses of the state, studied by Althusser, to reproduce the conditions of capitalist production even when these conditions conflict with the people who relate and reproduce themselves through them. In institutional logic, *social means and ends are inverted*, and relations between people reproduce social forms, not the other way around.

Merleau-Ponty approaches this process of autonomisation in terms derived from the Hegelian logic of the objective spirit (Hegel, 2003). For Hegel, the properly social dimension of subjectivity is not presented in intersubjective pacts or in moral conduct, sustained by the volition of individuals, but in the way the social subjectivity of a people or historical moment is imprinted on the materiality of the world – on those things that, while being human products, confront us as an environment or an exterior force. Similarly, the French phenomenologist proposes to think of the exterior or autonomous dimension of institutions in terms of their passivity, that is, in terms of how this 'durable dimension', which drives the meaning of subsequent actions, separates itself from human activity, coming to inhabit objects, protocols and norms that do not depend on our subjective acquiescence for them to continue to operate and inform functional normative regimes. The logic of institution thus combines the transformation of an event into a duration with a process of inversion, whereby the instituted duration becomes a passive and autonomous background that is autonomised from the volition and subjectivity of those who instituted it.

Now, an interesting perspective opens up here to question the common logic between Marx's theory of social forms – the process of autonomisation of "abstract wealth" (Rotta and Teixeira, 2016), which slowly separates money and capital from their immediate material traction (Paulani, 2011) – and Lacan's theory of the drive, where we also find this inversion between means and ends, the transformation of relations of desire into modes of perpetuation of an unconscious satisfaction and a complex dialectic between the discontinuity of a traumatic event and the continuity of forms of dealing with the Other (Lacan, 1985). It is no wonder, therefore, that it was precisely in the Hegelian theory of the spirit that the Slovenian philosopher Slavoj Žižek sought a point of contact between Marx and Lacan (Žižek, 2013): it is there that we find – as Merleau-Ponty suggests – the elaboration of a theory of autonomisation, of the way in which human actions, words and relations can become estranged from their support, inverting the game between background and figure. In the drive, the failure of satisfaction becomes satisfaction in failure, in the valorisation of value, human reproduction through consumption becomes consumption of the reproduction of humanity itself.

What is of great interest, however, is to realise that, as a logic, the process of institution is both ambivalent in its effects and hybrid in its individual or social character. The same is not true of the Marxist and psychoanalytic references to the logic of autonomisation. In Marx, the process of social autonomisation is largely univalent, always pointing to the estrangement of capitalist social forms in particular, and even Althusser is unable to elaborate his theory of ideological apparatuses *in general* – including, for example, socialist ideological apparatuses. In Lacan, on the other hand, the ambivalence is maintained, and clinical work is often about finding better paths for the drive's satisfaction, rather than treating it as an excess to be eliminated. On the other hand, autonomisation in psychoanalysis is part of a metapsychological theory, its domain of application is exclusively the dynamics of a subject's desire – and no large-scale social process is treated as if it could situate, in its own dimension, something of the 'real' drive. And indeed, there is no concept in Lacanian theory for the autonomisation proper to collective organisations, with their own processes of inversion of means and ends, their ambivalent detachments from the organised. The greatest example of this deficit, after all, remains the very dissolution of Lacan's school.

Organisational drives and social needs

There is a famous fragment in Marx's *Economic and Philosophical Manuscripts* which reads as follows:

> In order to supersede the idea of private property, the idea of communism is enough. In order to supersede private property as it actually exists, real communist activity is necessary. History will give rise to such activity, and the movement which we already know in thought to be a self-superseding movement will in reality undergo a very difficult and

206 Philosophy After Lacan

protracted process. But we must look upon it as a real advance that we have gained, at the outset, an awareness of the limits as well as the goal of this historical movement and are in a position to see beyond it.

When communist workmen gather together, their immediate aim is instruction, propaganda, etc. But at the same time, they acquire a new need – the need for society – and what appears as a means had become an end. This practical development can be most strikingly observed in the gatherings of French socialist workers. Smoking, eating, and drinking, etc., are no longer means of creating links between people. Company, association, conversation, which in turn has society as its goal, is enough for them. The brotherhood of man is not a hollow phrase, it is a reality, and the nobility of man shines forth upon us from their work-worn figures.

(Marx 1974, p. 302)

First of all, Marx distinguishes the "idea" from the "real activity": the idea of private property from its actual existence, the idea of communism from its real movement. As usual with Marx, this is not merely a distinction of registers, between the abstract and the concrete presentation of a given thing. The idea of communism can in fact work against the real communist movement, insofar as, from the standpoint of an idea that has no effective reality, "the real estrangement of human life remains and is all the greater the more one is conscious of it as such" (ibid.). The actual communist movement, however, does not overcome the actual relations mediated by private property so easily as its ideal version: communist practice, in reality, moves slowly, step by step, it undergoes "a very difficult and protracted process". But Marx suggests that the very shift away from the abstract realm of the idea to the harsh reality of concrete struggle is already "real advance": being aware of "the limits as well as the goal of this historical movement" constitutes our first victory as communists. There is a great sense of pragmatic realism here, a true conviction that being exposed to our real limitations is preferable to being trapped in a dream of great things, without actuality.

The second paragraph, however, introduces a strange twist into this orientation. Marx stops speaking of communist strategy in general terms and turns to the "communist workmen" gathered together for the purposes of accomplishing some tasks of importance for the political movement: agitation, propaganda, political formation. This active movement, a painfully difficult process of liberation – which is a hundred times more important than the work of philosophers, seating home, aloof, thinking of the idea of freedom – is nonetheless suddenly interrupted or distorted by the appearance of "a new need".

This new need has a very peculiar structure, because, unlike the "real estrangement of human life", which can only be superseded by the actual overcoming of private property, it can find satisfaction in the present, in the very process of socialisation of workers. This new need inverts the relation between means and ends: rather than organise in order to accomplish certain tasks of interest for the movement, the communist workmen take part in the harsh struggle for actual communism so that they can engage in "smoking, eating and drinking" (see also Dolar, 2013). In a sense, they become, in their pleasure in "company, association, conversation", like the lazy philosophers Marx had just criticised, who think of communism for the pleasure of thinking. However, here, the free association of men, unlike in the case of the philosopher, freely associating ideas, is a reality. A reality which Marx emphatically praises, even though it does not present itself as an effective contribution to the actually existing communist movement. This "new need", which in fact appears as a new satisfaction, an uncalled for pleasure, makes in fact a sudden and unwanted appearance. From the standpoint of those who, having abandoned the narcissistic satisfaction of wallowing in the ideal, dedicate themselves to the actual communist practice, with all its grit and frustrations, to suddenly have their hard-earned efforts of collective mobilisation turned into a "mere" means for people to gather and talk can only be experienced as a deviation, a stoppage or even a betrayal. But they are powerless against it. As Jacques Rancière puts it:

> Here is the problem that is likely to transform the enthusiasm of the communist into the despair of the revolutionary − the nobility of humanity already shining on brows that should have lost even the appearance of it in order to produce the future of humanity. [.] The obstacle to the transformation of Straubinger communists into revolutionary proletarians is not their status as artisans, but their status as communists − not the heavy weight of their journeyman past but the lightness of their anticipation of the communist future.
>
> (Rancière, 2003, pp. 82–3)

And so the revolutionary movement splits itself − which would be our unavoidable destiny, according to Althusser (Althusser, 1999) − between those moving in the direction of a future transformation of society, and those who, having suddenly acquired this "new need − the need for society", relish in its present satisfaction.

Psychoanalysis has greatly contributed to a renewal of Marxist theory in recent years, especially due to the work of Žižek. But the consideration of "enjoyment as a political factor" (Žižek, 1991) has, even in Žižek's own work, led to new developments mostly in two specific areas of political thought: the critique of ideology and the theory of political intervention. Lacanian psychoanalysis has helped us to understand ideology from the standpoint of the logic of fantasy, and to propose a theory of transformation which takes the unconscious into consideration, but not much has been developed apropos of the relation between the theory of the drives and the theory of collective organisation. There is, however, one fundamental reason for this: this relation has not been properly established within psychoanalysis itself (Tupinambá, 2015, pp. 159–179).

We would be looking in the wrong place if we were to blame Lacanian psychoanalysis alone for this practical and theoretical deficit. Rather, this particular lack marks the place of insertion of analytic thought in a much broader field – which includes a great part of emancipatory movements today, as well as most conservative thinkers – which shares this same unilateral treatment of the autonomous dimension of collective organisation. Rancière himself, who wrote extensively on the fragment of the *Manuscripts* quoted above, shares the same position, simply taking the side of immediate satisfaction of the workers, against the "institutional" revolutionaries who remain seduced by future objectives (Rancière, 2009, pp. 167–178).

Franz Kafka, a theorist of institutional autonomisation

But if psychoanalysis cannot facilitate the development of a theory of these organisational inversions, whereby means become ends, giving rise to previously inexistent or unrecognised lacks and needs, we can turn to a surprising ally here, to help us give form to these problems, Franz Kafka. Even though he is often presented as *the* writer to best capture the "absurdity" of bureaucracy and of totalitarianism, once we have the problem of institutional autonomisation in mind, a different side of Kafka emerges, a theorist of a form of life capable of accommodating the reversals between means and ends, future and present satisfaction, that Marx recognised in the French workmen organisations – reversals which still today are mostly understood only as signs of how the autonomy of the whole over the parts leads to corruption, betrayal and, ultimately, totalitarianism.

Žižek has brilliantly encapsulated the fundamental impasse which structures the narratives of *The Trial* or *The Castle*. Both novels revolve around an "election", as Calasso puts it, but this call does not simply interpellate the characters: "the Kafkaesque subject is the subject desperately seeking a trait with which to identify, he does not understand the meaning of the call of the Other" (Žižek, 2009, p. 43). In other words, it is a subject who suffers from the lack of determination which could socially locate him: its not simply that we have a debt, a penalty or an appointment due, but rather that there is no place for this lack to be situated in the Other, no channel through which to inscribe our fault in the very institution which has singled us out because of it. Josef is accused, K. has been called – but of what, by whom?

On the other hand, Kafka's short stories like *Josephine, the Singer* or *The Problem with our Laws*, which also focus on an otherness whose meaning eludes us, are narrated from a completely different standpoint. As Fredric Jameson puts it, a propos of *Josephine*:

The Logic of Institutions in Lacanian Psychoanalysis 209

nowhere is the icy indifference of the Utopia of democracy more astonishingly revealed (but revealed by way of nothing and no reaction) than
in the refusal of the people to grant her this form of individual
difference.

(Jameson, 1996, p. 126)

In many of these short stories we still find the problem of "individual difference" and its suffering to constitute itself as such in this world, but the crucial point is that this form of suffering − and its intrinsic conception of what
an appropriate social institution should be − is not mediating our entry into
the story. Rather, we are first introduced to the world, to its inconsistent
structure, and it is from within it that questions of identity and exception are
posed. In these short stories and parables, the narrative is less driven by the
need to explain what distinguishes Josephine from the other mice, or what
the true status of a country's laws, but by an anonymous character's attempt
to have this indeterminate aspect of his world inscribed as indeterminate "in
the eternal history of the people" (Kafka, 1971). The privileged form of suffering here − the one that finds compassion, that stirs debates and polemics
− is a sort of cold passion or fervor around something which the people
themselves don't consider essential or special. This is not only the case in the
polemics around Josefine, but also in the debate between parties concerning
the nobility, in *The Problem with our Laws*, or the Emperor, in *The Great
Wall of China* and even the townspeople in *The Castle*, who adore Klamm
even though they can't even distinguish his particular features.

It is not for nothing that the famous parable about the "door of the Law"
concludes with the admission that "this entrance was intended for you alone"
(Kafka, 2009, p. 155): this first entry point singles us out personally, focusing the
narrative at the individual level, at the cost of blurring everything else. From this
standpoint, the habitual detachment with which the remaining characters deal
with Josef's demands can only be understood as a sign of society's profound
"alienation" and "apathy" when facing a man's desperation, rather than a
"refusal of the people to grant [him] this form of individual difference".

The true challenge is, therefore, to propose this "parallax shift" from one
perspective to another, reading the universe of the main novels from the
standpoint constructed in the short stories. To realise that *Josef was always
already Josefine*. An appropriate place to test this hermeneutic approach is
with K.'s letter of employment. It's a short note:

Dear Sir, you are, as you know, taken into the count's service. Your
immediate superior is the village mayor as chairman of the parish council, who will communicate to you all further details concerning your
work and your remuneration, and to whom you will be answerable.
Nonetheless, I will keep an eye on you myself. Barnabas, the messenger
who brings this letter, will make enquiries of you from time to time, find

out what your requirements are, and impart them to me. You will find me always ready to oblige you as far as possible. I am anxious to have contented workers.

(Kafka, 2009b, pp. 23–24)

K.'s own analysis of its content is quite telling. He notices that "there were passages where he was addressed as a free agent whose autonomy was recognized" as well as others "where he was openly or by implication addressed as a common labourer, hardly worthy even to be noticed by the chief executive". K. considers these two passages to be in blatant contradiction: how could he be simultaneously recognised as a "free agent" and as someone "hardly worthy even to be noticed"? But the incompatibility here is less between the two aspects of the letter than between K. and the form of recognition that has been offered to him by the administration of the Castle. It is as if K. has been addressed by the mouse folk from Josefine, who would have no problem in imagining the coincidence of singularity and anonymity – since this is the destiny of "the numberless throng of the heroes of the people" (Kafka, 1971, p. 342).

In his subsequent talk with the village mayor, K. finds out that the initial request for a land surveyor had been cancelled long ago, and had found its way into his hands due to a sort of administrative fluke. However, the reason as to why this happened is presented by the mayor in a manner that cannot but recall Freud's theory of the psychic apparatus in the Project for a Scientific Psychology:

When an affair has been under consideration for a very long time, and even before assessment of it is complete, it can happen that something occurs to settle it, like a sudden flash of lightning at some unforeseeable point, and you can't pinpoint it later. The case is thus brought to an arbitrary, if usually quite correct, conclusion. It's as if the official mechanism could no longer stand up to the tension and the years of attrition caused by the same factor, which in itself may be slight, and has made the decision of its own accord with no need for the officials to take a hand. [...] these decisions are generally excellent, and the only disruptive aspect of them is that, as it usually turns out, we learn about them too late, so passionate discussion of an affair that was settled long ago still goes on.

(Kafka, 2009b, p. 63)

The explanation of this "particular feature of our official mechanism" must be carefully analysed. It is a complete exposition of the logic of autonomisation we have discussed before. On the one hand, the mayor describes something which interrupts the deliberation of a given matter like a "sudden flash" that cannot be retroactively discerned. This intervention leads the issue at hand to practically solve itself – not due because the solution appeared in an insight, but because "the official mechanism could no longer stand up to the tension". The mayor trusts the conclusion to be correct and "generally excellent", but the deliberative process has no discernible agent – the trust seems rather to rather concern the very fact that a decision has been reached. At the same time that this "official mechanism" moves on its own, according to a weird homeostatic logic, the "passionate discussion of an affair" also goes on irrespective of having met its official end. Marx writes of Capital as an "automatic Subject" (Marx, 1976, p. 255), but what we have here is something slightly different. It is not only the symbolic form which detaches itself from its material basis, rendering the latter paradoxically dependent on the self-propagation of the former, but rather a "double kenosis": the official mechanism decided the matter on its own, but the officials have also continued passionately debating on their own, like the horse Bucephalus, in Kafka's *The New Advocate*: "his flanks unhampered by the thighs of a rider, free and far from the clamour of battle, he reads and turn the pages of our ancient tomes" (Kafka, 1971 p. 261). The process of autonomisation, for a procedure to go on beyond its immediate aim, appears here "as substance as well as subject" – a transformation that is nowhere so telling as when Kafka writes: "'I do indeed suffer from it,' said K. slowly, smiling to himself, for just now he did not suffer from it in the slightest" (Kafka, 2009b, p. 227).

Bibliography

Althusser, L. (1998) *Ideology and Ideological Apparatuses of the State.* Lisbon: Editora Presença.

Althusser, L. (1999) *Writings on Psychoanalysis.* New York: Columbia University Press.

Dolar, M. (2013) Smoking Communism. Available at: http://vanishingmediator.blogsp ot.com.br/2013/06/mladen-dolar-smoking-communism.html.

Freud, S. (2010) *Psychology of the masses and analysis of the Self and other texts (1920–1923).* São Paulo: Companhia das Letras.

Hegel, G.W.F. (2003) *Princípios de Filosofia do Direito.* São Paulo: Martins Fontes.

Jameson, F. (1996) *The seeds of time.* New York: Columbia University Press.

Kafka, F. (1971) *The Complete Stories.* London: Schocken Books.

Kafka, F. (2009) *The Trial.* Oxford University Press.

Kafka, F. (2009b) *The Castle.* Oxford University Press.

Lacan, J. (1961–62) *The Seminar*, Book 9: Identification. Unpublished.

Lacan, J. (1976–77) *The Seminar*, Book 24: L'insu que sait de l'une-bévue. Rio de Janeiro: Jorge Zahar.

Lacan, J. (1979) *The Seminar*, Book 1: Freud's Technical Writings. Rio de Janeiro: Jorge Zahar.

Lacan, J. (1980) *Dissolution in The Seminar*, Book 27. Unpublished. Rio de Janeiro: Jorge Zahar.

Lacan, J. (1985) *The Seminar*, Book 11: The Four Fundamental Concepts of the psychoanalysis. Rio de Janeiro: Jorge Zahar.

Lacan, J. (2003) *Outros Escritos*. Rio de Janeiro: Jorge Zahar.

Lacan, J. (2005) *The Seminar*, Book 10: Anguish. Rio de Janeiro: Jorge Zahar.

Lacan, J. (2007) *The Seminar*, Book 23: The sinthome. Rio de Janeiro: Jorge Zahar.

Lacan, J. (2012) *The Seminar*, Book 19, ...or worse (pp. 160–172). Rio de Janeiro: Jorge Zahar.

Marx, K. (1979) *Economic and Philosophical Manuscripts*. London: Progress Publishers.

Marx, K. (2013) *Capital*, Vol.1. São Paulo: Boitempo.

Marx, K. (2017) *Capital*, vol. 3. São Paulo: Boitempo.

Merleau-Ponty, M. (2010) *Institution and Passivity*. New York: Northwestern University Press.

Paulani, L. (2011) The Autonomization of Truly Social Forms in Marx's Theory. São Paulo: Revista EconomiA, 12(1), 49–70.

Rancière, J. (2003) *The Philosopher and his Poor*. New York: Duke University Press.

Rotta, T. and Teixeira, R. (2016) The autonomization of abstract wealth: new insights on the labor theory of value. *Cambridge Journal of Economics*, 40(4), 1185–1201.

Tupinambá, G. (2021) *The Desire of Psychoanalysis*. Evanston, IL: Northwestern University Press.

Žižek, S. (1991) *For They Know Not What They Do*. London: Verso.

Žižek, S. (2009) *The Sublime Object of Ideology*. London: Verso.

Žižek, S. (2013) *Less than Nothing: Hegel and the Shadow of Dialectical Materialism*. São Paulo: Boitempo.

Index

Abraham, Nicolas 134
Althusser, Louis 42, 142–143, 148, 153, 155, 160, 164n18, 198–207
Althusserian 143, 154, 200, 201, 202
Anti-philosophy xi, 142, 188
Appiganesi, Lisa 69
Aristotle 1, 27
Atheism 2, 7–25
Autonomisation 204–205, 208, 210–211
Autonomy 88–89, 121, 203–204, 208, 210

Bachelard, Gaston 153
Badiou, Alain 1, 5–6, 95, 98, 138n1, 142–191, 192n45, 193n69
Barad, Karen 62, 67n4
Beckett, Andy 98
Bersani, Leo 84, 86
Besso, Michele 44n17
Bion, Wilfred 75, 79–81
Britton, Ronald 96
Brown, Wendy 106
Buddhism 15–23
Butler, Judith 83

Cantor, Georg 169–189, 194n84
Cantorian 169–171, 174, 177–178, 185, 187, 189
Capitalism 4–5, 71, 86, 96–98, 104–105, 199
Casas López, Andrea 98, 100
Causality 58, 144–145, 151, 160, 163
Cavell, Stanley 119, 125n23
Charraud, Nathalie 192n34, 192n38
Chiesa, Lorenzo 8–10, 12–14, 18, 25n1
Christianity 7, 9–11, 18
Cicero 92–93
Clark, John 15–16
Cohen, Paul 170
Communism 16, 43, 97, 102, 105, 205–207
Communist 42, 205–207

Coulthard, Glen 4, 84, 91
Countertransference 74, 89

Dachy, Vincent 70
Dahrendorf, Ralf 43n11
Dean, Jodi 4, 84, 87–89
Derrida, Jacques 2, 5, 29, 127–140
Descartes, René 1, 143, 185
Desire 16–23, 31, 33, 37–42, 55–56, 58–59, 63, 70–71, 73–75, 78, 82, 87–88, 92, 95–96, 100–101, 103–106, 111–116, 120, 134, 136, 171–173, 180, 198, 200, 205
Diamond, Cora 114, 117–120
Didi-Huberman, Georges 106
Discourse 2–5, 28, 36, 43–44, 58, 62, 64–66, 70, 84, 87–88, 96, 101, 113, 118, 125n10, 130–131, 135–137, 138n2, 139n2, 140n17, 143–144, 147–155, 168–169, 173, 176, 179–182, 184–187

Edelman, Lee 3–4, 83–93
Einstein, Albert 44n17, 103
Energy 57, 78, 124n6, 139n8, 161–163
Engels, Friedrich 198
Entropy 161
Epistemological 12–13, 16, 30, 153, 155
Epistemology 24, 143, 153
Ethics 3–5, 40–41, 67n4, 109–124, 124n1, 127
Exergy 161
Existentialism 143

Fantasy 4, 13–14, 19, 75–76, 78, 85, 89, 97, 99–102, 104–105, 107, 140n6, 150, 208
Feminism 2–3, 68, 75
Fink, Bruce 140n13
Fisher, Mark 95, 97–98

214 Index

Foreclosure 96, 100–101, 104, 152–153, 168
Forrester, John 69
Foucault, Michel 30, 35, 130, 144, 198
Freud, Sigmund 1–2, 9–10, 16, 19, 23, 27, 33, 37–39, 42–43, 51, 57, 61, 63, 66, 68, 72, 78, 82, 99, 101–103, 110–112, 114, 125n10, 133, 135, 139n8, 144, 148, 177–178, 186, 188, 197–198
Friedman, Milton 77
Frye, Northrop 129

Gifford, Sanford 102
Gitlin, Todd 89–90
Gould, Stephen Jay 37
Grigg, Russell 1, 100

Halberstam, Jack 88–89
Hegel, Georg Wilhelm Friedrich 1, 5, 13, 23–24, 28, 51, 61–62, 66, 142–143, 149, 153, 155–158, 160, 162, 164n6, 198, 204
Hegelian 2, 5, 9, 13, 21, 28, 31, 36, 41–42, 91, 143, 158–159, 161, 198, 204–205
Heidegger, Martin 31, 40, 148, 188
Historical Dialectic 159–163
Hunter, Virginia 79–80
Husserl, Edmund 36, 148
Hysteria 68–82, 95–96, 102, 139n8

Identification 70, 74, 104, 197–200
Ideology 52, 86, 97–98, 152, 198–200, 207
Imaginary xii–xiv, 6, 29, 33, 43, 98–99, 101, 103, 106, 110–114, 117, 146–149, 151, 162–164, 164n18, 198–200
Imbert, Claude 170, 192n27
Infinite 23, 36, 70, 76, 78, 97, 130, 134, 152, 174–175, 177–178, 181, 189–190, 193n69, 194n84
Infinity 13, 175–178, 190–191
Institution 3, 6, 56, 68, 70–71, 131, 135, 197–205, 208–209
Interpellation 200–201
Irigaray, Luce 83
Ivakhiv, Adrian 15–17

Johnson, Barbara 134
Johnston, Adrian 9
Jouissance 17–19, 31, 37–38, 51, 59, 70, 72–74, 76, 78, 84, 89, 114, 138, 155, 160, 162

Kafka, Franz 208–211
Kant, Immanuel 1, 13, 24, 28, 41, 109, 120–124, 124n1, 167, 169
Kantian 13, 28, 40–41, 109, 121, 124n1, 167, 169
Kernberg, Otto 68, 70
Klein, Melanie 135
Klein, Naomi 105
Knot 74, 163–165
Kojève, Alexandre 28,
Koyré, Alexandre 1
Kristeva, Julia 72
Kriszat, Georg 44n16
Krug, Wilhelm Traugott 28,

Lacanian xii–xiv, 1–6, 17, 19, 28–29, 36–38, 40, 53, 72, 83–84, 87, 99, 102, 104–105, 113, 121–122, 135–137, 140n16, , 153, 164, 176–178, 180, 185, 188, 193n69, 197–201, 203, 205, 207–208
Laclau, Ernesto 32
Laplanche, Jean 35
Lavendhomme, René 167
Leader, Darian 69–70
Lebrun, Jean-Pierre 67
Leibniz, Gottfried Wilhelm 147–148
Lenin, Vladimir 161
Leninist 42
Lévi-Strauss, Claude 138n5, 148
Levitin, Michael 89–92
Lewontin, Richard 37
Libidinal 19, 52, 102–104, 138, 200, 202
Linguistic(s) 1, 12, 19, 31–32, 35, 43n4, 73, 101, 110, 113, 115, 117, 121, 124, 127, 129–130, 134, 138n2, 138n5, 143, 144, 151
Loss, Robert 87

Man, Paul de 130
Mathematics 1, 5–6, 29, 31, 51, 168–191, 192n31, 192n44, 192n45, 193n65
Matheme 171–173, 178–183
Marx, Karl 28, 42, 51, 65, 102, 144, 148, 160, 198, 205–208, 211
Marxism 2, 5, 7–8, 31, 43, 144–145, 153, 164n18, 198
Marxist 7, 16, 28, 31, 37, 42, 98, 105, 198–201, 203, 205, 207
Melancholia 4, 100–101, 104–108
Melman, Charles 67n5
Melville, Herman 3, 83, 85–86
Merleau-Ponty, Maurice 197, 203–205

Index 215

Metaphysics 3, 29, 62, 67n4, 115, 118, 134, 156, 175
Metonymy 152, 155
Metzinger, Thomas 14–15
Miller, Jacques-Alain 128–129, 144–145, 147–153, 155, 157, 160, 164n18, 165n38, 165n48
Miller, Joseph Hillis 130
Molière 2, 67n1
Montrelay, Michèle 3, 68, 71, 76–78, 82
Muller, John 133
Muñoz, José 87–88

Nietzsche, Friedrich 51, 61, 125n23, 127, 142

Occupy Wall Street 3–4, 84–93
Ontology 5, 12, 24, 28, 41, 67, 101, 124n1, 152, 162, 168–170, 173, 175, 179–180, 184, 187–191
Overdetermination 66, 147, 150, 153

Pascal, Blaise 1
Phenomenology 13, 149
Plato 1, 93, 184–185, 192n45
Platonism 93
Poststructuralism 138
Poststructuralist 27, 30, 128–129, 138n2
Propaganda 206
Psychoanalysis xii–xiv, 1–6, 16, 28, 31, 33–34, 36–41, 43, 43n9, 43n10, 52–54, 58, 65, 68, 70–72, 76, 79, 82–83, 87–88, 95, 98–105, 111, 119–120, 127–128, 133–138, 138n1, 140n17, 144–145, 150–153, 164n18, 168, 171–172, 176–180, 182–183, 185, 187–188, 190, 196–197, 201–203, 205, 207–208
Psychosis 36, 64, 99, 101–106, 154

Queer Theory 2–4, 72, 84–85, 87, 88–89, 92

Ragland, Ellie 1
Rancière, Jacques 207
Real (the) xii–xiv, 2–6, 8, 10, 13, 15–16, 29–31, 35–41, 43, 70, 73, 81, 86, 99, 105, 109, 111–114, 118–124, 125n10, 146, 149, 154, 160, 162–164, 169–170, 172, 175–184, 186–190, 193n69, 198, 201, 203, 206
Regnault, François 152
Rhetoric 92, 108, 135–136, 138, 140
Richardson, William 133, 150

Roazen, Paul 114
Ronen, Ruth 1
Rotta, Tomas Nielsen 205
Roudinesco, Elisabeth 129, 141, 147, 138n1, 139n6
Russell, Bertrand 5, 167–170, 186–187, 192n31

Saito, Kohei 97
Salmon, Peter 131, 138n5
Sartre, Jean–Paul 1, 38, 139, 155, 160
Saussure, Ferdinand de 29, 35, 148, 151
Schizophrenia 36, 46–48, 67n2, 78
Scientific Discourse 144, 148, 152–153, 182
Socrates 1, 92–93
Soler, Colette 71
Structural Dialectic 169–161, 163
Structuralism 121, 138n2, 138n5, 142–145, 147, 154–155, 159
Structuralist 42, 101, 128–129, 138n2, 139n5, 154
Suture 6, 147, 151–152, 155, 164n18
Symbolic (the) xii–xiv, 2, 4–5, 10, 15, 31, 35–36, 74–75, 101–104, 110–114, 118, 134, 160–163, 177–179, 211

Teixeira, Rodrigo Alves 205
Theory of discourse 143–144, 147–149, 153
Török, Mária 134
Transference 2, 27–28, 50, 69–71, 73–74, 77, 81, 99, 132, 197, 203
Tustin, Francis 3, 68, 78–81

Unconscious 10, 27–42, 58, 63, 65–66, 73–78, 96, 101, 103, 110–111, 121, 125n10, 134, 136, 138n2, 138n5, 139n8, 144, 150, 152–153, 156–158, 177–178, 186–187, 200–202, 205, 207
University Discourse 3, 45, 62, 64–66, 113
Utopia 87, 209
Utopian 8, 87–88, 90–91, 97

von Uexküll, Jakob Johann 40

Wittgenstein, Ludwig 2, 4, 27, 109–125, 142

Žižek, Slavoj 1, 7–26, 84–88, 95–98, 105–106, 205, 207–208
Zupančič, Alenka 1, 100, 103–104, 120–122, 125n29